THE ELUSIVE DANIEL DEFOE

THE ELUSIVE DANIEL DEFOE

by
Laura A. Curtis

VISION
and
BARNES & NOBLE

Vision Press Limited
Fulham Wharf
Townmead Road
London SW6 2SB

and

Barnes & Noble Books
81 Adams Drive
Totowa, NJ 07512

ISBN (UK) 0 85478 435 7
ISBN (US) 0 389 20063 8

For Michael

Printed and bound in Great Britain by
Unwin Brothers Ltd.,
Old Woking, Surrey.
Phototypeset by Galleon Photosetting,
Ipswich, Suffolk.
MCMLXXXIV

Contents

Preface

This book has had a long period of gestation; Chapter 4, on Defoe's sense of humour, was written in its earliest form in 1970–71, and Chapter 2, on fortresses and prisons in *Robinson Crusoe*, in 1971–72. In the meantime I was working on *The Versatile Defoe* (1979), which project required my familiarizing myself with most of Defoe's writing (557 items, according to the final calculations of his best-known twentieth-century bibliographer). For Chapters 1 and 3 of this work, I read carefully the twenty-two volumes of Defoe's long-lived journal, the *Review*.

I want to take this opportunity to thank Professors Louis Landa of Princeton University and Paul Fussell of Rutgers University for reading the first draft of this book and for offering helpful suggestions for rewriting it. Dr. David Liebling of Princeton, N.J., read the last draft and assured me that my interpretation of the way Defoe's mind worked was congruent with contemporary psychiatric theory. I am deeply grateful for the perspicacious editorial criticisms made by Professor Robert Adams Day of Queen's College and the Graduate Center of C.U.N.Y.

Finally, I want to thank my husband, Professor Michael Curtis of Rutgers, to whom this book is dedicated, for his unstinting moral support of this project.

Introduction

In the early eighteenth century Jonathan Swift anathematized Defoe as a stupid, illiterate fanatic, and Joseph Addison dismissed him as a false, prevaricating rogue. To our own day Daniel Defoe remains misunderstood and frequently underestimated, thanks largely to the power that the myth-like *Robinson Crusoe* exerts over our imaginations and our consequent tendency to identify its protagonist with its author. When we conceive of Defoe himself as emotionally simple and intellectually of a primarily practical bent, we find ourselves unable to harmonize a recurrent strain of sophistication, even cynicism, with the major strain of simplicity and directness in his writings. The result, as we have seen in the lively and continuing debate over *Moll Flanders*, is to leave us not much further advanced toward a conclusion about the meaning of the work than the ideas that prejudices like those of Swift or Addison suggest about its author. 'Did Defoe merely blunder into writing a great novel when he wrote *Moll Flanders*?' asks the publisher of an influential compilation of criticism on that fiction.[1]

More than most other major literary figures, Defoe needs to be understood as a personality; all of his fictions are first person narratives, and he wrote before the development of the novel as a literary genre. An innovator, Defoe had no support from a tradition showing how to differentiate the author's point of view from that of his fictional protagonist. More important, Defoe's point of view was far from consistent; the man himself possessed all of the attributes listed by Wayne Booth in his *Rhetoric of Fiction* as contributing to problems of interpretation: 'excessive complexity', 'subtlety', and 'privacy of norms to be inferred'.[2]

Because Defoe's fictional characters are not completely detached from their creator and because their creator himself

7

was a secretive person with a predilection for disguising himself as a crackerbarrel philosopher, understanding how his mind worked is essential for reconciling differences in interpreting his writing that have arisen from incomplete acquaintance with the elusive Defoe. Such an approach requires not only a thorough knowledge of the works of this most prolific of English writers but also an awareness of the historical and biographical context in which he wrote. The magnitude of Defoe's canon and the diversity of his interests have thus far been the major impediments to undertaking the exploration needed: an analysis of the mental characteristics of this complex writer.

The method by which I have reconstructed Defoe's consciousness is not entirely new. It consists of recognizing amidst the diversity of works, non-fiction as well as fiction, repeated ideas, images, characters, actions, and styles of writing, and of permitting them to organize themselves into a pattern. As Jean Starobinski explains, the critic does not reduce the writer's work to a network of unconscious drives defined by some antecedent system of psychology; instead, he stays with the words of the writer in order to question their meaning until he can see a coherence of intention not perceived by the writer.[3] Yeats was perhaps expressing the same idea when he said, 'There is some one Myth for every man, which, if we but knew it, would make us understand all that he did and thought.'[4]

My thesis about Defoe's consciousness has emerged in the course of twelve years of reading Defoe's writing, first the fiction and then the non-fiction. The instability perceptive readers frequently sense in his fictions arises from contradictory drives in Defoe. On the one hand he grasps at an ideal world of order and rational control; on the other hand he is irresistibly drawn to a real world of disorder and impulse. Elements from the ideal and the real world are present in Defoe's fiction and in his non-fiction, and frequently the mixture is unstable, as in *Moll Flanders*. When the real world impinges too far on the ideal the horizon darkens, and a world of nightmare emerges, as in *Roxana*.

In fiction Robinson Crusoe represents Defoe's ideal self. Crusoe works indefatigably, producing tangible objects of domestic use. He relies upon common-sense reasoning, he represses emotion, he is comforted by simple Protestantism of the Low-Church variety, and he acquires a helper who serves as a responsive audience for his didacticism. As a hermit, he experiences no difficulty reconciling ethical principle with daily practice. He expresses himself in the concrete and vigorous language Defoe advocated as a medium for communication in the well-known definition of his *Complete English Tradesman*:

> If any man was to ask me, what I would suppose to be a perfect style or language, I would answer, that in which a man speaking to five hundred people, of all common and various capacities, idiots and lunatics excepted, should be understood by them all, in the same manner with one another, and in the same sense which the speaker intended to be understood, this would certainly be a most perfect style.
>
> All exotic sayings, dark and ambiguous speakings, affected words, and as I said in my last, abridgments of words, or words cut off, as they are foolish and improper in business, so indeed are they in any other things. . . .[5]

Above all, he conquers his island, becoming absolute monarch and paternalistic ruler of his animal entourage. Similarly, in the non-fiction, the plain-dealing Mr. Review represents Defoe's ideal self, a personality of great public interest during the heyday of the *Review*, which was read eagerly by members of Parliament and government ministers as well as by the lower and middling ranks of the London middle classes to whom much of it was addressed.[6] The Mr. Review familiar to most readers is moderate, honest, candid, plain-dealing, plain-speaking, sensible, unemotional, and knowledgeable about agriculture, trade, and commerce. He is remarkably similar to Robinson Crusoe, if more loquacious, but remarkably dissimilar from Daniel Defoe, who behind the scenes was bustling around in political intrigues, despairing over the prospects of success, or amusing himself by taunting political opponents into furious outbursts while on stage the calm and moderate Mr. Review was chiding them for bad temper.

The major difficulty Defoe encountered in trying to live up to his vision of the ideal world and the source of the contradictory elements in his writing was the restlessness he could never entirely control, no matter how busy he kept himself at no matter how many different activities at the same time. This malaise was recognized by his contemporaries, one of whom referred to him disparagingly as 'restless Daniel'. It would be difficult to imagine social snobbery expressing itself in the same form a hundred or so years later and denigrating Dickens as 'restless Charles' for an idiosyncrasy of the creative temperament similar to Defoe's. In a self-confident moment (*A Vindication of the Press*, 1718), Defoe minimized his restlessness as a characteristic of writers, people of 'more than ordinary vivacity than the common herd', who should therefore be excused a few more 'extraordinary actions' than average people. He could have been referring to any one of a number of business gambles that led to lawsuits and bankruptcy or of political hoaxes and ironies that led to prison. His insatiable intellectual activity inspired him with so many kaleidoscopic perspectives on any particular issue of politics, economics, religion, and ethics, that probably even he didn't always know what he really believed, and his hyperactivity frequently took the form of covert aggression against society. 'It was the pleasantest thing in the world', he writes in his *Minutes of the Negotiations of Mons. Mesnager at the Court of England during the Four Last Years of the Reign of Her Late Majesty Queen Anne* (referred to in my discussion as the Mesnager *Minutes*), to witness the frenetic activity aroused in England's wartime allies by their alarm about rumours set off by Defoe himself for the ministry he was serving. And in an autobiographical passage in *Religious Courtship*, he describes the mischievous activity of a man who secretly distorted the meaning of pious books belonging to his wife by changing a word here and there. The method was similar to Defoe's own sly editorial practices as a political propagandist, and the motive he supplies for the man in *Religious Courtship* is a general contempt for virtue and a desire to make fools of his readers. Defoe's contemporaries resented this quality in him; they accused him of 'setting the nation by the ears', and Addison, who dismissed him as a rogue, had reason to know more about his political activities than did Swift, whose egotism led him to underestimate Defoe.[7]

The restlessness Defoe could never entirely control appears

even in the idyllic world of Robinson Crusoe, who no sooner succeeds, after immense effort, in barricading himself in against a potentially hostile environment than his domesticity starts to feel like imprisonment, and he begins making plans to escape from his fortress. H.F. of *A Journal of the Plague Year*, another ideal creation of Defoe's imagination, does the same thing, venturing out imprudently into a plague-ridden city from no material necessity, simply in search of life outside his fortress. Beyond the restlessness and fear of others that invade even the perfectly controlled ideal world of Robinson Crusoe are covert attacks in Defoe's other fictions and in his non-fiction on his naïve characters and on his readers. The attacks reveal that Defoe harboured a half-conscious, affectionate contempt for the straightforward, unimaginative, and stolid types he posited as models of proper conduct.

The real world that so attracted Defoe is characterized by compromise with all of the values represented by Crusoe. In fiction Moll Flanders figures as Defoe's 'real' self, in the sense that she is an outsider striving to get on in the real world. She is industrious and practical like Crusoe, but a great deal more impulsive and lively, good natured and unmalicious though not honest—she rationalizes away her unethical conduct. She enjoys the good things in life, nice clothes, money, a gentle-manly husband. Her religion is not deeply felt, and she is interested only intermittently in domestic arrangements. She is secretive, not didactic like Crusoe. Her diction may often be concrete, but her syntax is frequently more spontaneous and disorganized than Crusoe's. Above all, her narrative is marked by irony and innuendo. (We should note that Defoe was recognized by fellow journalists as a master of innuendo.) Although she eventually finds herself an acceptable niche among the middling classes, unlike Crusoe she does not become an absolute monarch, not even a materfamilias.

Above all, Moll differs from Crusoe in her exuberance about disguising herself and playing various roles. Like Defoe's Quaker William, the prosaic adventurer in *Captain Singleton*, Moll Flanders is a creation of the comic spirit, which stresses more 'the energy of impulse than . . . its evil'.[8] The comic spirit, delighting in its own energy and revelling in masquerade, occasionally losing control of its activities, was very much a side of Defoe, who got himself pilloried for impersonating a High-Flying Churchman in his *Shortest Way with the Dissenters*, and who described his activities as agent in Scotland to his employer, Robert Harley, with delight:

> Tho I will Not Answer for Success yet I Trust in Mannagemt you shall not be Uneasy at your Trusting me here. I have Compass't my First and Main step happily Enough, in That I am Perfectly Unsuspectd as Corresponding with anybody in England. I Converse with Presbyterian, Episcopall-Dissenter, papist and Non Juror, and I hope with Equall Circumspection. I flatter my Self you will have no Complaints of my Conduct. I have faithfull Emissaries in Every Company And I Talk to Everybody in Their Own way. To the Merchants I am about to Settle here in Trade, Building ships &c. With the Lawyers I Want to purchase a House and Land to bring my family & live Upon it (God knows where the Money is to pay for it). To day I am Goeing into Partnership with a Membr of parliamt in a Glass house, to morrow with Another in a Salt work. With the Glasgow Mutineers I am to be a fish Merchant, with the Aberdeen Men a woollen and with the Perth and western men a Linen Manufacturer, and still at the End of all Discourse the Union is the Essentiall and I am all to Every one that I may Gain some.[9]

How different this spirit is from the staid common sense of the Daniel Defoe recognized by the majority of readers can best be illustrated by contrasting this letter with a passage from his *Complete English Tradesman*, addressed to retail shopkeepers, where the voice we hear is the one most readers would immediately identify as Defoe's:

> Trade is not a ball, where people appear in mask, and act a part to make sport; where they strive to seem what they really are not, and to think themselves best dressed when they are least known. But 'tis a plain visible scene of honest life, shewn best in its native appearance, without disguise; supported by prudence and frugality; and like strong, stiff, clay land, grows fruitful only by good husbandry, culture and manuring it. (p. 117)

The voice in this passage expresses Defoe's nostalgia for an ideal world where everything is ordered and controlled. Paul Fussell explains that polite writers like Swift and Pope used images of buildings to suggest stability[10]; Defoe also used buildings, but he concentrated upon images of trade and agriculture because the plain and concrete objects that made up their stock and the numbers and figures in which these activities could be described suggested stability to him. Perhaps, too, the fundamental processes of trade and agriculture and the classes of people associated with them were associated in his mind with values absorbed in the course of his childhood.

In any case his own restlessness and the opportunities offered by the intensely political age in which he lived combined to catapult him into the lively yet sinful world of journalism and politics, in spite of his having been trained for the Presbyterian ministry. But frequent business and political misfortunes—repeated bankruptcies, his public pillorying in 1703, the active malice of enemies—and the shortcuts with principle he had taken in his accommodation with the real world must have exacerbated the doubts he himself seems to have harboured about both his moral rectitude and his failure to live up to the standards of his ideal world.

Accordingly, while life in the real world is frequently treated in a comic spirit in fictions such as *Moll Flanders* and in political hoaxes such as the Mesnager *Minutes*, at certain points in Defoe's writing a nightmare world of total depravity begins to impinge upon the real world of compromise. This happens occasionally in *Moll Flanders* and in didactic writings such as *Religious Courtship* and the 1718 *Family Instructor*. *Roxana*, a psychological novel in embryo, is the fiction most fully depicting Defoe's world of nightmare. Loss of control of self and of environment are the basic characteristics of this world, illustrated by a number of recurrent features. Luxury, even sensuality, reigns in an absence of purposeful activity by upper-class characters. Objects gain power over imaginations dominated by the emotions of fear and of guilt. Dreams and disembodied voices become prominent. Characters rebel against Protestantism or submit to Catholicism, renounce their domestic affections and obligations, or reject the Protestant succession in favour of the Stuarts. Characters depicted as complementary pairs in the ideal or real worlds are depicted as satanic doubles in the nightmare world. Language becomes characterized by abstract diction, and frequent recourse to ambiguous expressions serves to disguise instead of to reveal the motives and meanings of the speaker. The characters who people this ominous world are predominantly upper-class: members of the gentry and even the aristocracy.

In order to clarify my thesis of a Defoe divided between an ideal world of order and rational control and a real world of disorder and impulse, I have reconstructed two Defoes, a plain dealer and a sophisticated trickster, from his longest non-fiction work, the *Review*. The journal, which runs to twenty-two books and over 5,000 double-columned pages, was written over a period of nine very busy years, from 1704 to 1713. A compendium of most of Defoe's ideas, emotions, and styles, it is the one work in which this highly secretive man revealed at length the different sides of his personality.

In Chapter 1, I describe the characteristics of the plain-dealing Mr. Review's ideal world and touch upon some of the disturbances he encounters in this realm. Chapter 2, 'Trouble in Eden', is devoted to *A Journal of the Plague Year* and *Robinson Crusoe*, two fictions inspired by the perspective of the plain dealer. Here I concentrate upon the disturbances shown in Chapter 1. Chapter 3 returns to the *Review* in order to describe another side of Defoe; here I discuss the characteristics of the real world as perceived by the sophisticated and tricky alternate Mr. Review. Chapter 4, '*Moll Flanders* as Hoax', analyses that fiction as the creation of the worldly Daniel Defoe, not the plain-dealing Defoe who wrote *Robinson Crusoe*. Chapter 5 treats motifs from the real world of Mr. Review, masks and doubles, that appear in Defoe's fictions. Chapter 6 deals with the pivotal point between the real and nightmare worlds of Mr. Review, tracing in Defoe's fiction and non-fiction the process by which accommodation with imperfection, at first appearance funny, becomes increasingly frightening.

The purpose of this organization is to provide a context, not of Defoe's ideas, which have been admirably described by Maximillian E. Novak, G. A. Starr, and J. Paul Hunter,[11] but of his temperament, in order to help readers of the individual fictions to understand better Defoe's contradictions and ambiguities. His fictional imagination appears to have developed as he shaped historical, geographical, and economic facts to his own design, gave his characters objects to fashion or to manipulate, and endowed his narrators with imagined emotions. The reluctance to relax his grasp on objects and facts and to strike out boldly in a general design and the resort to mimicking the styles of other writers, are not surprising in a writer so gifted with empathy that he could easily enter other situations and psyches, yet so plagued by guilt, fear, and anger that he had to invent a fictional medium allowing him to conceal his unstable sense of self, fluctuating between nostalgia for an ideal controlled world of plain characters and fear of a nightmare uncontrolled world of satanic characters. Excited and attracted by the activities of the real world, versatile in interests, hyperactive, Defoe never stopped to analyse himself well enough to forge a viable compromise between his ideal and real selves, his ideal and real worlds. In addition, the public success of plain-dealing speakers in his non-fiction writing, not to mention the immediate popularity in 1719 of *Robinson Crusoe*, served to fix him in adherence to the Dissenting and lower middle-class values he had outgrown. As a result, he never succeeded in creating a fictional character who fully embodied both the devious and the direct sides of his own consciousness. This literary failure is what in my opinion has led one school of critics to under-estimate Defoe, dismissing him on the grounds of deficiency in understanding and in artistic seriousness, while a newer school, better acquainted with his non-fictional writing and more appropriately respectful of his intellectual abilities, has responded by over-emphasizing consistency of pattern in his fiction. The interpretations of both groups are based as much on preconceived notions of the author as they are on independent examination of his writing. In addition, they perpetuate a simplified picture of a solemn Defoe, divested of all the mercurial, playful, and unstable characteristics discerned by his best biographer, James Sutherland: humour, the incurable urge for excitement and adventure, the love of secrecy and mystification, the assumed innocence, the desire to *épater les bourgeois*, the penchant for bluff, and the restlessness.[12]

NOTES

1. *Twentieth Century Interpretations of 'Moll Flanders'*, ed. Robert C. Elliott (Englewood Cliffs, N.J.: Prentice-Hall, 1970), publisher's blurb on back cover.

2. Wayne Booth, *The Rhetoric of Fiction* (Chicago: University of Chicago Press, 9th impression, 1970), p. 320.

3. Jean Starobinski, *J.-J. Rousseau: La Transparence et l'obstacle* (n.p.: Gallimard, 1971), p. 285.

4. Cited by Justin Kaplan, 'The Naked Self and Other Problems', in *Telling Lives: The Biographer's Art*, ed. Marc Pachter (Washington, D.C.: New Republic Books, 1979), p. 46.

5. 1725, Letter III. All citations from Defoe's works that have neither been edited at all nor edited in the twentieth century are taken from first editions, unless otherwise indicated. I have modernized the texts of all these writings.

6. It was quoted in Parliament during the Sacheverell trial of 1709; more to the point, in 1705 Defoe explains that 'the publisher finds that the sale of the *Reviews* differs much from the common method of such public papers; and above one half of them are bought by gentlemen, that lay them up to bind together in volumes, many of the coffeehouses in town have them not at all, and the countries hardly see them; but gentlemen and men of reading collect them, and as for such they were designed, such will still approve it . . .' (3: Supplement II, 4–5, *Review*).

   Based on my collation of series of arguments of totally different levels of difficulty and style in the *Review*, I am accepting Defoe's assertion. Thus I differ from most scholars, who take it for granted that they hear one consistent speaker in the *Review*. See, for example, Marjorie Nicholson's introduction to *The Best of Defoe's Review*, ed. William L. Payne (New York: Columbia University Press, 1951). James Sutherland, aware of the upper-class readership of the journal, gentry and government officials, aware of the changes in Defoe's style according to his audience, nevertheless stresses as audience for the *Review* the poorer types of freeholders.

   Pat Rogers adumbrates an important direction for Defoe scholars when he discusses the question of audience. Speaking of the 1707 *Caledonia*, Rogers points out that its subscription list of eighty-four names includes thirty-three peers. He observes, 'Over a third of those listed figure in the *Dictionary of National Biography*, a higher proportion than Pope, Gay or Prior achieved with their sumptuous subscription volumes in the next two decades. If we were to judge Defoe's public by this example, we should be forced to conclude that he aimed for a special and localised audience on each occasion. Most of his writing, in fact, must have sought a wider base of support; but the evidence should warn us not to imagine that he was always preaching to a converted middle class' (p. 103, *Robinson Crusoe*, London: Allen & Unwin, 1979).

7. Addison worked closely with Arthur Maynwaring, who supervised the Whig press from 1710–12 and was closely concerned with it earlier. Maynwaring knew Defoe well enough to speak harshly of him in later

years, but in July 1710 he praised Defoe's *Review* highly in his *Four Letters to a Friend in North Britain*. See my *Versatile Defoe* (London: George Prior Publishers, 1979), pp. 128–29, for a discussion of the possibility that Defoe had tricked Maynwaring in the writing of *A Letter from a Gentleman at the Court of St. Germains*.

8. Martin Price, *To the Palace of Wisdom* (1964; rpt. Garden City, New York: Doubleday Anchor Books, 1965), p. 276.
9. *The Letters of Daniel Defoe*, ed. George Harris Healey (Oxford: Clarendon Press, 1955), pp. 158–59. Henceforth, citations from the *Letters* will appear within the text rather than in footnotes.
10. Paul Fussell, *The Rhetorical World of Augustan Humanism* (Oxford: Clarendon Press, 1965), p. 264.
11. J. Paul Hunter, *The Reluctant Pilgrim* (Baltimore: Johns Hopkins Press, 1966); Maximillian E. Novak, *Defoe and the Nature of Man* (London: Oxford University Press, 1963) and *Economics and the Fiction of Daniel Defoe* (Berkeley: University of California Press, 1962); G. A. Starr, *Defoe and Spiritual Autobiography* (Princeton: Princeton University Press, 1965) and *Defoe and Casuistry* (Princeton: Princeton University Press, 1971).
12. James Sutherland, *Defoe* (Philadelphia: J. B. Lippincott Co., 1938), pp. 45–6, 66, 125, 143, 149, and 157.

1

The Ideal World of the Plain Dealer

In December 1705, during an all-too-brief interlude of relative domestic peace between warring factions during the stormy reign of Queen Anne, Daniel Defoe, in the character of Mr. Review, describes the harmony among Crown, Lords, Commons, and people of England. He concludes that the country is now calm because all involved agree on pursuing one basic goal, the common good of the nation:

> To agree, is the effect of a rectitude of measures, and a rectitude of principle; for the first is seldom found without the last. Men generally take wide and eccentric steps in prosecuting secret dark designs, the ways of honesty are all laid out in straight direct lines, pointing fairly at their discovered end, *viz.* justice and truth.—
>
> There is no need of intrigue and cabal-party, and combination to carry them, it only wants that all men should pursue the same just end, and they would immediately concur in the means. Honest designs pursued with wise consultations, would direct all men the same way, there would be harmony in the proceedings, men would all go hand in hand, if their actions were right, and there wants nothing to make a universal peace in the world, but a general rectitude of principle; to have all men honest would be at once to make them all friends.
>
> 'Tis true, honest men may differ in the means, though they aim at the same end, but they would never differ, so as to destroy the end; whenever they discovered their mistake, they would rejoin their reason, and seeking only truth and right, they would of course come in to the general road of it at last,

18

and in the meantime there would be no fatal shocks, n(
destructive of the general interest wilfully practiced on
hand.

The conduct of the rest depends upon trick, sham, and
sharping. 'Tis all intrigue and artifice, the effects of human
policy; the lines are oblique, and of all sorts of indirect angles,
confused and concealed; their ways are full of darkness, and
tend to it in general.

From hence come division of councils, jarring of interests,
dissensions, wrath, strife, envyings, contention, and every evil
work.

I could enlarge on this subject, but think 'tis needless; the
substance of the whole is this, that the present harmony of the
government proceeds from, and is a very happy demonstration
of a clear regulated rectitude in both the motions and designs of
the whole, that the general good is singly at the bottom of all
their designs, for without that it would be impossible they could
so unanimously concur. (5:475–76)[1]

I have quoted the passage at length because of all Mr.
Review's descriptions of an ideal world, this is most explicit
about essentials; the general principle of the common good is
clear to and accepted by everybody, and such agreement
makes it easy to reconcile disputes about means of reaching
the goal. Furthermore, men of principle always do agree about
the common good; individual honesty automatically engenders
general peace and harmony. The image dominating Mr.
Review's description is linear; the map of the ideal world
consists of straight lines along which good men proceed
directly to truth and justice.

The opposite condition—private goals, diversified means of
reaching these goals, and self-interested and dishonest individuals—creates a maze of eccentric paths, oblique lines, and
indirect angles. Intrigue and artifice create a world of strife
and contention. In contrast to the clarity and simplicity of the
map of an ideal world, the confused labyrinth of evil is dark
and complex.

Details in harmony with this vision of heaven on earth can
be found in other descriptions by Mr. Review. They serve to
furnish his ideal realm; like those in the above passage, they
consist of generalized concepts provided by Mr. Review's own
vision and by his occasion as political polemicist: moderation, .

Christianity, Protestantism, constitutional monarchy, the Revolution, the Union between England and Scotland, subjection of military to civil authority, the rule of law, security of property, trade, tolerance, liberty, gratitude, and forgiveness (4:294; 6:147; 7:414–16; 8:455; 9:87; 10:324, 343; 14:11, 72; 15:366; 18:343–44; 19:158, 239; 22:100; and so forth).

He links the ideal world of clarity, directness, honesty, peace, and human community explicitly with the Protestant faith, with heaven, and with God, as he links the opposite world with the Devil. The continuation of the Union between England and Scotland is assured while a peaceable temper prevails in the nation: ' 'tis a divine preparation which is wrought in the minds of every nation and people whom Providence resolves to make mighty; everything that tends to breaches and contention, is of the Devil, and tends to mere confusion, the emblem, and in part the essence of that horrid place' (11:502). The Devil is 'the author of confusion'; he promotes 'all sorts of disorder in the world', whereas people who 'meet in the name of God, meet for peace, for he is the God of peace, of order, and of government in the world . . .' (21:662).

As readers have inferred from the endings of Defoe's fictions, where a virtuous Robinson Crusoe returns home while a vicious Roxana remains in exile, Defoe as Mr. Review regards England as an earthly paradise. When a citizen of another nation grows rich in a foreign country,

> he settles there, establishes his family, and his posterity become natives of that country, he is lost to his own country.—But if you speak of England, if any of her subjects grow rich abroad, whether in East or West Indies, Germany, France, Italy, or Spain, he always depends upon coming home to enjoy it, all their earthly heaven is there and then their native climate is sure to possess their wealth and their posterity are restored to their country. (10:402–3)

During the 1710–14 ministry of Robert Harley, later Earl of Oxford, civil dissension became more and more intense. As Mr. Review's vision of the ideal world came to appear less practicable, he began to express himself in images of circles and fences when he discussed the hotly debated questions of the Succession, the British Constitution, and the legal Toleration of Dissenters. The proliferation of circle and fence, or fortification imagery, at a time when the political values most cherished by Daniel Defoe were under their hottest attack is significant to consideration of *Robinson Crusoe* in Chapter 2, 'Trouble in Eden', for circles and fences are prominent in that fiction, which I regard as in part the dramatization of a successful struggle against the fear of others. Circles and fences in *Robinson Crusoe*, as in the *Review*, suggest an attempt to barricade oneself and one's values from attack.

When, to the dismay of Defoe, a law was passed forbidding Occasional Conformity to Dissenters who wished to hold public office, Mr. Review advised Dissenters to secure themselves against the world, to be careful not to make friends as easily as they had done in the past, when they allied themselves with the Whigs who then betrayed them on their cardinal issue. 'But I am for the Dissenters retiring to their safe entrenchments, fenced round by the laws of God and man, and retrieving the just character their fathers had, of conscientious, not politic Dissenters', he writes (21:695). The link between fences and retirement from the world is drawn explicitly by Mr. Review in the following passage, in which the description is similar to that of the fortification built by Robinson Crusoe:

> In their politic circumstances, as above, like a resolute garrison, the outworks and palisadoes of their fortification being taken, they retire within the body of the place, make coupres, retrenchments, and barricadoes within, as the last refuge, resolving to maintain themselves there, till relief comes, or the enemy, weakened by their furious and unskillful attacks, grow faint in their pushing on the siege, and then they sally out, and recover their outworks again.
>
> These retrenchments, and this last resort of the Dissenters, I call their religious concerns, and their forming themselves into a body, as Dissenters, enquiring what is their proper interest, as such, and pursuing it by the harmless, lawful, proper, and necessary means, which God, and the Constitution of the government they live under, gives them leave to make use of; if this will restore their circumstances, their character, their reputation, and the figure they formerly made in the world, then, if the Dissenting interest sinks, it is their own fault and their own neglect which is the cause. (21:710)

The ideal world associated in the *Review* with the reign of Defoe's cherished William III, is by the last book of the journal almost exclusively confined to the past. The Whigs of the good old days are not like the party Whigs of today (22:66, 172); foreign commerce has debauched itself by concentrating on luxury items (22:83–4); King William led a happy life before he encountered hellish factions in England (22:43). .

Yet in Book 22, Mr. Review still insists that the natural state of human emotions is calm, using an extended simile to describe the English:

> The people of this nation seem to me like the great ocean of waters; the original surface was smooth and fair; it was created calm and still; when the sun shines upon it in its native posture, it smiles again, and reflects back the rays of light with a brightness, and kind of pleasantness very delightful to behold. But its nature being fluid, its particles easily separated, the least aggression of wind puts it into motion.

He goes on to describe the disorder that ensues when winds blow hard and when the violence increases to a storm, concluding, 'And yet after all the fury of the waves, let but the winds abate, the storm cease, and a calm come on, the sea returns to its native beauty, bright and smooth as at first' (22:187).

In spite of the optimism of Mr. Review's final statement about the temper of his countrymen, Daniel Defoe probably believed privately that individual peace of mind was all one could reasonably hope for in the tumultuous England of his day: 'He that cannot live above the scorn of scoundrels, is not fit to live; dogs will bark, malice will rage, slander will revile— and they shall; without lessening one moment of my tranquillity' (15:341–42). The emphasis in *Serious Reflections during the Life and Surprising Adventures of Robinson Crusoe* would indicate that such was the case, judging from the first essay, 'On Solitude', where Defoe describes the ideal state of mind, explaining, 'The business is to get a retired soul, a frame of mind truly elevated above the world' (p. 9), and asserts that 'next to good company, no company is best' (p. 11). He defines good company as 'religious and good men' (11),[2] which would suggest a very limited approval of society in general.

The Ideal World of the Plain Dealer

Even as early as the fourth book of the *Review*, the language of the usually optimistic Mr. Review suggests that he may sense that peace in life is as closely connected with death as it is with religion. Heaven is not to be found in this world; the cessation of conflict and the clear and accurate perception of truth is reserved for those who are looking into eternity:

> I believe nothing would contribute more to making us good Christians, than to be able to look upon all things, causes and persons here, with the same eyes as we do when we are just looking into eternity. Death sets all in a clear light, and when a man is, as it were in the very boat, pushing off from the shore of the world, his last views of it being abstracted from interests, hopes, or wishes, and influenced by the near view of the future state, must be clear, unbiassed, and impartial. . . .
>
> To quarrel among ourselves, has always the same unreasonableness, and tends to the same ruin and destruction; the difference only lies in this, that while we put the evil day far from us, we do not see the necessity of union with the same eyes.
>
> Now as realizing these mischiefs would make a true representation of the sordid, unreasonable humour of private dissension, and party strife among us, so, though the disasters were never to come, the discovery would have this use, that strife and ill nature would be represented in their native colours; we should see the easiness of public agreement, *and the necessity too*, for the business would be *not to form a thing that was not*, but to remove the clouds and mists from a thing *that is*, that it might be represented in its own shape, and that the beauty of peace being shown, *joined to the necessity of it*, all men might be in love with the picture, and sincerely join in the practice. (4:201–2)

Truth as Foundation of the Ideal World

To readers who identify Daniel Defoe with Robinson Crusoe and regard him as a plain-dealing and plain-speaking individual with a simplistic notion of the world, it will come as no surprise that 'truth' is referred to in the *Review* as if it were a concrete object. Defoe uses the word 'foundation' in alluding both to truth in general and to the particular gamut of 'truths' he espouses—the English Constitution, the Union between England and Scotland, the legal Toleration of Dissenters, and so forth.

For Mr. Review truth is self-evident and unchangeable; it always 'upholds itself' or prevails against error. Mr. Review's task is merely to set it in a clear light, opening eyes blinded by fine words or unruly emotions, to describe, explain, and defend it. The ultimate aim of the ingenuous Mr. Review is very modest: to 'put plain things in a plain form, that a clear view may undeceive the people, and we may come all to understand the matter in the same way' (19:199).

Describing or Demonstrating Truth by Citing Proofs

Yet in spite of Mr. Review's loud iterations of faith in the irresistible power of truth, the plain-dealing journalist is compelled to cite ever more indisputable proofs and to devise ever more irrefutable arguments to make it prevail. Many of his proofs are familiar to readers of Defoe's fiction—objects, money, actions, facial expressions, gestures—all the specific, preferably tangible things associated with the realistic, non-emotional style of the Defoe of fiction. As Mr. Review points out in the very first book of his journal, he is not interested in motives or 'secret reasons' for political actions, because they are 'not visible enough for me to treat of, and for speaking by guess, 'tis not my custom, especially in this book, which I pretend to call a history' (1:118). Since he is writing as a historian, he cannot be certain about the motives of political figures and will depend for his analyses on the external evidence of their actions. At a later date (May 1708) he again stresses his preference for historical or factual evidence when he eschews literary inventiveness in describing the High-Flyers of the Church of England: 'I could answer . . . by giving a Character of a High-Flyer; I could dress him up à la Scaramouche, put the cap upon his head, and paint the Devil upon it to make him look frightful . . .' (12:101). Instead, he chooses to portray them not only with the accuracy of history, but with its dignity and gravity, recounting 'a little of the men in a more serious view of their past and present conduct . . .' (12:101).

Truth is demonstrated by two kinds of objective proof, tangible and abstract. The latter kind of proof—historical, economic, and geographical facts, written sources of information, quoted or paraphrased accurately, on-the-spot reports, Biblical statements—is as much used in the *Review* as are objects and quantities of money. Mr. Review tends to use tangibles when addressing less educated readers, abstract proofs when addressing more educated readers.

The difference between proving with facts and proving with objects comes up often in the *Review*. In one striking instance Mr. Review points out that the benefit of the Duke of Marlborough's victories over the French, so difficult to prove to the educated, does not need to be demonstrated by fact to the uneducated, even those in the hinterlands of England:

> I know no better way to speak to the common understandings of the people, than to come home to their own doors, and let every man feel the effects of the victory in his pocket. There's not a poor country clothier in those parts, but can tell you there is something happened abroad, that has made them a brave trade; he does not know what it is, but this he knows, that his cloth sells well. . . . (8:479)

Defending Truth by Argument: Deduction from Facts

But the aid of factual or concrete proofs to demonstration proved insufficient to establish truth in spite of Mr. Review's confidence: 'There wants nothing to set these people to rights in this affair, but a little history, narration of fact, and fair stating things; and when this is done . . . none, that will open their eyes, and let in demonstrations, can be any longer blind' (13:441). Defoe as journalist was obliged continually to explain and defend the self-evident, and for this purpose repeatedly set forth his principles of correct reasoning.

As his emphasis upon concrete proofs would suggest, Mr. Review was opposed to arguments that started from abstract premises. In the January supplement to Book 3 of the *Review*, disagreeing with a letter he has received, he writes, 'As for the mathematical or philosophical account given in this letter of the machine of the sensitive body and life, 'tis owned, 'tis finespun by Schoolmen's art, but seems very empty of demonstrations, and little more than the collection of words into mathematical order' (3:26–7).

Frequently he aims at first establishing factual truths and

deducing his arguments from these facts by means of common sense, judgements of self-interest, reasonable probabilities, history, experience, Scripture, and so forth. He refers to this process of arriving at conclusions that seem self-evident as 'natural reasoning, agreeable to our constant opinion' (4:146) or 'general received notion' (21:607).

Analysis of specific issues rather than synthesis of many issues into one argument is the hallmark of reasoning in the ideal world of Mr. Review: 'Generally all our mistakes in argument . . . arise from a want of distinguishing right of the subject we are upon', he writes (6:57). Accordingly, in the controversy between Whigs and Tories over the commercial agreements of the Treaty of Utrecht opening up trade with France, Mr. Review rejects discussing party principles and instead proceeds directly to considerations of economic benefit: 'In my last I stated the first principle of all argument in the affair of a trade with France, (*viz*), Is it worthwhile for us to open a trade to France, or is it not? Will the French trade be a market for our manufactures, or will it not?' (22:197). The twenty-two books of the *Review* are filled with examples of his clarity and incisiveness in defining a subject and breaking it down for discussion.

Mr. Review is convinced that most important questions are clear in their essentials, with only the lesser side issues doubtful, a conviction also illustrated by Robinson Crusoe's discussions of the essential elements of Protestantism, and by similar discussions in Defoe's 1715 and 1718 *Family Instructors*.

The dislike of scholastic argumentation, the emphasis upon empirical premises and common-sense reasoning, along with the power in analysis will seem obvious to readers of *Robinson Crusoe*. In a passage on political emissaries Mr. Review deprecates the opposite type of reasoning from his own, the 'placing things to be looked at obliquely'. He deplores the subordination of fact to party policy, the praising of actions without intrinsic merit, and the distortion and exaggeration of arguments. The design in that kind of reasoning is to deceive rather than to illuminate the truth. As we will see in Chapter 3, oblique reasoning is embraced with gusto by the worldly Mr. Review, less familiar to readers than his plain-dealing brother, and it is common in Defoe's fictions, where characters frequently place 'things to be looked at obliquely, not directly, that shadows may deceive your sight, and misrepresentations may state actions, not as they are, but as they would have them be . . .' (11:586).

The final significant characteristic in reasoning of the plain-dealing Mr. Review is his emphasis upon distinguishing between generals and particulars. In discussing the concepts of truth and liberty, for instance, he remarks, 'I confess, these are great words and as all generals are liable to different explications, so it seems to remain here for me to examine, and indeed to determine, what I mean by Truth and Liberty, or in short to explain the terms' (10:457). Mr. Review's scrupulousness about the distinction permits him a certain optimism about avoiding the fate of John Tutchin, who was beaten to death in retaliation for what he had written. Mr. Review explains he has

> never run into such extremes of personal insults, as some men have done; I assault crimes, not persons, I reprove vice, oppose tyranny, and condemn parties; but I do not call men rogue and rascal *by name*, just as if on purpose to provoke men beyond the government of their own passions; if I did this, I might expect the worst. (12:183, my italics)

Judges of Truth

Confident that he has faithfully described, explained, and defended truth, Mr. Review anticipates its easy reception in an ideal world. In the first book of the *Review* he declares his readiness 'to submit [his] remarks to any impartial judge' (1:84).

On matters of trade in particular, writing to an audience that understands the subject, Mr. Review speaks with great self-assurance. His appeal to the less educated, as we have seen above, is marked by the appearance of concrete objects, in this case bodily parts:

> Were my head, if cut off, of any use to the state, or were it good for anything where it is, I would gage it to a meaner trifle, if that could be found, that I would make out all the following particulars to be true, in relation to the present state of our English trade; and I appeal to the whole nation; I appeal to the Parliament; nay, I'll appeal yet higher. (2:346)

27

Aware that an audience more interested in being pleased than being instructed is catered to by some rival journalists, Mr. Review nevertheless continues to appeal to the impartial. This remains so whether he is discussing a simple or a complicated subject and whether he is addressing more or less educated readers.[3] When the subject is constitutional rights, he envisions the House of Commons as a God-like judge of a right cause, fortified against partiality, the 'sanctuary of British privileges' (16:478), and he compliments the House by comparing actions God cannot take because they are inconsistent with his Being with those the House cannot take for the same reason (16:486).

Effective Action in the Ideal World

In the end, however, proper methods of deductive reasoning based, wherever possible, on factual premises, and addressed to the impartial, are insufficient to fortify oneself in the ideal world of the plain dealer. Control of emotion, mental alertness, and effective action are essential to the attainment of this ideal state of life. The plain-dealing Mr. Review has much to say about these matters, and what he says is directly relevant to the conduct of Defoe's protagonists in *Robinson Crusoe* and *A Journal of the Plague Year*, and intermittently true of characters in the other fictions.

On the larger scene, periods of hysteria and violent agitation alternate cyclically with periods of apathy in the nation at large. During these periods it is impossible for the rare person who remains in control of himself to stem the tide (17:21). As we will see in Chapter 2, these two general emotions are the poles between which Robinson Crusoe and the characters in *A Journal in the Plague Year* alternate, with Crusoe restlessness and apathy, with characters in the *Journal* desperation and 'Mahometan predestination'.

The pragmatic Mr. Review himself has not always been immune to emotional storms. He speaks from his '*own unhappy experience* . . . in the rolling of the passions, the boiling of the blood, the furious agitation of the animal spirits'. In this case he is referring to a third emotion to which he is vulnerable, the emotion of anger: '. . . if conscience presumes to give a pinch in the dark, or put in a word, *the inflamed organ* answers, come what will, I cannot go back, I cannot live. . . . I cannot bear it, I cannot help it . . .' (22:68).

Nevertheless, emotion must be controlled, particularly the emotions most threatening to Mr. Review, those of restlessness and of dejection. 'What evils do men undergo, by the slavery they are in to their passions?' he asks.

> I have not more contemptible thoughts of a dog, a bear, or any brute, than I have of a man, whom I see easy to be provoked, or soon dejected; those two things render a man perfectly un-capable of managing himself, either in prosperity or adversity. In the first he runs out to all the excesses of a tyrant, and commits the most extravagant things in the world; in the last, he is the most soulless, dispirited thing in the world, and is fit for nothing but to despair, or perhaps, at last, die for fear of death. (21:722)

Any object or interest that tempts a person into excess, Mr. Review despises so heartily that he classifies it as one's whore (22:213). One cause of his disgust is that excessive love provides a handle by which others can manipulate a foolish idolator. Mr. Review expresses his disgust in a Swiftian image: 'You may even . . . see, how you are used in the world, and who underhand, screws and works you up, as if you were mere engines or machines, and makes you subserve to their vile projects . . .' (15:413). Calling for an appropriate antidote in the form of the machine described in Defoe's 1705 *Consolidator*, Mr. Review explains: ' 'Tis an engine composed of abundance of curious parts, and is properly employed to *screw a man into himself*, that is, to reduce his wandering delirious head to sedate and regular thinking' (9:94, my italics). The violence of the consolidator's action is appropriate to express the anger that lies hidden under the plain-dealing Mr. Review's ostensibly dispassionate calls to right reason. While he claims to be simply restoring the misguided to truth and impartiality, the method by which he proposes returning to the direct lines of his map of the ideal world is by no means gentle.

Excessive emotion, says Mr. Review, leads others to mis-prize the intrinsic or true value of events, objects, and people, as in the cases of victory and defeat in war, stocks, or statesmen. In addition, excessive emotion is counterproductive in reaching any goal desired by an individual. Mr. Review never tires of using the example of James II's failure to restore Roman Catholicism in England because the king could not content himself to do it gradually, so that 'time would have brought that to pass, which impatience and immoderate councils, ruined and prevented' (4:287). Excessive emotion in others is equally destructive of their goals. ' 'Tis the subtle, smiling, wheedling, cautious enemy that is the dangerous enemy', warns Mr. Review, for 'the furious, hasty, precipitant enemy always splits himself upon the rocks of his own passion, and throws his cause down the precipice of his own rage' (16:515).

He offers some cures for emotionality. One is moderation in judging others, since overestimation terrifies us into despair and under-estimation exalts us in conceit (1:25–26). Another is preparing oneself in advance for all contingencies (10:332). A third is trying to see wholes, analysing them into parts, and comparing the parts with each other, instead of jumping to gloomy conclusions on the basis of one insight (5:461). A fourth remedy is using one's reason to direct the imagination, so as to block out an undesirable fancy with a desirable one. Here he uses the example of a man whose religious devotions are distracted by visions of his mistress. Mr. Review advises the man to think about death while praying in order to forget his mistress (5:26, *Little Review*).[4] Above all, Mr. Review disapproves of crying over spilt milk (10:395).

Most of the time, however, Mr. Review is less interested in offering remedies than in castigating overly emotional opponents, usually with an arrogance and contempt that must have seemed insufferable to his enemies, especially when they were on the losing side, as in the case of the High-Flyers, who lost the election of 1705. About these he wrote: 'I would advise them to furnish themselves with a good *stock of patience*, that when the disappointments they must most certainly meet with in this case shall come, they may not fly out into any fatal excesses against themselves; such *as hanging themselves*, or the like unnatural violences' (5:362).

If excessive emotion, especially anger or despair, is the most important impediment to clear reasoning in the world of the plain-dealing Mr. Review, lack of alertness is also a danger to be guarded against. 'If you sleep, Gentlemen,' warns the journalist assure yourselves the other gentlemen do not; if you are secure of your peace, and think yourselves safe, that your point is gained, and the danger is over, I pretend to assure you, the other people do not think so; I therefore cannot but think, that as 'tis their maxim never to despair, it ought to be the maxim of every English Protestant, to be ever on his guard for his country's good. (6:210)

Throughout the *Review*, lack of alertness is identified with sloth, dozing, lethargy, sleep, and dreaming. Those who promote this state are accused of employing the sinister arts of magic. England as well as the rest of Europe has supinely dozed in the face of the French menace (8:454; 14:15, 19, 38, 71). In domestic elections voters are plied with liquor by contending candidates for the purpose of stupefying their senses. The pernicious doctrines of non-resistance to tyranny and of the divine right of kings gained currency in England during the reigns of Charles II and James II because 'from the Restoration to the Revolution, [the people had] been wheedled and chimed into a lethargic state slumber, they had swallowed the gilded pill, they had been charmed with Court syrens—till they were brought into bonds' (16:445–46). Dissenters are asleep to the danger of an impending bill to prevent Occasional Conformity: 'Whence is this opiate? How are we dozed? Who has cast this charm or tied this philter? Are we awake, or has Heaven demented this generation, that they should not see when His judgments impend?' (20:475).

The emotions most deplored by Mr. Review seem to have been restlessness (in the form of violent agitation), despair, and anger. One judges from comments in the *Review* that a combination of repression and appropriate activity was Defoe's prescription for controlling these emotions. Different kinds of activity are recommended; decisive action where possible, but, in most cases, slow and patient work.

Decisive short-term action is advocated or praised in the *Review* in cases where it is practicable, for instance in Louis XIV's strict measures to eliminate duelling, in suggestions for eliminating play-acting or gaming booths at Bartholomew Fair, for dealing with the growing menace of a pirates' nest at Madagascar, for using conscription to raise a larger army, and for deciding whether or not to continue the war with

31

France. The plain-dealing Mr. Review expresses perhaps his most typical no-nonsense attitude in the case of the Mohock gangs ranging the streets of London in March 1712. His prescription is simple: rather than the angelic moralizing of the *Spectator*, the application of a Protestant flail (21:614).

One of the anecdotes that seems best to suit the personality of the plain-dealing Mr. Review is about a Civil War general who, in spite of unfavourable odds, stoutly advises fighting:

> And now I am talking of fighting and praying, it puts me in mind of an old soldier, I think it was Major General Skippon, in the Civil Wars here, when King Charles I had couped up the army of the Parliament in the West, and the generals made a most dishonourable escape by sea, and left the army to surrender at discretion; when at a council of war it was proposed to do so, the old Major General, who commanded the infantry, refused to leave his charge, but would take part and share with the soldiers, and exclaimed against Essex and others, that were for going away.
>
> Why what would you have us do? said some of the Generals— Do, says the old lad! Do like Christians and Englishmen, pray well and fight well, and I'll warrant, says he, we break through them—the old man was for charging through and through, and fighting his way out, but he was for praying to God at the same time. (10:251)

When Defoe reworks the same anecdote years later in *Captain Singleton*, he gives it an ironic twist that makes it more appropriate to the outlook of the worldly Mr. Review we will meet in Chapter 3: 'Brave old *Skippon* proposed to fight through with the Foot and die, as he called it, like *English* Men, with Sword in Hand; but the rest of the Officers shook their Heads at it; for, being well paid, they had at present no Occasion for dying' (p. 222).

In most cases of action decisive measures are impractical, and Mr. Review advocates prudence, patience, and slow, often discouraging work. 'The Shortest Way', the title of the ill-fated pamphlet that earned Defoe pillorying and jail in 1703, is a phrase used frequently, usually in a contemptuous tone, in the *Review* (i.e., 3:411; 9:57; 10:383, 440; 11:686; Supp. 518 and 94–5; 14:151). Mr. Review knows from experience that the shortest way is often the worst way to get anything done, but men of much haste and little experience advocate it as a panacea for every kind of political, economic, or social problem.

Co-operating with the times is important in getting things done. After English credit has been restored, in spite of the efforts of some to destroy it, Mr. Review refers to useless attempts to struggle against the tide (19:61), an image Defoe used in *Robinson Crusoe* in describing the protagonist's struggle to get to shore and his co-ordination of his own efforts with the shoreward flow of the waves. Co-operating with others is as important as co-operating with nature, Providence, or the times. Writing to Whigs after a Tory victory, Mr. Review asserts,

> The thing is plain, we are all in a bottom; though I don't like the crew, I won't sink the ship, though I think I am wronged, or injured, I'll rather be oppressed, than have all drowned; I'll do my best to save the ship; I'll pump, and heave, and haul, and do anything I can, though he that pulls with me were my enemy; the reason is plain, *We are all in the ship*, and must sink and swim together. (17:240)

Ethics in the Ideal World: Principles and Practice

In questions of ethics, the plain-dealing Mr. Review is concerned above all with the congruity between professed principle and actual practice. His basic position is stated in Book 4 of the *Review*:

> Honest designs are carried on by honest methods; they that mean fairly, act fairly, and there is always something of sympathy between the means and the end.
>
> Trick, cheat, violence, drunkenness, bribery, and all sorts of villainy, are seldom made use of to bring to pass just designs, but the nature of the business has, generally speaking, something of it seen and explained in the introduction: the purpose and the practice are adequate. The Spaniards say, he that goes to rob a house, never goes out of his way to church; the people that have no design to do well, seldom pursue that vicious end, by virtuous and honourable methods. . . . (176)

Quite simply, good principles are manifested by 'virtuous and honourable methods', bad principles by trickery or violence. Mr. Review explains more specifically on a later occasion that 'virtuous and honourable methods' include 'legal designs' and 'moderate proposals', whereas bad principles include 'dangerous experiments, furious, illegal, and exotic methods' (5:370).

Defoe's interest in Quakers (William Walters in *Captain Singleton*, the Quaker landlady in *Roxana*, and several non-fiction pamphlets in the Quaker dialect) is explained by Mr. Review's admiration for their practice: '. . . they have, generally speaking, stuck closer to their professed principles than most, if not than any sort of people among us; you get men off from them to other persuasions with more difficulty; nor if a man be proselyted from them, is he easily or often brought to fly in the face of his former principles . . .' (12:132).

If people must differ with him, Mr. Review prefers an open opponent to a disguised one. In his mind 'a man that professes bad principles is better than he that covers bad principles with a mask of virtue' (21:779). He proclaims again and again that open non-jurors and Papists are superior to Jacobites who have taken the oath abjuring the Stuarts (8:487, 12:305, 13:355). In fact, he claims he would not 'disturb or disrespect any man for his firm adherence to his principle, let it be what it will' (14:69). His tolerance goes so far that he is willing to admit and sometimes to extol honesty of practice in those whose principles he dislikes, in an Irishman, even in a Turk (12:310).

Disguised opponents, however, he cannot abide. Oath-taking Jacobites are scorned and abhorred by 'the down-right honest Jacobites', for their practice is 'all doubling with God and man'. These traitors and hypocrites are 'double-tongued, side-shifting, underhand-acting knaves' (16:514). 'Ambo-dexters' or those who say one thing and act another are not permitted in the ideal world of Mr. Review: 'They are a sort of people nobody can defend, nobody can excuse, nobody can plead for' (16:459). Shapelessness and indefinability are attributes of these people. A High-Flyer 'is a man whose character is neither to be found in his pretensions, or in his practice; you can gather no definition of him, either from what he is, or from what he seems' (18:429). In sum, the inconsistency of saying one thing and doing another is regarded as downright diabolical by Mr. Review: '. . . the fraud is capital,

34

indeed it is the superlative of hypocrisy and dissimulation, it is in its nature so black, that nothing can be worse, the nature of man is not capable of a crime more hellish, nor has the Devil a clan in the world so like himself . . .' (18:422).

Personality: The Emphatic Plain Speaker

Frequently attacked for causing dissension while claiming to be simply exposing the truth, Mr. Review was forced to justify his journalistic practices. In July 1710, just before the ministerial revolution that returned Harley and the Tories to power, Mr. Review was warning that the rumoured dissolution of Parliament was designed to further the notions of hereditary right and non-resistance to the Crown and to repeal the toleration of Dissenters. To a complaint about this incendiary argument and the words in which he has couched it, Mr. Review replies that his is the best way to open the eyes of the common people of England and accuses the complainer of speaking so politely and temporizing so long, that the nation is now in a state of acute danger. He goes on to defend his plain style as the only effective method of opening the eyes of the common people:

> If these things require similes and allusions, to explain them to the people; if a dark way of ambiguous doubtful speaking, will open the poor people's eyes, *I am not your man*, gentlemen, you must turn another way.—When this paper ceases to speak *plain English*, and *apply it home* to the very persons, you may conclude this author has laid it down. (17:191–92)

Mr. Review's emphatic manner is the result of his attempt to touch the senses of his readers. As we have seen, he draws a distinction between demonstrating truth by citing facts and naming objects and defending truth by argumentation. The former method is surer, not only because facts are irrefutable, but because demonstration appeals to the senses and thus has a more powerful impact than appeals to reason.

In spite of its being clear, from the variety of styles and levels of argument, that the *Review* was addressed to different social classes, depending upon the topic under discussion, the Mr. Review of the ideal world professes to favour plain folks.

His 5 June 1707 issue is an important pronouncement on the question of readership. Speaking about the disputes over the Union in Scotland, he explains that those who complain that it is being violated belong to two different categories. In the first category are knaves. The second category, much less clever, consists of honest people who are made tools of by knaves; they are the 'gunpowder', the knaves are the 'fire' (9:199). Mr Review asserts:

> For my part, I value the instructing and informing one honest meaning ignorant person, more than the detecting and confronting a thousand knaves, and 'tis for the sake of these I write; for their sakes I dwell upon a subject sometimes longer than the rules of language allow, for their sakes I repeat and repeat, and quote myself over and over, and can with ease bear the foolish banters of the envious critic and reproacher; I had rather say the same thing over twenty times, than once omit, what may this way be useful.
>
> I am, *without vanity*, neither ignorant of the rules of writing, nor barren of invention, that sometimes I repeat and quote what I have formerly said, which I know, those, *this paper reaches*, never saw; 'tis for their sakes I bear the reproach of the scurrilous, who upbraid me with printing in this paper, what I had in other pieces printed before; thousands see this, that never saw the other, and what is it to them that it has been said before; do not our ministers preach the same sermons to different auditories? If it does good here, 'tis not the worse for having been thought of before, let the railers rail on. (9:199)

Preferring to instruct 'honest meaning ignorant person[s]' rather than to detect knaves implies more than a choice among temperaments. In effect, the plain-dealing Mr. Review is seeking a less educated readership and thus a reader of lower social class than the knaves; at the same time he is opting for a strongly didactic rhetoric. Accordingly, when he lectures tradesmen, Scottish Presbyterians, citizens of London, Dissenters, or simple country people, his voice sounds like the familiar voice of Robinson Crusoe, so often equated with the voice of Daniel Defoe.

When he argues in favour of a new law against treason for Scotland, for instance, Mr. Review reasons slowly for the benefit of slow minds:

Now there may be disadvantages which such may come under by this law, *which before they were free from.*—And at the same time there are advantages which they will reap by this law, *which they* had not before.—It remains then to set these one against another, draw a fair balance between them, and see, whether really the people in Scotland are losers or gainers by this law.—And this, I conceive, is the directest method to end the dispute.— (14:86)

He goes on to draw up an actual balance sheet of advantages and disadvantages, making his argument graphically clear (14:95).

Turning from the difficult subject of credit, where he was addressing an educated audience, to the less difficult and more concrete question of settling the Palatine refugees in England, and addressing himself, presumably, to Dissenting tradesmen at first, he remarks, 'Before I enter upon the discourse of these, I shall explain them more particularly, that I may make everything clear as I go; my study being to speak in the things, the meanest people are employed about, so as I may be understood by the meanest capacity' (14:135). When he asks for charity to the Palatines, Mr. Review probably means also to address country people below the level of the gentry, perhaps small farmers and yeomen, if we may judge from the humble products he names in quantities of one when he reports on Palatines settled in country areas. He asserts that 'people live round them as secure, as if there were no such folks there; not an apple or pear out of their orchards, nor a hen or a chicken lost, that I can possibly hear of' (15:216).

Speaking to citizens of London, who understand and remember what they know from their own experience, not what they have read in books, Mr. Review points out that this is why he avoids historical allusions:

> I could give you similes, and allegories to represent the case to you, and read you long lectures upon the Roman affairs under the government of their consuls and tribunes; from which you might see readily what I mean, and might make application to yourselves—But I have chosen a downright plainness, and to speak home both in fact and in style: a method, *however less safe to myself*, yet more generally instructing and clear to the understanding of the people I am speaking to.

> Nor is our present times without examples, from whence to
> fetch our instruction, as well as the ages of the Roman or
> Grecian government—from which examples a man may speak
> more directly to the understandings of our readers, and may bid
> the citizen of London rather remember what they have seen,
> than what they have read. (17:149) (My italics)

In addition to driving his instruction home my demonstration, and resorting to proofs that attack the senses of the
ignorant, Mr. Review counts upon anecdotes (10:325–26) and
repetition (18:589) to clarify his message to his readers.
Finally, he takes great care to furnish background information
wherever necessary for understanding.

The emphatic tone of the plain-dealing Mr. Review, then,
arises naturally from his journalistic mission to make truth
prevail. He projects so strong a personality in his writing because
he claims to prefer honest, ignorant, and simple people as readers
and therefore must resort to relatively heavy-handed tactics in
order to touch their senses and to make ideas explicit for them.

The servant of univocal truths addressing himself to simple
and honest readers must not only be emphatic; he must also be
sincere.[5] His allegiance is solely to truth of fact and to calm
reasoning; he is always prepared to show to any inquirer
authorities and proofs for what he has written in the *Review*. He
always signs his name to his works, and anything he writes in
the future will 'have his hand fairly set to it, that everybody may
know it' (2:179). Finally, he never writes or will write against
his principles.

Above all, Mr. Review feels strongly about the writing style
appropriate to the plain dealer who eschews fiction as forgery
and falsity, allied with the devil. 'Does not every forgery and
falsity undermine the honour, the character, and the interest of
the party that makes use of them?' he asks. Declaring his
allegiance to truth over fiction, he writes:

> Truth is the glorious support of itself, and relating it, is an
> honour, not to him that makes it public only, but to the cause it
> relates to. . . . The business is, to let the world see the truth, and
> it leads them by consequence to reproach the contrivers of the
> sham, as a people who have no other way to keep their cause
> alive, but by the assistance of the Devil, and the mean resort of
> fiction and forgery. (20:426)

Further analysis of the style of Mr. Review follows in the next section. It is sufficient to note here that Mr. Review proclaims repeatedly that he esteems 'plainness to be the perfection of language, and being explicit, the true design of Providence in giving men a voice and words to speak by'. He dismisses a non-colloquial or learned style as affectation, asserting, '. . . he that studies to speak deeply, studies, and takes a great deal of pains to do just nothing, and as Job says, darkens counsel by words without knowledge' (18:589). Indeed, his tone is self-congratulatory when he proclaims himself a plain, blunt fellow (19:221), always decent, of course, never reviling enemies, but never a flatterer (17:258, 18:477).

The unadorned style he affects, like the congruity in ethics between honest means and ends, is appropriate to the character of the sincere plain dealer. As G. A. Starr points out, opposition to the tradition of rhetoric rested on the same grounds as opposition to casuistry: 'to be good . . . one's words and actions alike should be spontaneous and uniform, not calculated and variable.'[6] Mr. Review makes his moral superiority clear when attacking stock jobbing: 'I profess to be a plain dealer, I shall never cover such practices with fine names' (14:203). The idea of using fine language to disguise devious aims sometimes causes him to deprecate in theory even the use of similes and allusions, which in practice he is free in using, as a dark, ambiguous, doubtful way of speaking.

Near the end of the life of the *Review*, during the turbulent ministry of Robert Harley, Earl of Oxford, he was sorry to acknowledge that peace and Christian love were marked mainly by their absence from England. As a result, Mr. Review found himself isolated, with only truth and the general good as his supports. The boundaries of his ideal world, as we have seen before in this chapter, had become constricted to one person, and that person alone remained unchanged amidst general strife:

> He that writes against the sense of two potent, contending, and violent parties, is likely to be censured by both, and certain to be crushed by one.—As I thank God I have never written for any party yet, so I find myself almost writing against every party now; and doubt not I may be a sacrifice to both, or at least to the fury of that which shall prevail, let it be which it will.

But while I am convinced I am writing for the general good, and upon a right foundation of truth, *that truth and I against you all,* let the venture be what it will; though Whig and Tory are both against me, I am the same, and so I hope to remain. (20:449)

Style

Some of the stylistic characteristics of the plain-speaking Mr. Review have already been discussed in this chapter: his predilection for facts in general and for tangibles like objects and bodily parts. These and other characteristics are discussed by James Boulton in the excellent introduction to his anthology, *Daniel Defoe.*[7] Accepting Defoe's assertions, in the Baconian tradition, that language ought to be strictly functional, Boulton explains Defoe's plainness as appropriate to this tradition, to the desire to instruct ordinary men in daily life, and to the morality of honesty and sincerity, or plain dealing. He discusses Defoe as a popular writer, referring to his robust, sometimes vulgar, expressions, his colloquialism, his delight in speech mannerisms, his penchant for dramatization, his interest in human behaviour and in the world of things. Boulton lists many of Defoe's popular literary devices— the aphorism, the fact, the figure, technical terminology—as well as his formal stylistic devices—antithesis, apostrophe, and rhetorical question. On imagery he points out that in fiction and non-fiction Defoe drew on the world of 'natural phenomena or commonplace activities, from, in other words, that everyday existence which is at once the source and the test of proverbial wisdom' (p. 14). The images Defoe relied on came from trade, agriculture, war, the sea, the Bible, and proverbs.

It would be redundant to supply examples from the *Review* to support Boulton's summary of Defoe's style, especially since I shall be arguing that Defoe himself did not have an identifiable style, but that out of his many styles the plain-speaking Mr. Review's, which Boulton among many other scholars equates with Defoe's, became the most successful. For my purpose, therefore, probably the most significant characteristic of the plain dealer is his diction. When we consider this diction from the perspective of Defoe's intellectual interest in generals and particulars, the technical problem that most occupied him seems to have been the fine discriminations in wording one can make, from the most general to the most particular term. Defoe's agility in this matter was one of the secrets of his great ability as a polemicist and why the plain-speaking Mr. Review came to be regarded by contemporaries as a fake. Juggling generals and particulars, Defoe—and Mr. Review himself—managed to conceal innuendoes and reservations, and to argue for or against any issue under discussion at any particular moment. This was certainly the case in successive definitions offered in the *Review* of the term 'just and honourable peace', when peace negotiations with France were in progress, as it was with many other definitions.

Presenting himself as a man of simple certainties, Mr. Review confines his didactic activity with diction to translating general words or notions into specific ones, denying that he is thereby not only narrowing down but also reducing and sometimes even distorting their meaning. In fact, in many cases, clarity does seem to be his aim. On the other hand, anger or humour, or both at once are often as important as the desire for clarity in dictating Mr. Review's choice of specific nouns and verbs over general ones. As an example, here we have Defoe's 1705 *London Post* spokesman, 'Truth and Honesty',[8] a reduction to dullard level of the plain-speaking Mr. Review, discussing a nonjuring journalist rival with a parson:

'Well, Sir,' said T. and H., 'in what pray does he dissent from the government?'

Parson 'Why, he cannot take the oaths.'

T. & H. 'That is, he does not acknowledge the Queen to be his rightful sovereign. Don't you mean so?'

P. 'Yes, yes.'

T. & H. 'That is, in English, he looks upon the late King James and his Perkinite race to be the true line.'

P. 'And that he is bound by his oath to them.'

T. & H. 'Or in truth and honesty, that the Q———n is an usurper, and sits in a throne she has not right to.'

P. 'You are always for putting things in the worst terms you can, softer words would do it as well.'

T. & H. 'I am always for speaking truth, according to my name, my faculty and practice. . . .' (6 June 1705)

Even Mr. Review's familiar predilection for concretes and tangibles can often be seen less as a translation from general ideas or actions to particular meanings, than as a means of expressing anger, contempt, or humour. When he professes himself unable to determine whether with Henry VIII 'the motion [of religious conversion] began in the head or the tail' (9:106), for instance, his choice of concrete and specific nouns conveys contempt, innuendo, and humour. The same can be observed of his comment about the complaint received by the *Review* 'against a certain magistrate, for that he having been made a trustee for some moneys appropriated to better uses, had misapplied it, and bestowed a large sum of it in the laudable practice of eating and drinking, *Anglice*, feasting and drunkenness' (2:239). He goes on to discuss the meaning of the verb 'appropriate', stating that the mayor did not understand it, asking that the Scandal Club of the *Review* speak plain English, not Latin, to him. Much of the humour of the plain-speaking Mr. Review rests on the same technique; one of the cleverest is the naming of a tangible object in lieu of a general answer to why the English are so slow about developing the potentially rich fishing trade in Scotland:

> Remove this, and I'll answer for it, there can be but one reason more, why we should not remove all our Newfoundland trade to the northwest of Scotland.—The fish is the same, the voyage shorter, the shore better, the curing easier, and the quantity as great.—But what is this objection, says one now? Oh, a very material one indeed, 'tis a party cause, and why not parties in our trade, as well as in our religion; 'tis a strong objection, Presbyterian fish. (11:635)

We have already noticed the tone of moral superiority assumed by Mr. Review when he declares himself to be a plain speaker. He points out again and again that double meanings suggest double faces or double dealing, that to speak ambiguously in any way is a sign of fraud in intention and hypocrisy in the speaker (5:338). An honest way of dealing is indicated by a plain manner of speaking; means should be in harmony with their end. Mr. Review does not care for affectation, objecting, for instance, to the use of French words, especially in reporting on military affairs, when perfectly good English words are available. He objects to fiction, equating it with forgery and lies, with the one exception of fiction created to illustrate some valid moral precept. The word 'allegorical' is equated in the *Review* with 'figurative', usually when some moral is being illustrated (10:425–28, 12:82, 17:221–23). It is worth emphasizing this definition in order to understand what Defoe meant when he justified writing the fiction of *Robinson Crusoe* because it was an 'allusive, allegoric history'. The meaning of 'allusive' is explained in Book 10 of the *Review*, 16 August 1707. Mr. Review, then in Scotland, was asked to comment on the significance he attached to a prodigious shower of flies that had just appeared in London. Mr. Review pretends to report many whimsical suggestions he had actually received: the flies might signify something about the war, about the Union, or about High-Flyers. In offering his own theories, he supplies three religious 'allusions', or morals.

The shower of flies issue of the *Review* is significant as an example of Mr. Review's humour about drawing generalizations from particular events, even when these events occur in the form of special providences favoured by popular Christian apologists. It illustrates how the same shower of flies may signify to some that the English should not fight the French, to others that they should, and to still others, that if English armies enter Paris, bodies of English soldiers will be strewn about its streets as thickly as flies. He goes on to ring up alternative interpretations of what the flies might signify about the Union or about High-Flyers. Only at the end of the issue, in offering three religious generalizations, 'allusions', or morals, does Mr. Review's tone become serious. Nevertheless, his discussion shows that although a religious moral might be the most instructive of all, he himself can think up three possibilities right on the spot, and therefore one might attach any number of religious as well as political interpretations to one specific event. He himself prefers a scientific explanation, with no particular moral. Thus we see that even the limited acceptance of fiction as parable occasionally professed by Mr. Review is subject to his reservations at other times.

The concept of decorum, discussed by critics as a matter of course when they deal with polite writers of the eighteenth century, is rarely associated with a popular writer like Defoe.

Yet it is a key to understanding his discriminating sense of what language is appropriate to what social class, and on what occasion. His disapproval of swearing is often cited as an example of his adherence to the Baconian tradition of language as a tool for conveying useful information; since swearing has no meaning, it is worthless. Furthermore, it offends the religious sensibilities of the plain dealer.[9] Although Mr. Review of the ideal world does object to swearing on those grounds, he also objects to it on grounds of decorum or of literary sensitivity: '. . . you hardly ever find a man that has any taste of eloquence, any politeness of diction, or regard to cadence in speech, who can be a common swearer', he asserts (19:247). He points out that repeating oaths frequently has the effect of stripping them of their solemnity (22:141–42). Mr. Review objects to the style of High-Flying churchmen because it resembles street talk or 'Billingsgate' and is totally inappropriate to the majesty of the pulpit and the solemnity of preaching (16:467).

Sometimes Mr. Review offers his readers alternative levels of diction, as, for instance, when discussing English trade to Africa, he says, 'Supposing the House [of Commons] never so strongly enclined to sacrifice the African Company to them [a new company], *or to speak more mannerly*, to dissolve the Company, and lay open the trade' (22:79). In deploring the displacement of a shop selling woollen goods by a tavern, Mr. Review supplies three levels of diction: 'What succeeds him? A most noble, and to be sure, a much more valuable vintner's warehouse, *Anglice*, a tavern, *more vulgarly*, a bawdyhouse' (22:86).

Analysing diction is one key to distinguishing between Defoe's many styles of writing. Listening to speech rhythms is another. Especially in his colloquial styles, words fall into seemingly inevitable places within their phrases, even when hurried writing occasionally causes Defoe to lose control of the syntax of the sentence as a whole. This statement is true of all Defoe's styles, those of the plain dealing Mr. Review as well as of the worldly Mr. Review (see Chapter 3 below). It is important when reading Defoe to pay attention to the tempo or rapidity of his 'speech', because it is varied in pace according to the social class and level of understanding of the audience he is addressing. For example, military reports in the *Review* move at a fast clip, and Defoe uses many present participles to emphasize the qualities of action and manliness he wishes to convey to sporting country gentlemen by his language. Writing more 'characteristic' of Mr. Review, addressed to small retail shopkeepers (or readers even lower in the social scale), moves at a slow pace and contains a good deal of explanation. The series of issues dedicated to the problem of settling the Palatine refugees in England, addressed at first to such an audience, could well have served Swift as the style he parodied in his *Modest Proposal*. Defoe had a poor visual sense, at least insofar as one can judge from his writing, where although objects abound in name, visual descriptions are rare. But he seems to have had a phonographic ear. In reporting dialogue he is able to reproduce the speech rhythms of many of the classes of England of his time. Discussing style in the *Review*, Defoe emphasizes the 'cadence of speech', and 'the . . . music of words' (19:246–47, 253), as much as 'politeness of style' (19:253), and he points out elsewhere that he counts nobody an accomplished writer who lacks ability in dialogue.

The following passages are taken from a letter to the Glasgow mob, printed in the *Review* on 2 January 1707 (8:625–28). Beginning with a compliment to Glasgow Presbyterians for their past history of resistance to Episcopalian and Popish tyranny, Mr. Review admonishes them for rioting against the Union between England and Scotland:

> . . . and I could write a long history of your former conduct, very much to the honour of your city.
>
> But where are you going now? What's become of all the zeal for religion, the warmth of your spirits for liberty, the forwardness and boldness with which you asserted the Protestant Church of this nation to be the only true reformed and purely constituted church in the world?—What, have you forsaken your old principles, and are you pulling down all your fathers have built? For God's sake, Gentlemen, and for your own sakes, look before you a little, look down the dreadful precipice before you take the fatal leap in the dark. Can you see the bottom of this pit? Can you see the rocks and clifts against which you will be dashed in the fall? Did ever people run thus rashly upon destruction but you?

See but how your present behaviour flies in the face of your former, and condemns you either for betraying the cause of Christ's church, or your followers for suffering for it.

Were ever such strange preposterous things done? Was ever people so unaccountably distracted? For GOD's sake, Gentlemen, look about you a little, and see what company you are in, for they say, *Men are known by their company*. I am persuaded, when you see what a wretched hellish society you are got into, you will blush, and come to yourselves.

Perhaps you think, you are standing up for the Church. Well, Gentlemen, and did ever the Church get any good by such methods as you take, or such people as are joined with you?— Let's see their character, all the Jacobites are in league with you, the Papists are on your right hand, the Prelatists on your left, and the French at your back; *Have these any inheritance in Jacob, or part in the lot of Jesse! To your tents O Israel*, for shame, abandon such a wretched cause, and fly into the arms of your friends, before you put forth your hands to blood, and bring destruction upon your families. (8:626)

I have chosen this passage as one example of the style of the plain-speaking Mr. Review, because of the rhetorical questions following the refrain, 'Where are you going?', the same refrain with which Robinson Crusoe's parrot greets him on land after his narrow escape from the sea during a dangerous attempt to leave the island. Although Crusoe does not speak in the hortatory tone of this letter, it is a sermon appropriate to his level of literary sophistication. The audience at whom it was directed consisted not only of a mob of the poor and the manual labourers of Glasgow but also of Scottish Presbyterian ministers, who were helping to inflame the 'rabble' against the Union. Defoe points out, in a letter of 9 December 1706 to Robert Harley, that although the title says his exhortation is addressed to the mob, he 'presume[s] [it] may be usefull to all the rest . . .' (*Letters*, p. 169). He also classifies it in a letter of 12 December as 'a plain but course Expostulation' (p. 170).

What marks it as the writing of the plain-speaking Mr. Review is a combination of diction, of rhythm, of Biblical references and quotations, and on the part of the speaker of an assumption of equality with his audience. Above all, the personality of Mr. Review intrudes on our consciousness so insistently that many commentators on Defoe have objected to him on the grounds of his personality, believing it to be the same as the one displayed in the Glasgow letter.

In spite of the familiarity of the writer with sermon style, seen in his careful construction of parallels (for instance, 'the zeal for religion, the warmth of your spirits for liberty, the forwardness and boldness with which . . .' and 'the Papists on your right hand, the Prelatists on your left, and the French at your back'), and the rhetorical questions, the writing seems relatively simple, partly because the phrases and sentences are relatively short, so that the audience can comprehend what is being said. Also, the ideas, not at all complex, are expressed in such concrete terms that they seem almost childish. As an example, Mr. Review wishes his audience to stop opposing the Union; without explaining why it is good, he simply orders his uneducated hearers to take dramatic action, to abandon their cause 'and fly into the arms of your friends, before you put forth your hands to blood, and bring destruction upon your families.' We note also the informal and very active verbs 'pulling down', 'dashed', 'run', 'flies in the face', and 'standing up for'.

The *Letter* in its entirety (not reproduced) is a fine piece of writing of its kind, especially notable, I think, for the interesting variations in pace and in syntax at the beginning of each paragraph, as the speaker anticipates questions from his audience:

> 'But where are you going now?'
> 'See but how your present behaviour flies in the face of your former.'
> 'Were ever such strange preposterous things done?'
> 'Perhaps you think you are standing up for the Church. Well. . . .'

Much less dramatic is the following selection chosen from the 9 July 1709 issue in Mr. Review's series on the Palatine problem, much of which sounds like the honest but monstrous projector of *A Modest Proposal*:

> I presume, my last would in part clear up a point that has been pretty much debated among us, and which sometimes gives our people uneasiness enough, viz., that the encreasing the numbers of our people shall lower the price of our wages;

the contrary of which I affirm.—I shall say but a little more to it.—And hope to put it out of question.

I readily grant, if you were to bring over a hundred thousand butchers or shoemakers—they would be ready to butcher one another for work, and the shoemakers would ruin those we have already, and themselves; *the reason is plain*, because they would multiply that particular occupation, more than they would encrease the employ, by just so much as these hundred thousand could kill, and dress more flesh than they could eat; or make more shoes than they could wear.

Again, if a hundred thousand people were to come over here, and plant upon land, and everyone to do their own work—they would not have employment enough for themselves, and would want to be employed in the service of those that were here before them—and by consequence would want to do some work, that some other body did before; and this is what we call by that ill-natured phrase, of *eating the bread out of the mouths of our poor*.

Again, barely planting a number of people upon our land, who should produce the provisions they eat, and manufacture the clothes and household stuff they wore; if that were probable, would not perhaps answer, all that is alleged of encreasing wealth to a nation—Nor would a colony so considered, make good what I have said, of numbers of people making more employment than they could perform, and so by consequence assist to the employment of others—There is no doubt, but a hundred thousand people planted in any country might subsist themselves, and do all the necessary works they should want, without employing anybody.

But when we talk of people, and planting them in a nation, we are to consider this nation as concerned in trade; trade, which is now the consequence of peopling a country; and this trade is to be considered in its full circulation, by which it employs perhaps ten times the hands, which the same things produced in another manner would employ, and which circulation is the life of general commerce.—'Tis for want of this distinction, that most of our vulgar errors about trade are midwifed into the world. *For Example.*

I wear a suit of clothes.—They are made of cloth, lined with shalloon, stitched with silk, the buttons are of one work, the buttonholes of another; the pockets are of leather, the waistcoat is lined with flannel, the breeches with dimmety, and the like.

I will make it appear, that from the first principles of the clothes to my wearing them, 100 families have a part of their subsistence out of this one suit of clothes, as the things are handed on in the course [of] trade, and as they circulate from one place to another. (14:165–66)

Again, most readers would identify the style as Mr. Review's, mainly because of the laborious, even slow-minded way he works out his computations, leaving nothing to the imagination of his readers. The style is humdrum, with no striking images, no hint of wit or humour, and little variation of rhythm. The trades mentioned are menial (performed by classes Defoe specified elsewhere as 'mechanics' or skilled labourers)—butchers, shoemakers, poor farmers. The self-assurance of the know-it-all speaker about a field not worth understanding could well seem offensive to a literary person: ' 'Tis for want of this distinction, that most vulgar errors about trade are midwifed into the world.' We should note that the verbs are mostly as flat and boring as their context, so that 'midwifed' and 'butchered' are the only words in the whole passage that command attention. The details about the suit of clothes are typical of the kind of details supplied about making pots, for example, or domestic arrangements by Robinson Crusoe, and although they are interesting to us today, they would have seemed low to polite writers of Defoe's period.

After reading the two selections above, we might well come to conclusions about Defoe's style that would lead us into the same error as his London subscribers of 1707 regarding the *Review* he was writing from Scotland. Reading passages like the one that follows below, they concluded that a new writer had taken over the journal. Defoe assured them he was indeed still writing it, pointing out in a notice he ran for several issues, '. . . the judgment of the gentlemen that spread this report, must be very good; that can neither guess at the style, nor guess by the story or manner of it both, whether it be the author's and where the author is' (8:624).

The passage that follows, in Mr. Review's high style, is an explanation of a complicated point: why the Presbyterian Church of Scotland, which did not have representatives in the Scottish parliament as the Episcopalian Church of England had in theirs, was protesting against the Union. Bishops of the

Church of England sitting in the House of Lords would have the right to legislate upon Scottish church matters, whereas, having no bishops, the Church of Scotland would have no special representatives in the House of Lords to legislate upon English church matters. The Church of Scotland was protesting a lack of reciprocal rights for them under the proposed Union of England and Scotland; their intention, Mr. Review argues, is not to gain power over the affairs of the Church of England, but to object that the Church of England might by the Union be gaining power over the affairs of the Church of Scotland:

> By the Union and the establishment of the respective churches, the spiritual Lords retain their seats in Parliament, and by those seats have really a vote upon everything relating to, or required by the Church of Scotland; except only such things, as being established by the Treaty, are reserved from even Parliamentary jurisdiction by the Treaty. If this be so, let no man wonder, that the Commission of the Assembly protests, since it cannot, nor by men of reason is not expected, that the Church of Scotland should be in anything subjected to the Church of England by the Union, or the Church of England to the Church of Scotland; but that either constitution reserving its authorities, should subsist on its proper foundation independent and entire.
>
> And thus in the English Parliament, my Lords the Bishops themselves protest against being denied a vote in matters of blood, though at the same time, they do not at any time attempt to give their vote, nor perhaps desire it.
>
> In like manner the Church of Scotland protests against the Bishops sitting in their British Parliament of Britain, as against their having any legislative authority over the Church of Scotland, as inconsistent with their independency; at the same time it does not follow, that in things relating to their own Church, they do not leave England and the English Church, to do what they please with their own Church affairs.
>
> For example; suppose by the constitution of Scotland, the Church of Scotland had enjoyed the privilege of a representative in Parliament, besides their Assembly, and 26 ministers or ruling Elders had a right to sit there in either house; suppose then the Church of England, either by the Convocation of their own representatives, or by the spiritual Lords in Parliament, should declare, that they did not submit to be in anything

prejudged by, or subjected to the authority of those men, whose ecclesiastical authority they disowned and rejected.

Would it follow now, that because the Church of England thus protested or objected, that therefore they designed the destruction or subversion of the Church of Scotland, and would not be at rest, till they had brought it to pass?

I cannot but think, that the attempts of these people by way of scandal is a plain evidence, that they do not argue for the safety of either church, but really against the prosperity of both. (8:574)

It would be impossible to judge, from the university lecturer's style of the above excerpt, that it had been written by the plain-speaking (and slow-minded) Mr. Review. The nouns are almost totally abstract, the verbs are appropriate but not dramatically active, the rhythm is of written, not spoken language. There are no aphorisms, no Biblical quotations, no images from everyday life, and no proverbs. The example supplied for explanation is no less abstract than the general discussion—it consists of supposing the shoe to be on the other foot and the Church of England to be objecting. Yet it makes the point clear: that it is simply not logical to conclude that such a protest was anything else than self defence. The argument is closely reasoned, its logic convincing, its transitions almost mathematically clear: 'If this be so . . . since it cannot . . . is not expected . . . and thus . . . in like manner . . . at the same time it does not follow . . . for example . . . would it follow now?' Above all, the argument is made objectively to intelligent readers whom the writer does not know personally; far from being obtrusive, the personality of the writer is notable for its absence.

Judging from the style and from the historical background of the excerpt, Mr. Review appears to have been addressing legislators, government ministers, and others of the same educational level, which would mean the two top classes of society as he once defined them, the 'rich' and even 'the great'.[10] But the rather antiseptically logical tone he assumed in the Scottish issues of 1706–7 was not necessarily occasioned by awe at the social level of his readers. A second excerpt I have chosen to illustrate Mr. Review's high style is a great deal livelier than the first, although it is addressed to the House of Commons on the issue of the Succession to the throne of England raised by Sacheverell's inflammatory sermon of 1709. In January 1710 the House was debating these issues:

> Passive obedience, non-resistance, and the divine right of hereditary succession, are inconsistent with the rights of the BRITISH NATION (not to examine the rights of nature), inconsistent with the constitution of the BRITISH GOVERNMENT, inconsistent with the *being* and *authority* of the BRITISH PARLIAMENT, and inconsistent with the declared essential foundation of the BRITISH MONARCHY.—These abhorred notions would destroy the inestimable privileges of Britain, of which the House of Commons are the glorious conservators; they would subject all our liberties to the arbitrary lust of a single person, they would expose us to all kinds of tyranny, and subvert the very foundations on which we stand.—They would destroy the unquestioned sovereignty of our laws, which for so many ages have triumphed over the invasions and usurpations of ambitious princes; they would denude us of the beautiful garment of liberty, and prostitute the honour of the nation to the mechanicism of slavery.—They would divest GOD Almighty of his praise, in giving his humble creatures a right of governing themselves, and charge Heaven with having meanly subjected mankind to the crime TYRANNY, which He himself abhors. . . .
>
> It is well known to your honourable House, that notwithstanding the self-evident testimony of the rights of the people of Britain, as above, there are not wanting men among us who broach again, and vigorously promote, both in printing, preaching, and conversation, the said exploded principles of passive obedience, non-resistance, and divine right, with manifest design to render odious and contemptible our legal Establishment, to overthrow the foundations of our present government, unravel the Revolution, and invalidate the just title, which Her Majesty derives to these crowns by the principle of Parliamentary limitation. . . .
>
> This is the substance of the author's humble application, viz., that the sense of the House, as to the principles of passive obedience, non-resistance, and Parliamentary limitation, might be so declared, as that this wicked party may be no more at liberty to insult the government, the QUEEN, and the Parliament, or to disturb the peace, or debauch the loyalty of Her Majesty's subjects.
>
> I hope, in this humble representation I cannot have offended.—

52

I protest to have designed neither to lead, direct, or reflect.—But from a true principle of, and, I hope, a rightly informed zeal for the general good, the peace, the privileges, and the prosperity of Britain, I have presumed thus far; and for myself, I entirely submit to the justice and censure of the Parliament, in which every honest man is safe, his property and person secure, and over which, I hope, no prejudice shall ever prevail. (16:473–76)

What makes the above so lively is the heavy use of parallelism in syntax, emphasized by alliteration and assonance (in the second paragraph especially, the long *o* assonance in 'broach', 'promote', 'exploded', 'obedience', 'odious', 'overthrow', interwoven with the sounds 'un' and 'in' in 'unravel' and 'invalidate'—the alliteration, especially with p's and b's—'broach', 'promote', 'printing', 'preaching', 'principles', etc.). In the first paragraph, the parallelism is marked by repetition of the word 'inconsistent'.

Although the nouns are abstract ideas in the main, the verbs are highly active ('destroy', 'subject', 'expose', 'subvert', 'triumphed', 'denude', 'prostitute', 'divest', 'overthrow', 'unravel', 'insult', 'debauch'). Mr. Review even resorts to adjectives, a rare practice with him, to lend weightiness and dignity to some of the abstract nouns: 'inestimable privileges', 'exploded principles', 'odious and contemptible . . . Establishment'.

Indeed, the highly worked style of the above passage makes it rather difficult to follow its logic, which may be one reason why Defoe refrained from such tricks in the Scottish pieces, intended as explanations of issues with which English readers were unfamiliar. The address to the House of Commons above is hortatory rather than didactic.

Although the speaker mentions himself, his personality is not that of the know-it-all Mr. Review, nor is he at all obtrusive. What one hears in reading the address as a whole is a speaker of great intelligence and education who feels very strongly about the issues under discussion, yet who is more interested in destroying pernicious ideas than in displaying his own personality.

Now that we have seen examples of Mr. Review's high and low style we can better understand his comment as he speaks of parliamentary matters: 'If I am not explicit enough in this to everyone's understanding, I am yet very easy; the gentlemen to whom I write, understand me well enough; and all that know anything of parliamentary affairs will agree to the truth of fact' (5:390). Evidently he had discovered from experience that the more educated the audience he was addressing, the less explicit he had to be. This observation will be helpful to us later in recognizing the style Defoe used to describe the satanic world of the rich and the great, a style the very opposite of the one admired by Mr. Review for its clarity and explicitness.

I have avoided until now supplying examples of Mr. Review's middle style so as to make very clear the difference between low and high styles of writing. Before going on to examples of the middle style, I should like to point out that the plain-dealing, plain-speaking Mr. Review occasionally parodied his own plainness, as we saw in the excerpt from the *London Post* (see page 41 above).

Truth and Honesty's style Defoe usually reserved for children, savages, countrymen, and 'honest' plain people—or slow-minded people with good principles and hearts. Its use seems to be based on his observation that uneducated people do not know how to deal with abstract ideas; instead of supplying particulars to explain the idea, they simply repeat the noun that names it. One of many such observations concerns the popular aversion to Popery or to the Pretender. In most of these remarks, scattered through Defoe's writing, he supplies the abstract noun, adding that the ignorant do not know whether the word signifies a man or a horse:

> Should they [Jacobite supporters] but once offer the Pretender themselves to the people, the very same mob that has huzzaed them into favour, would tear them all to pieces—for the Pretender is the nation's aversion; not that every poor plebian of the country, knows what the Pretender means, but the Pretender, like Popery, is the direct object of popular hatred, even by its outside, by the very name.
>
> I have often said, and believe it to be very true, that there are an hundred thousand stout fellows in this nation, that would fight to the last drop against Popery, who do not know whether it is a man or a horse; so as many would rise up against the very name of the Pretender, who know nothing at all who he is, what his design is, where he is, or what he is like to do if he comes hither; his name is become the nation's aversion.... (21:759–60)

Here is an example of the very low style of Mr. Review, speaking with an ignorant but well-meaning Scottish Presbyterian about the Union:

> One honest good man, but frightened at the Union, comes in just as I am writing this, and not knowing what I am upon.— Well, says he, you English people are a politic nation.—If you go on thus, you will make our people like the Union in spite of their own resolutions.
>
> Well, Sir, says I, but are they not an honest nation too? Indeed, says the good man, they have been more than honest in this, for they have been very kind.—Well, Sir, said I, has it reconciled you to the Union? Indeed has it, says the gentleman; if you will always treat us in this manner, you shall have us, we will be all your own to the end of the chapter.
>
> Well, said I, you ought from this beginning to believe they will, till you find it otherwise. That's true indeed, says he, and I promise you , I begin to hope well of it now, which I never did before. (9:191)

The limited vocabulary, the monotony of a conversation where the linguistic abilities of the speaker are insufficient to convey more than platitudes, we will meet again in an important scene from *Moll Flanders* discussed in Chapter 4.

The following is an example of Mr. Review's middle style, the easy, colloquial style that made his journal so popular, if we may judge by complaints from readers when he launched into his formal style in Scotland. It is addressed to country gentlemen, upper middle class in twentieth-century terms, 'the rich' in Defoe's social classification. These isolationist country gentlemen were lukewarm about Continental entanglements, so they favoured sea warfare with France over land warfare. The Tories argued that England, an island, had the advantage at sea, whereas they were at a disadvantage on land, needing to raise and equip huge armies at great expense:

> Nor can you revenge yourselves on the French *or pay them in kind*; because their ships are so few, you cannot make it worthwhile, and yours are so many, they cannot miss of a prey. It is noted, that at the first of this war you took a great many French privateers, and they got but few prizes; the *first* was owing to your diligence, 'tis true, but the *last* was, because their fleet being fitted out for two year together, their privateers were called in to

man the navy, and they were fewer than now; you have had no French fleet out, *I mean their grand royal navy*, now for two years, and for that reason the seas swarm with their privateers, *and* I must own, the worst way the French can make war with us, is to plague us with their privateers, and lay their navy up, *and never say I tell them how to hurt us*, for you see they have made the experiment already.

And now, *to you gentlemen, who tell us, the best way to reduce France is to ruin their naval power*, pray tell me how will you ruin their privateering trade, I'll tell you one way, if you will tell me another: about 2 year ago the Duke of Marlborough was our admiral, and he shewed us the way, he ruined a whole nest of privateers at once—

If this be a riddle to you, I'll soon explain it; the Battle of Ramellies cleared the sea of a matter of 42 privateers, that did us a great deal of damage, and took abundance of our ships. If it be still a riddle to you, remember, that the only way found out to deliver us from the Ostend privateers, was by taking the town. This the Battle of Ramellies procured, and the Duke of Marlborough was our best admiral for that expedition; and what could a hundred sail of men of war have done towards this? Little enough GOD knows, witness our fruitless attempts to bombard Dunkirk and Calais, and our many vain expeditions to lie before Dunkirk to keep them in. But if you will effectually ruin the naval power of France, bring down your armies, and take the seaport towns, and 'tis done at once. This is the *Shortest Way* with the French.

I assure you, Gentlemen, we have not lost one ship by an Ostend privateer, since the Duke of Marlborough took that town from the French, and do but pull Dunkirk about their ears, do but unroost them there, beat them out of that nest of thieves, and put a good garrison of bold Britons into it, I warrant you, I procure you good merchants to ensure you, that as long as you can keep possession of the town, you have no more damage by Dunkirk privateers.

On the other hand, dismiss all your armies, and employ 7 millions yearly in men of war, and fit out a thousand cruisers, *if you can find men for them*, and when you have done all, the French shall be every day snapping up your merchants' ships, even at your own doors, but take the towns, and the work is done at once.

If you will effectually ruin France, you must push at him by land, beat him out of his arsenals and magazines by land, and then he will be quite undone.

56

When the hounds have run a fox to earth, they can do no more, 'tis the spade and the mattock must dig him out; indeed the terriers will run *in* a little way, and bark at him, but these are but yelping curses, and can only make a noise, the crafty devil lies close—But dig him out, and you catch him *in a poke*, or force him to his heels again, and then the hounds come in with him fairly.

Your fleet royal is *the pack*, which runs the French navy down with *full cry*, and they take *to earth*, that is, run into harbour, run into Brest, or Dunkirk, or Thoulon, and then we can do no more with the fleet; if you will drive them to sea again, you must come with your spade and pick axe, that is, bring your armies, and besiege them there, dig down their bastions, and throw open their defences; the bomb ketches, *like the terriers above*, may creep into the ports, and bark at them, but though they spit fire at them, they lie still, lay themselves under water, *or the like*; but taking the town brings them all into a poke, or drives them to sea again upon the article of desperation, and then you have them.

The affair of Thoulon illustrated this simile but too plainly, where for want of digging out this fox, the pack of hounds, huntsmen, and all were fain to go home without him.—So insufficient is all your naval power without the superiority by land. (11:570–1) (My italics on the two 'ands' in the first paragraph)

The line of argumentation here is clear, for Mr. Review explains more than he exhorts, probably for several reasons. The first is personal: he cannot claim to be a country gentleman, so he has to avoid haranguing his readers. The second is practical: the argument for war by sea was plausible and therefore required serious refutation. The third is probable: fox-hunting country gentlemen are not likely to have been overly intellectual, so that although Mr. Review could rely on their patriotism, he could not rely on their intelligence. For that reason he may have felt obliged to explain his simile very carefully.

Mr. Review uses several methods of explaining: first he points out that the danger to English ships is from French privateers, not the royal French navy. Then he discusses the arithmetic of English and French fleets in general terms of few and many. Next he propounds a riddle: the Duke of

Marlborough, commander-in-chief of the army, is really commander-in-chief, or admiral, of the navy. On the basis of his explanation of this riddle, validated by recent historical experience, he proposes two courses of action, demonstrating that war by sea, the second course, spells disaster for English merchant ships. Finally he states his solution: 'If you will eventually ruin France, you must push at him by land, beat him out of his arsenals and magazines by land, and then he will be quite undone.' To drive the point home, he supplies a simile from fox-hunting appropriate to the experience of country gentlemen.

The use of proofs from history and from generalized arithmetic, the riddle, the appropriate simile, are examples of the striking and colourful details for which Mr. Review's (and Defoe's) style is valued. His appeal this time is to the love of action and the patriotism of country gentlemen, so he boasts about the glorious victories of Marlborough and uses highly active verbs to suggest beating the French: 'do but pull Dunkirk about their ears', 'unroost them', 'beat them out of', 'push at him', etc. The appeal to patriotism suggests the phrase 'put a good garrison of bold Britons into it [Dunkirk]'.

The syntax here is of spoken, not written language, and it is the informal, lively, and colloquial speech of the upper middle class, not the slower, less lively speech of the lower middle class, for example, the Palatine speaker. The slight confusion with pronouns at the end of the next to last paragraph, as well as the run-on sentences in the first and second paragraphs, do not impede rapid understanding of the argument, which Mr. Review is careful to state succinctly at the beginning of his paragraph. We should note that the first paragraph consists of two sentences. The first states the point clearly. The second, which goes on for the rest of the paragraph, is jumbled. The jumble is due mainly to the parenthetic remark, 'I mean their grand royal navy', and to two uses of the conjunction 'and' (marked with my italics) where careful writing would dictate beginning a new sentence. In spite of the jumble, the meaning is clear; indeed, the rush of clauses is appropriate to convey the feeling that the speaker, like his audience, is a man who likes action.

Again, the personality of the speaker is very strong. He is

not fiery and indignant; like his readers, he is a man of action, eager, interested in hunting and in military affairs. Yet he remembers to remind his audience that in spite of the interests they share, he is still the Mr. Review they know from his journal; he speaks from his acknowledged position as business-man acquainted with other businessmen, when he says that if the English conquer Dunkirk, 'I warrant you, I procure you good merchants to ensure you, that as long as you can keep possession of the town, you have no more damage by Dunkirk privateers.'

What is common to all these passages? Not the style, which I have shown ranges from very low to very high in diction, from colloquial speech to the syntax of formal writing, from concrete to abstract proofs in argumentation. Not the sentence rhythms, which range from the rapidity of a man of action to the deliberateness of a writer who is willing to take time to explain a complicated issue of ecclesiastical rights in Parlia-ment to his readers. Not the Scriptural and proverbial refer-ences, which are reserved for religious fundamentalists. Not the everyday imagery, like hounds for country gentlemen, suitable to special groups of readers. Not even the personality of the plain-speaking Mr. Review, for the Palatine plodder is very different from the manly, patriotic and quick witted advocate of war by land, and the personality of the writer is almost totally absent from the argumentations and exhorta-tions about abstract issues of political and constitutional theory.

What marks them all as belonging to the plain-dealing Mr. Review is the presence behind all variations of style and of personality of a consciousness engaged in exerting control over its world. Whether the subject matter consists of concrete objects or of ideas, the organizing mind of Defoe's spokesman of an ideal world seeks to tidy up all disorder arising from inadequate understanding or unruly emotions, to eliminate disputes, and to unite contraries. The ultimate aim of his ordering is to construct an ideal world of peace and of clarity, the world described at the beginning of this chapter.

NOTES

1. All citations from Defoe's *Review* come from the complete facsimile in twenty-two books edited and introduced by Arthur Wellesley Secord (New York: Columbia University Press, 1938). I have followed the practice of William L. Payne, compiler and editor of *The Best of Defoe's Review: An Anthology* (New York: Columbia University Press, 1951), in modernizing spelling, some of the punctuation, and in supplying missing letters. Since I am stressing recurring patterns in Defoe's writing, I do not, except when it is pertinent, supply the volume number or date of citation from the *Review*. My references are to book, not volume number, and to page number.

2. *Serious Reflections during the Life and Surprising Adventures of Robinson Crusoe with His Vision of the Angelic World*, ed. G. H. Maynadier (New York: Crowell, 1903).

3. The target reader of both Tory and Whig propaganda during this period was the impartial man of property, probably because of the appeal to the 'floating voters who, as W. A. Speck observes, decided elections and mirrored the changes which occurred in the public consciousness'. See T. N. Corns, W. A. Speck, and J. A. Downie, 'Archetypal Mystification: Polemic and Reality in English Political Literature, 1640–1750', *Eighteenth-Century Life*, 7 (May 1982), p. 23.

4. As William L. Payne explains succinctly, the amusing section of the *Review* (modelled on John Dunton's *Athenian Mercury*) in which Defoe answered questions from his readers, ran only for the first two years of the life of the journal. (The *Review* itself ran from 19 February 1704 to 11 June 1713.) At first this section was entitled 'Mercure Scandale: or, Advice from the Scandalous Club (translated out of the French)'. Then it became 'Advice from the Scandalous Club' (February 1704–April 1705). From May to August 1705 the section was published separately twice a week in the *Little Review*. From September 1704 to January 1705 the section appeared as five monthly numbers called 'A Supplement to the Advice from the Scandalous Club'. With the introduction to the 1706 volume of the *Review*, the Club was replaced by an irregularly appearing end essay called 'Miscellanea'. This was a shorter essay than the main one of the issue, but not always much less serious. Defoe abandoned his Scandalous Club with relief for lack of time, and Addison and Steele picked it up and developed it in their own inimitable way.

5. Rachel Trickett analyses the techniques by which major figures like Dryden, Pope, and Johnson attempted to satisfy the increasing demand of the times, first for public honesty, eventually for private sincerity, in writers who claimed to speak with moral authority. See *The Honest Muse: A Study in Augustan Verse* (Oxford: Clarendon Press, 1967).

6. G. A. Starr, *Defoe and Casuistry* (Princeton: Princeton University Press, 1971), p. 8.

7. J. T. Boulton (ed.), *Daniel Defoe* (London: B. T. Batsford, 1965), pp. 1–22.

8. My information about the 'Truth and Honesty' column written by

Defoe for the *London Post* (but not all my citations) comes from J. A. Downie, 'Daniel Defoe's *Review* and Other Political Writings in the Reign of Queen Anne', Master of Letters thesis, University of Newcastle upon Tyne, 197.

9. Defoe's objection to swearing was not necessarily, as some critics have maintained, the result of his Puritanism or of his middle-class origins. According to Corns, Speck, and Downie (p. 3 and *passim*), swearing was 'given a surprising prominence' in anti-Cavalier propaganda and continued to be stressed in its descendant, anti-Tory political propaganda.

10. In his *Review* of 25 June 1709 (14:142), Defoe divides the people of England into classes: (1) the great, who live profusely; (2) the rich, who live very plentifully; (3) the middle sort, who live well; (4) the working trades, who labour hard, but feel no want; (5) the country people, farmers, etc., who fare indifferently; (6) the poor, that fare hard; (7) the miserable, that really pinch and suffer want.

2

Trouble in Eden

In Chapter 1 we saw that the ideal world sought by the plain-dealing Mr. Review resembles the island world constructed by Robinson Crusoe in its emphasis upon order, directness, clarity, simplicity, repression of emotion, and slow and patient work. In every area—Mr. Review's ideal world, his notion of truth, his method of describing and proving, and above all in his style, whether low, middle, or high—appeared the same drive to force the world into an acceptable shape. He longed for a machine like the Consolidator, that could screw men's heads into sedate and regular thinking, ensuring that principles and practice, means and ends were in accord, and that people might 'come all to understand . . . matter[s] in the same way' (19:199).

Yet in his imagery of circles, fences, and barricades, and in the associations he made between the peaceful ideal world and the past, the remote, the static, and the dead, we find hints of the challenges to ideal order that will be seen more clearly in *A Journal of the Plague Year* and in *Robinson Crusoe*: the restlessness that feels confined by an ordered world, and its opposite tendency, passivity. The anger of which the plain-dealing Mr. Review was accused and to which he even occasionally confessed, is repeated in Crusoe's occasional anger toward cannibals and other invaders of his island and reversed in his more habitual fear of such invaders.

Imposing Order: Repressing Emotion

The following scene from *Robinson Crusoe* occurs shortly after Crusoe has been shipwrecked on his island:

... at my coming back, I shot at a great Bird which I saw sitting upon a Tree on the Side of a great Wood, I believe it was the first Gun that had been fir'd there since the Creation of the World; I had no sooner fir'd, but from all the Parts of the Wood there arose an innumerable Number of Fowls of many Sorts, making a confus'd Screaming, and crying every one according to his usual Note: but not one of them of any Kind that I knew: As for the Creature I kill'd, I took it to be a Kind of a Hawk, its Colour and Beak resembling it, but had no Talons or Claws more than common, its Flesh was Carrion, and fit for nothing. (p. 53)[1]

Defoe's description evokes Crusoe's feelings of mystery and awe about his own solitude and about the concept of immeasurable tracts of time having passed in a place remote from and indifferent to human existence. Visual details are characteristically scarce in this passage (Defoe rarely visualizes scenes clearly in his writings), but their relative absence is in this case overshadowed by Defoe's effective concentration upon sound. The sound of Crusoe's gun, the many different kinds of bird cries responding to this sound, the community of the birds in cacophony, contrasted to the isolation of the man, Crusoe's observation that of all this 'innumerable Number' not one bird was of a kind familiar to him, his inability to penetrate into the community even by eating one of its members, emphasize the strangeness and solitude of Crusoe's 'silent Life' (pp. 63, 156 and others). (Defoe must have liked this scene, for he repeated it, less successfully, in *Farther Adventures of Robinson Crusoe*.)

In striking contrast to the scene from Robinson Crusoe is a passage from one of its analogues cited by Arthur Secord in his *Studies in the Narrative Method of Defoe*:

'I saw ... an exceedingly large bird. ... I shot him. ... His bill was curved like an eagle's beak, but was blood-red. His head and breast were of a golden yellow, and on his head he had a very beautiful red tuft. His neck ... was green and blue. ... His legs were very large and black, and on them were very thick and red curved claws. His wings were exceedingly large. ...' The boy found him excellent eating, and for several days fed himself and his dog from the carcass.[2]

Hendrik Smeeks's description (from *Krinke Kesmes*, Amsterdam, 1708) of the same scene is certainly more clearly visualized than is Defoe's, but in spite of all the colours he employs (and only partly because of the monotony of the sentence structure and rhythm), his description is utterly prosaic, lacking in any sense of the mystery and awe evoked so simply by Defoe.

What I wish to emphasize in Defoe's description, however, is not the lack of visual, or reliance upon aural, detail. Neither is it his evocation of a sense of mystery and awe. Rather, it is Crusoe's resolute rejection of this mood. Crusoe's reaction to his momentary recognition of a world existing outside of, independent of, inconceivably larger than, human activities, is the almost immediate assertion of his own independent existence. He begins to analyse the characteristics of the bird he has shot, to classify it in the family of hawks familiar to his English readers, to take an intellectual possession of the bird. Like Adam, he assumes that to bestow a name is to become master over what one names.[3] Having analysed its physical characteristics, categorized as precisely as possible the species of this unknown bird, exhausted its unfamiliarity, Crusoe has no further use for it, rejecting it as 'fit for nothing'.

Another passage illustrating the imposition of order on the world through the rejection of emotion is the famous description of Crusoe's discovery of a mysterious single footprint:

> It happen'd one Day about Noon going towards my Boat, I was exceedingly surpriz'd with the Print of a Man's naked Foot on the Shore, which was very plain to be seen in the Sand; I stood like one Thunder-struck, or as if I had seen an Apparition; I listen'd, I look'd round me, I could hear nothing, nor see any Thing. I went up to a rising Ground to look farther, I went up the Shore and down the Shore, but it was all one, I could see no other Impression but that one, I went to it again to see if there were any more, and to observe if it might not be my Fancy; but there was no Room for that, for there was exactly the very Print of a Foot, Toes, Heel, and every Part of a Foot; how it came thither, I knew not, nor could in the least imagine. (pp. 153–54)

One of the most remarkable things about the footprint is the disparity between its meagre, even prosaic description: 'For there was exactly the very Print of a Foot, Toes, Heel, and every Part of a Foot', and the torrent of emotion it releases in Crusoe. Frightened beyond measure, he fancies at first that the mark may have been made by Satan. After reflection, however, he dismisses the possibility of a supernatural cause, deciding that the footprint must have been made by a savage. His reasoning is significant; it reveals him engaged in the same characteristic mental action as when he attempted to classify the unknown bird he had shot. Crusoe is rejecting the strangeness introduced into his comfortable little world by the unwelcome footprint, whittling down the size of this new world, and of his newly magnified fear, by divesting the footprint of mystery. His determined attempt to reduce Satan to the embodiment of common sense empiricism is only a prelude to dismissing the supernatural entirely from his consideration of possible causes of the mark.

After Crusoe deduces that the footprint must have been made by visiting savages, he manages to compose his mind. The external sign that his mind is at rest is his ability once again to pray to God—when he is anxious, he has difficulty in praying. Indeed, he calms himself so successfully that he becomes bold enough to go back and re-examine the footprint. If his first attempt to domesticate it was to reject intellectually a diabolical agent as its possible source, his second attempt is at physical reduction: he attempts to measure the mark against his own foot. To his consternation, the footprint refuses to be reduced by this gesture. It is, unfortunately, a good deal larger than the mark of his own foot.

Thrown into a frenzy by this reaffirmation of the power of the inexplicable, its resistance to his control, Crusoe is tempted to destroy the work of fifteen years:

> O what ridiculous Resolution Men take, when possess'd with Fear! It deprives them of the Use of those Means which Reason offers for their Relief. The first Thing I propos'd to my self, was, to thrown down my Enclosures, and turn all my tame Cattle wild into the Woods, that the Enemy might not find them; and then frequent the Island in Prospect of the same, or the like Booty: Then to the simple Thing of Digging up my two Corn Fields, that they might not find such a Grain there, and still be prompted to frequent the Island; then to demolish my Bower, and Tent, that they might not see any Vestiges of Habitation, and be prompted to look farther, in order to find out the Persons inhabiting. (p. 159)

After a good, sound sleep, he reconsiders his apocalyptic resolutions, reasoning, as after his first encounter, that the footprint indicates merely that savages from the mainland occasionally visit his island, that all he has to do is disguise the evidence of his habitation and, on the occasion of such visits, conceal himself. Thus he seems to have succeeded in domesticating the mysterious footprint, at least in his own mind.

Although Crusoe's deduction about visits to the island by mainland savages is correct, for the reader of *Robinson Crusoe* the footprint remains mysterious, its significance elusive, its meaning irreducible to rational explanation or control. Unobliterated by winds, tides, animals, or by Crusoe's rationalizations, it remains uncompromisingly there in the sand, larger than life, single in number and therefore lacking an efficient cause. It is an expressionistic symbol, embodying Crusoe's fears. It symbolizes danger from surroundings Crusoe was certain he had domesticated, and is terrifying because the danger it represents had been present but unnoticed all the time as a result of his complacency about having mastered himself and his surroundings. It symbolizes a threat from other people, savages, anarchistic forces, to the civilization he has so painfully constructed, with his food animals, his crops, his fortress and country seat, his family, and his table equal to that supplied by Leadenhall market to London consumers. Finally, the footprint, symbolizing as in a nightmare an ever-present but overlooked danger, is connected to two opposite forces in Defoe's own mind: the secret desire to relax all effort, to surrender to his environment by lapsing into fearful inertia, and the opposite urge to run amuck with restlessness and anger, becoming himself the instrument that smashes his own civilization. As George Starr points out about Defoe's imaginative projections,

> Such mastery as the Defoean hero achieves over himself and his world is quite precarious: it involves insulation and repression rather than openness and liberation, an imposing of order on everything alien and threatening rather than that benign acceptance of the facts of otherness and disorder (or order beyond man's contriving) which we find at the conclusion of a Sophoclean or Shakespearean tragedy.[4]

Dissatisfaction with Order: Fortresses into Prisons

Defoe's ambivalence about order and rational control is best exemplified by his creation of prosaic fictional characters, driven out of the domesticity that seems natural for them into the quest for adventure by mysterious and undefined motives.[5] The transmutation by which painstakingly constructed protective enclosures become prisons, constricting the freedom of these fictional characters, illustrates how difficult it is to pin down Defoe's consciousness and yet how consistently this consciousness varies. On the one hand, the contours of enclosures or fortresses blur disconcertingly before our eyes to reconstitute themselves as prison walls. On the other hand, the limits of their metamorphoses are fixed; if protective enclosures become constricting, constricting enclosures in turn become protective. Thus, ambivalence in Defoe is not inconsistency; rather, it is variation along a predictable path.

The discussion of 'shut' or quarantined houses that runs through *A Journal of the Plague Year* is a clear illustration of the consistent path taken by Defoe's ambivalence. On the one hand, H.F. approves highly of the actions of Dutch merchants, who laid in stores of provisions in anticipation of the plague and then imposed their own quarantines on their families, keeping 'their Houses like little Garrisons besieged' (p. 55). (In *Due Preparations for the Plague*, a non-fiction work, Defoe provided detailed instructions on preparing for self-quarantine.) H.F. contrasts the prudence of these merchants to the 'supine Negligence' of most, which 'during the long Notice, or Warning they had of the Visitation', was apparent in their failure to make plans for it 'by laying in Store of Provisions, or of other Necessaries' (p. 75). Literal imprisonment in quarantined houses is the fate of those who have failed to make rational provision for themselves and their families in the face of the plague: 'Here were just so many Prisons in the Town, as there were Houses shut up; and as the People shut up or imprison'd so, were guilty of no Crime, only shut up because miserable, it was really the more intollerable [*sic*] to them' (p. 52). Thus, to lay in provisions in advance, to choose one's own quarantine, is to construct a fortress or citadel; to have quarantine imposed by others is to allow oneself to be imprisoned.

On the other hand, H.F. finds it difficult to make up his mind about state-enforced quarantine. He recognizes the objective need for such a policy, but most of the time his emphasis upon individual suffering leads H.F. to stress the opposition. Desperation at being quarantined drove the afflicted out of their beds 'to wander abroad with the Plague upon them' (p. 71). He finally concludes against it, as much on the score of the severities it occasioned as for the fact that state-enforced quarantine did not 'answer the End' for which it was designed, preventing the spread of the plague (p. 170). (H.F. observes that many of the sick were unaware of their illness until they suddenly collapsed from it; there was no way to prevent such cases from carrying the plague among others unawares.)

H.F. himself is late in equipping his household as a fortress against the plague. He takes some measures and can therefore choose to barricade himself inside during the period when the disease is at its height. No Dutch merchant, however, he feels his fortress rapidly becomes a prison to him. He is subject to occasional unrestrainable fits of impatience at 'being pent up within Doors without Air' (p. 104), going so far on one of his excursions as the wildly improvident adventure of viewing in person the bodies 'shot . . . promiscuously' into the great burial pit at Aldgate (p. 62).

Prison in *A Journal of the Plague Year* is a metaphor for intellectual passivity. The tenor of this metaphor is the attitude against which H.F.'s central battle is waged, the attitude expressed by the term 'Mahometan predestination', a phrase repeated three times in the course of the *Journal*. The first time is when H.F.'s brother attempts to persuade him to take refuge in the country before London is overrun by the plague:

> Then he proceeded to tell me of the mischievous Conse-quences which attended the Presumption of the *Turks* and *Mahometans* in *Asia* and in other Places, where he had been . . . and how presuming upon their profess'd predestinating Notions, and of every Man's End being predetermin'd and unalterably before-hand decreed, they would go unconcern'd into infected Places, and converse with infected Persons, by which Means they died at the Rate of Ten and Fifteen Thousand a Week, whereas the *Europeans*, or Christian Merchants, who kept them-selves retired and reserv'd, generally escap'd the Contagion.

The second time is during H.F.'s consideration of the controversy over whether the plague is transmitted through contagion or through infected air, and the third time occurs during H.F.'s description of Londoners' rash behaviour when they hear that the plague is abating; like the second, it equates the miasmatic theory with Mohammedan notions of predestination: 'Not the *Mahometans*, who, prepossess'd with the Principle of Predestination value nothing of Contagion, let it be in what it will, could be more obstinate than the People of *London* . . .' (p. 230).

It seems apparent from these references that 'Mahometan predestination' refers to an attitude of surrendering without struggle and relinquishing the responsibility to choose every action and every belief, consciously sorting out the arguments for and against it. Louis Landa, in his excellent introduction to the Oxford edition of the *Journal*, relates Turkish predestinating notions to the traditional Christian question of conscience in the problem of whether or not to flee the plague.[6] I think the notion clearly has psychological connotations for Defoe and that the struggle against this attitude can be traced in the position H.F. takes on many of the issues he discusses.

On the question of whether it was 'natural to the infected People to desire to infect others' (p. 70), H.F. refuses to accept such perversity as natural. He attributes the propagation of this false report to other causes. Those who broke out of quarantine and ran about wildly from one place to another, not caring whom they injured, were out of their minds with illness and desperation (p. 70). In addition, many of the people transmitting the infection were unaware that they themselves were not perfectly sound in health (p. 199). In the incubation stage of the disease it was often 'impossible to know the infected People from the sound; or that the infected People should perfectly know themselves . . .' (p. 191).

Unable to accept the notion of widespread gratuitous, and therefore irrational, malice among the sick, H.F. makes certain to report that he himself knew good, pious, and religious people who forbade their own families to see them in their illness and, to avoid infecting them, 'even died without seeing their nearest Relations' (p. 70). He is unwilling to believe that maliciousness or gratuitous evil, such as the impulse to murder, might be a basic human motivation (pp. 199–200).

The rumoured cruelty toward Londoners fleeing the plague by inhabitants of towns adjacent to London is another ignorant exaggeration. 'Where there was room for Charity and Assistance to the People, without apparent Danger to themselves, they were willing enough to help and relive them', H.F. reports (p. 153). But in face of the terrible danger to themselves, rational self-interest required caution, which explained cases of ill usage of Londoners.

Was murder of the sick by their nurses as common a crime during the epidemic as many have since maintained? 'Robberies and wicked Practices' H.F. will allow, for he is willing to admit that 'the Power of Avarice was so strong in some, that they would run any Hazard to steal and to plunder' (p. 83). But murder is another matter entirely; admission of its widespread practice would be tantamount to accepting violence as intrinsic to human nature, something none of Defoe's protagonists, viewing it always as the exception, is willing to do.[7] H.F. uses his powers of analysis to allay the danger that people might accept such violence as normal.

That H.F.'s bent of mind is characteristic of Defoe's own continual concern with ejecting uncontrollable emotions from his ideal world, is illustrated by his non-fiction. In *The Storm* (1704), Defoe's first venture into reporting, an elaborate compilation, with narrative commentary, of eyewitness reports of the greatest storm in English history, he attests with horror to observed incidents of robbery, commenting upon the baseness of human beings who would take advantage of the distress caused by a natural calamity to cause more distress to others. The enormous distance Defoe travelled from his early historical work to the later fiction, which also deals with a great natural disaster and is built upon facts, is revealed by the contrast between the *Storm* and the *Journal*. In the latter work, facts are subjected to Defoe's narrative design to use them in structuring his account of the rise, spread, and decline of the plague, and to his rhetorical design to do battle with 'Mahometan predestination'.

It is possible to predict H.F.'s position on all the issues he discusses in the *Journal*, simply by considering his antipathy to and fear of the kind of attitude he characterizes as Mahometan predestination. Accepting the miasmatic over the contagion theory of infection means accepting the notion that individual effort to avoid the plague makes no difference at all. Accepting the notion that God's wrath alone accounts for the plague, without considering natural causes, again renders individual effort superfluous, inspiring such practices as running wildly to conjurers, astrologers, and other quacks, rather than praying soberly to God for forgiveness of sin, asking for compassion, and taking practical measures to protect oneself and one's family.

Yet H.F.'s interest in the natural causes of the plague, those accessible to human logic through scientific and medical information, does not cancel out the sense of mystery that pervades the *Journal*. Despite all the rational activities, mental and physical, projected and performed by H.F. and some Londoners in the account, the plague at its height mocks all their efforts, defies any attempt of human reason to control it. The frustration of reason is illustrated by the action of the Lord Mayor who, exhausted by conflicting arguments of physicians for and against the efficacy of fires in purifying the air, orders no more fires. All the prescriptions of medicine are of no avail, and Londoners give up their efforts in despair. Because of the ineffectuality of all human effort, the sudden slackening of the plague appears clearly the result of supernatural intervention.

Despite the victory of the plague at its height over all efforts of human reason, fortitude, and energy, the final effect of the *Journal* is not (as it will be in *Roxana*) to present the gradual domination of inexplicable and mysterious forces over measures dictated by rationality. London does not remain a deserted city, gradually turning back to pasture, with grass growing in its streets, its populace sequestered in the little prisons of their houses. For one thing, the plague does recede. For another, H.F., reporting after the event, is concerned with analysing rumours and reports, sifting out evidence as accurately as possible. His position as historian requires that he avoid being unduly swayed by the hysteria and despair so prominent in the scenes he is describing, that he keep a proper distance from his subject matter. Indeed, at the time when the plague rages at its height, H.F., with his brooding concern for London, his deep piety under God's chastisement, and his intellectual scepticism, provides the only source of stability in the *Journal*.[8]

This attitude of qualified scepticism, of intellectual restraint, runs counter to the subject he is describing, sets up a tension between H.F. and most of the Londoners in the account, and serves to enrich the tone of the *Journal*. Further, it illustrates Defoe's habitual unconscious desire to have things two ways at once, for the rationalistic technique by which H.F. bears witness to what is felt as essentially a divine visitation, beyond the control of human will, attests to Defoe's accommodation of two contemporary views of the plague as 'on the one hand a divine visitation and on the other a natural calamity'.[9]

The narrative of *Robinson Crusoe* is the account of how a single man gradually masters his own compulsions and extends his control over a huge, indifferent, even potentially hostile environment, learning to harness its inhuman forces and to put them to use for his own benefit. In this process, which is essentially that of rationalizing the unknown, the immeasurable, and the inexplicable, the forces that are being tamed stand in imminent danger of disappearing altogether. Once they are completely mastered, when Crusoe becomes infallible, *Robinson Crusoe* dwindles to the dimensions of a do-it-yourself and an adventure story, as in the final section, after Friday has been domesticated, or a travel story, as in the *Farther Adventures of Robinson Crusoe*.

One of the chief impediments to Crusoe's mastery of his environment is his own restlessness. Just as H.F.'s fortress home is transformed by his impatience and restlessness into a prison, Crusoe's prospective comfortable middle station in England, his life as a successful Brazilian planter, his comfortable fortification by the seaside of his island, the island itself, the whole civilization he has constructed on the island, are repeatedly transmuted by his 'rambling Thoughts' into constriction and bondage.

Crusoe's restlessness is the personal trait by which he is first introduced to his readers. His 'wandring Inclination' (p. 4) for going to sea drives him to reject all the advice, entreaty, and command of his father, his mother, and his friend's father, captain of the ship in which he makes his first abortive voyage.

In speaking of a series of voyages that preceded the ill-fated one to Guinea, Crusoe deplores his having preferred the role of leisured gentleman to that of novice sailor and as a result learning nothing about navigation.

Once he begins to settle into the life of a Brazilian planter, he reflects bitterly:

> . . . I was coming into the very Middle Station, or upper Degree of low Life, which my Father advised me to before; and which if I resolved to go on with, I might as well ha' staid at Home, and never have fatigu'd my self in the World as I had done; and I used often to say to my self, I could ha' done this as well in *England* among my Friends, as ha' gone 5000 Miles off to do it among Strangers and Salvages [*sic*] in a Wilderness, and at such a Distance, as never to hear from any Part of the World that had the least Knowledge of me. (p. 35)

Nevertheless, he perseveres in his efforts, and after several years of hard work at his new occupation, begins to be very successful. At this point, 'increasing in Business and in Wealth, my Head began to be full of Projects and Undertakings beyond my Reach; such as are indeed often the Ruine of the best Heads in Business' (pp. 37–8).

Crusoe attributes his decision to direct a slave-buying expedition to the coast of Guinea to a 'rash and immoderate Desire of rising faster than the Nature of the Thing admitted' (p. 38), the kind of remark that leads Ian Watt to assert that Crusoe's original sin 'is really the dynamic tendency of capitalism itself'.[10] But Crusoe also observes:

> . . . All these Miscarriages were procured by my apparent obstinate adhering to my foolish inclination of wandring abroad and pursuing that Inclination, in contradiction to the clearest Views of doing my self good in a fair and plain pursuit of those Prospects and those measures of Life, which Nature and Providence concurred to present me with, and to make my Duty. (p. 38)

Here it is clear that Crusoe believes that considerations of economic advancement would have dictated his staying at home and tending to his business, rather than rushing off all over the world at the bidding of his wanderlust. The accuracy of his insight is confirmed by the conclusion of his narrative; he learns that while he has been toiling on his island to provide himself with necessities of life, back in Brazil a fortune has been piling up for him from the production of his plantation, quite independently of any effort on his part. In Crusoe's case wanderlust conflicts with economic advantage—idiosyncratic temperament takes precedence over economics.

After his recovery from a severe illness on his island, Crusoe reflects with annoyance upon one result of his restlessness when he lived in Brazil. Making an exploratory survey of the island, he finds he is unable to recognize the plants he comes across:

> I . . . came back musing with my self what Course I might take to know the Vertue and Goodness of any of the Fruits or Plants which I should discover; but could bring it to no Conclusion; for in short, I had made so little Observation while I was in the *Brasils*, that I knew little of the Plants in the Field, at least very little that might serve me to any Purpose now in my Distress. (p. 98–9)

One of Crusoe's major activities during the island portion of his narrative is fortification, or the construction of walls and enclosures.[11] These structures are described as circles and fences, the same figures Defoe employed in writing for the *Review* after 1710. The seaside home Crusoe constructs is a camouflaged fortress protecting him from sun, rain, man, and beast, although it does not in the end secure him from his internal enemy. His home also provides Crusoe with contentment; a domestic Eden, it supplies in an orderly manner the necessities, even comforts, of life. Crusoe grows to love this place so much that he looks forward to returning to it after his many explorations of the island: 'I cannot express what a Satisfaction it was to me, to come into my old Hutch, and lye down in my Hamock-Bed; This little wandring Journey, without settled Place of Abode, had been so unpleasant to me, compar'd to that . . .' (p. 111).

Yet in spite of the security and comfort provided by Crusoe's seaside abode, his old restlessness soon reasserts its sway. The calm produced by his religious conversion at first causes an instantaneous transformation of his island in his eyes, if not changing it into a castle or fortress, at least softening its prison contours:

Before, as I walk'd about, either on my Hunting, or for viewing the Country, the Anguish of my Soul at my Condition, would break out upon me on a sudden, and my very Heart would die within me, to think of the Woods, the Mountains, the Desarts I was in; *and how I was a Prisoner lock'd up with the Eternal Bars and Bolts of the Ocean, in an uninhabited Wilderness, and without Redemption. . . .*

But now I began to exercise my self with new Thoughts; I daily read the Word of God, and apply'd all the Comforts of it to my present State. . . . (p. 113, my italics)

In the same way the re-emergence of Crusoe's restlessness will transform the island instantaneously, first into an ambiguous structure—fortified castle/prison—and then back in a twinkling to a refuge.

When Crusoe's imagination is fired by a glimpse of the mainland he has caught, he begins thinking about escaping there, without according sufficient attention to the possibility of falling into the hands of the cannibal inhabitants. After overly ambitious efforts to restore and to fashion a big boat, he finally succeeds in making a 'little Periagua' and sets sail for a tour around his island on the sixth of November, 'in the sixth Year of my *Reign*, or my *Captivity*, which you please' (my italics, p. 137—this is the ambiguous state, neither fully fortress nor prison, to which I referred above). In a twinkling all the fortifications of five years' labour, all the domestic comforts, have become intolerable bonds of captivity in Crusoe's eyes.

As a substitute for the security and comfort he is about to cast off, Crusoe equips his boat in a decidedly domestic manner with food, drink, clothes, ammunition, and an umbrella for shade. Once on the water, however, he is caught in an unanticipated current and driven out to sea. Death, not from the calm sea, but from hunger, seems inevitable. Now, Crusoe reports, 'I look'd back upon my desolate solitary Island, as the most pleasant Place in the World, and all the Happiness my Heart could wish for, was to be but there again . . .' (p. 139).

Upon his unexpected deliverance from danger and return to land, Crusoe finds himself within walking distance of his 'country house', a second dwelling he had previously constructed for himself in a 'delicious vale'. His original rejection of this dwelling as his principal residence had been based upon the fear that removing from the seaside to bury himself in a valley would have been 'to anticipate [his] Bondage' (p. 101). Defoe's decision to have Crusoe return to his country seat rather than his seaside residence after a harrowing sea journey therefore suggests the extremity of Crusoe's emotional recoil from adventure. A voice calling, '*Robin, Robin, Robin Crusoe, poor Robin Crusoe*, where are you *Robin Crusoe*? Where are you? Where have you been?' (p. 142) awakens a terrified Crusoe abruptly from his deep sleep of exhaustion. (Refer to pp. 45–7 above for a letter addressed to a Scottish mob, which uses a similar refrain.) Although he realizes that the apparently supernatural voice is only that of a parrot he had trained to speak, it is a good while, he reports, before he is able to compose himself. No wonder he experiences this difficulty; the resonance of the questions posed by the mysterious voice seems to suggest something more general than Crusoe's recent death-defying voyage. (The same questions in Mr. Review's letter to the Glasgow mob did indeed refer to something more general than rioting.) Providence itself, or God, the tender father, seems to be asking his restless son to consider where his rambling thoughts have been leading him.

After this high point Defoe has Crusoe perform certain activities that suggest he is at last fully at home on his island, his internal restlessness subdued. Some external stimulus will now be required to reawaken Crusoe's desire for adventure. Such a stimulus is provided by the portentous footprint, which serves as the prelude to another movement of Crusoe's narrative. Again his 'unlucky Head, that was always to let me know it was born to make my Body miserable' (p. 194) is 'fill'd with Projects and Designs' for getting away from the island:

> All my Calm of Mind in my Resignation to Providence, and waiting the Issue of the Dispositions of Heaven, seem'd to be suspended; and I had, as it were, no Power to turn my Thoughts to any thing, but to the Project of a Voyage to the Main, which came upon me with such Force, and such an Impetuosity of Desire, that it was not to be resisted. (p. 198)

The footprint serves as catalyst, demonstrating that Crusoe's restlessness and precipitation have been only temporarily and conditionally exorcized by his harrowing excursion around the island. If indeed Crusoe has managed to quell the enemy within, his victory is conditioned by the proviso that no external ally come to its aid. The appearance of the footprint tempts Crusoe to destroy the whole civilization he has so painfully constructed in fifteen years of labour, 'to throw down [his] Enclosures', to 'demolish [his] Bower, and Tent' (p. 159).

Crusoe's restlessness makes him feel guilty of some original sin in disobeying his father and in not being able to content himself with the good things God has allotted him. It prevents him from being attentive to his surroundings, learning from them, and putting them to some useful purpose. Not being able to appreciate its particular qualities, he is frustrated in his attempts to master and to enjoy his environment, and consequently feels himself imprisoned by it. Furthermore, his sense of imprisonment goads him into rash undertakings like the Guinea voyage or the abortive tour around his island, in which the only escape from imprisonment is death, or into the temptation to destroy all his work of civilization.

Restlessness, or the desire for adventure, however, is not the only temperamental impediment to Crusoe's happiness, or his mastery of his environment. If his laboriously constructed fortified castles keep changing their contours and becoming prisons, if he is constantly tempted to climb over the walls he has built, or even to raze them to the ground, he is also tempted by the opposite tendency, to relax his strenuous efforts, to sink into pleasure and enjoyment, to allow himself to become absorbed by his surroundings, which annihilate 'all that's made/ To a green thought in a green shade'.[12] This second temperamental affinity is sometimes expressed by means of cave imagery and fear of being buried alive; Crusoe's seaside fortification, as we will recall, consisted of a cave as well as of a tent.

On 10 December Crusoe reports in his journal, 'I began now to think my Cave or Vault finished, when on a Sudden, (it seems I had made it too large) a great Quantity of Earth fell down from the Top and one Side, so much, that in short it frighted me, and not without Reason too; for if I had been under it I had never wanted a Grave-Digger' (p. 74). An earthquake and hurricane follow, and Crusoe considers moving his habitation to an open place. Yet in the end he remains where he is:

> The fear of being swallow'd up alive, made me that I never slept in quiet, and yet the Apprehensions of lying abroad without any Fence was almost equal to it; but still when I look'd about me and saw how every thing was put in order, how pleasantly conceal'd I was, and how safe from Danger, it made me very loath to remove. (p. 82)

In this quandary the pleasures of domestic comfort and of concealment carry the day. Paradoxically, however, the enclosure and cave are located at the seaside,[13] with its opportunity as well as danger of meeting others.

Crusoe's discovery that while he has been strenuously wresting the bare necessities of life from his island a fortune has been piling up for him in Brazil, independently of any effort on his part, serves to suggest an unspoken longing for this alternative pattern of reposeful life in his creator's consciousness. Indeed, in retrospect Crusoe's life upon the island appears to him an emblem of such a pattern, at least in the sphere of economics:

> I was now to consider which Way to steer my Course next, and what to do with the Estate that Providence had thus put into my Hands; and indeed I had more Care upon my Head now, than I had in my silent State of Life in the Island, where I wanted nothing but what I had, and had nothing but what I wanted: Whereas I had now a great Charge upon me, and my Business was how to secure it. *I had ne'er a Cave now to hide my Money in*, or a Place where it might lye without Lock or Key, 'till it grew mouldy and tarnish'd before any Body would meddle with it. . . . (pp. 285–86, my italics)

The last sentence of the preceding paragraph crystallizes Defoe's characteristic metaphor of the fortress, the metaphor one senses growing under the surface of the last few sentences, after the verb 'secure': 'My old Patron, the Captain, indeed was honest, and that was the only Refuge I had.'

The temptation to relax and to become absorbed by his environment occurs intermittently in Crusoe's narrative. Its most arresting appearance is in the scene in which Crusoe shoots the unknown bird. In that scene Crusoe resists the temptation to reverie by resorting to physical violence—he shoots and kills a bird—and intellectual exercise—he analyses and attempts to fix and classify the unknown fowl, dismissing it finally by concluding, 'Its Flesh was Carrion, and fit for nothing' (p. 53). Having broken the spell of his surroundings, Crusoe again falls to work conveying and disposing of the cargo he had previously stripped from the wrecked ship.

Another occasion on which Crusoe's surroundings tempt him to reverie occurs in the course of his exploration across the whole of his island. When he comes within view of the sea to the west, the sight of land offshore awakens his characteristic restlessness. Crusoe allays his impatience with the consideration that the land he descries is probably inhabited by savages, that if he had landed there he would have been in a worse condition than he was now. But immediately he recovers from one temperamental infirmity, he is threatened by the other, its opposite:

> With these Considerations [that he is better off on his island than on the mainland] I walk'd very leisurely forward, I found that Side of the Island where I now was, much pleasanter than mine, the open or *Savanna* Fields sweet, adorn'd with Flowers and Grass, and full of very fine Woods. I saw Abundance of Parrots, and fain I would have caught one, if possible to have kept it to be tame, and taught it to speak to me. I did, after some Pains taking, catch a young Parrot, for I knock'd it down with a Stick, and having recover'd it, I brought it home; but it was some Years before I could make him speak. (p. 109)

Despite the absence of visual detail, Crusoe's leisurely walk suggests a sense of reverie, a semi-hypnotic mood of absorption in his surroundings. His sudden gesture, knocking down the parrot with a stick (the only solid object in this generalized description), acts as an abrupt intrusion upon this mood, dissipating it by an act of violence in the same way that Crusoe's shooting the bird dissipated the mood of that scene. Significantly, however, the action itself occurs 'after some Pains taking', and the future process of teaching the parrot to talk is to be so arduous as to require 'some Years'. Thus Defoe dramatizes in miniature the only successful pattern of action by which Crusoe can rescue his tools from the ship, build the walls of his two habitations, make boards and boats, bake bread, and in general, master his island environment.

Only after Crusoe has proved that he can build by continuous effort a substitute civilization, that he is in no danger from his own impulses of lapsing into sloth, can he permit himself to appreciate whole-heartedly the delights of a natural earth cave he discovers:

> When I was got through the Strait, I found the Roof rose higher up, I believe near twenty Foot; but never was such a glorious Sight seen in the Island, I dare say, as it was, to look round the Sides and Roof of this Vault, or Cave; the Walls reflected 100 thousand Lights to me from my two Candles; what it was in Rock, whether Diamonds, or any other precious Stones, or Gold, which I rather suppos'd it to be, I knew not.
>
> The Place I was in, was a most delightful Cavity, or Grotto, of its kind, as could be expected, though perfectly dark; the Floor was dry and level, and had a sort of small lose Gravel upon it, so that there was no nauseous or venemous Creature to be seen, neither was there any damp, or wet, on the Sides or Roof. . . . (pp. 178–79)

The description of the grotto stresses its delightfulness and the pleasure it arouses in Crusoe, the almost tactile sense of being securely included, instead of being separated from his surroundings. When Crusoe decides to remove his gunpowder to this delightful and secure place, he discovers that water has penetrated a few inches into the barrel of powder, 'which caking and growing hard, had preserv'd the inside like a Kernel in a Shell' (p. 179), a detail particularly appropriate to this episode.

The element of visual detail in the above description is rare in *Robinson Crusoe*, where such detail is reserved economically for the exotic: Friday's physiognomy and Crusoe's extraordinary-looking outfit. In addition to Crusoe's uncharacteristic appreciation of the visual aesthetics of his grotto, the security it affords inspires him to an unusual bout of fancy:

> I fancy'd my self now like one of the ancient Giants, which are said to live in Caves, and Holes, in the Rocks, where none could come at them. . . .
>
> I was now in my twenty third Year of Residence in this Island, and was so naturaliz'd to the Place, and to the Manner of Living,

that could I have but enjoy'd the Certainty that no Savages would come to the Place to disturb me, I could have been content to have capitulated for spending the rest of my Time there, even to the last Moment, till I had laid me down and dy'd, like the old Goat in the Cave. (pp. 179–80)

Envisioning himself now as a creature of fable, he is willing to allow himself to become merged with his environment, accepting its shelter like other (non-human) living creatures. Crusoe's willingness to consider himself and a goat on the same level is highly significant, for it is the first instance I have encountered in Defoe's fiction where a comparison drawn between a human being and an animal is not uncomplimentary, sometimes even terrifying.

Other signs which indicate that Crusoe has learned to live harmoniously with his environment, neither failing to put it to fruitful use because of restlessness, nor sinking passively into subjection to it because of sensuousness, idleness, or atavism, include the following:

Crusoe succeeds in reaching land after the ship's boat founders, by swimming with the incoming waves. (pp. 44–6)

He lands his raft by co-operating with the tide in order to harness its force. (pp. 51–2)

He learns to observe the proper seasons for planting. (p. 105)

He prunes the trees at his 'Country Seat' to make 'the more agreeable Shade'. (p. 152)

He succeeds in making a tobacco pipe, an article that contributes to a sense of peace with oneself. He weaves more baskets; he entraps and encloses goats; he strengthens the enclosures of both his residences. In a mock heroic vein, he sits down to dinner in his fortified castle as father and as benevolent despot:

It would have made a Stoick smile to have seen, me and my little Family sit down to Dinner; there was my Majesty the Prince and Lord of the whole Island; I had the Lives of all my Subjects at my absolute Command. I could hang, draw, give Liberty, and take it away, and no Rebels among all my Subjects.

Then to see how like a King I din'd too all alone, attended by my Servants, *Poll*, as if he had been my Favourite, was the only Person permitted to talk to me. My Dog who was now grown very old and crazy, and had found no Species to multiply his

81

> Kind upon, sat always at my Right Hand, and two Cats, one on
> one Side the Table, and one on the other, expecting now and then
> a Bit from my Hand, as a Mark of special Favour. (p. 148)

He encases his body in protective coverings, whose exotic
appearance is described fully by Defoe, almost as if he were
striving to localize and fix Crusoe to the utmost in his island
environment before the next section of his story, beginning
with the footprint and filled with fear and frenetic activity,
begins to unroll.

After Crusoe's next bout of restlessness has been exorcized
by finding himself a companion, Defoe's description of Friday
reveals his protagonist's continual attempt to shape or to
prune potentially inimical elements in his environment:

> He was a comely handsome Fellow, perfectly well made; with
> straight strong Limbs, not too large; tall and well shap'd, and
> as I reckon, about twenty six Years of Age. He had a very good
> Countenance, *not a fierce and surly Aspect*; but seem'd to have
> something very manly in his Face, and *yet he had all the Sweetness
> and Softness of an European in his Countenance too*, especially when
> he smil'd. His Hair was long and black, *not curl'd like Wool*; his
> Forehead very high, and large, and a great Vivacity and
> sparkling Sharpness in his Eyes. *The Colour of his Skin was not
> quite black*, but very tawny; and *yet not of an ugly yellow nauseous
> tawny*, as the *Brasilians*, and *Virginians*, and other Natives of
> *America* are; but of a bright kind of dun olive Colour, that had in
> it something very agreeable; tho' not very easy to describe. His
> Face was round, and plump; his Nose small, *not flat like the
> Negroes*, a very good Mouth, *thin Lips*, and his fine Teeth well
> set, and white as Ivory. (pp. 205–6, my italics)

I have tried to indicate with italics the effort to edit, or to
soften, features that must have been terrifying or repulsive to
English readers of Defoe's day.[14] The unacceptable, the visual
signs of some terrifying or alien power, are deliberately softened
by Crusoe, in the same way that he shaped pieces of wood or
pruned trees for his physical and aesthetic needs. Friday too
belongs to the environment around Crusoe, and the same
ingenuity that harnessed the tide is now to be employed in
fashioning Friday as a servant, companion, Christian, and son
who would have been dear to the heart of the plain-dealing
Mr. Review.

Responding to Charles Gildon's charge that *Robinson Crusoe* was a fiction, not a genuine autobiography, Defoe insisted that his contemporary was mistaken; in some sense the story was autobiographical. He never explained why the marooning of Alexander Selkirk had proved so powerful a catalyst to his own imagination, but he undoubtedly felt something about his literary offspring was more true than fact itself. (See pp. 100–3 below for his attitude about truth and fiction.) To a modern reader, it seems clear that Defoe regarded himself in some essential way as an outcast from society. As a result of the observations he made about Sacheverell in the *Shortest Way*, he writes in the *Review*, 'I suffered the overthrow of my fortune and family, and . . . I remain a banished man to this day' (16:455). Talking about the fate of debtors, he observes from experience that it was 'as if the debtor, immediately upon his being insolvent, became divested of all his birthright or claim to the title of subject, and was actually outlawed, and left like a wild creature, at the mercy of the next pack of hounds that came in his way' (16:535–36).

Robinson Crusoe feels himself an outcast from the time he defies his father's wish that he not go to sea. He is treated like an outcast at the end of his first disastrous sea voyage by the captain of the ship, whom he tells about his father's opposition. The captain reacts too strongly, if one considers only the literal level of Crusoe's story, blaming the young man for the sinking of the ship.[15] A planter in Brazil, Crusoe complains to himself that he 'had no body to converse with but now and then this Neighbour', and that he 'liv'd just like a Man cast away upon some desolate Island, that had no body there but himself' (p. 35). On the island itself, his most painful affliction is

> that I seem'd banish'd from human Society, that I was alone, circumscrib'd by the boundless Ocean, cut off from Mankind, and condemn'd to what I call'd silent Life; that I was as one who Heaven thought not worthy to be number'd among the Living, or to appear among the rest of his Creatures. (p. 156)

Yet in spite of Crusoe's longing for company, he is frightened of other people.[16] The footprint represents his fear of others, and cannibalism takes on the larger significance in Crusoe's narrative of man's brutality to man. Eating people is mentioned so frequently in *Robinson Crusoe* that although most of the references are literal descriptions of savage practice or of survival tactics in lifeboats, cannibalism seems extraordinarily widespread as a custom. In *Farther Adventures of Robinson Crusoe*, a travel narrative giving occasion for frequent contact with others, the motif of fear and the connotations of cannibalism become overt. Fear to the extent of paranoia is seen in the reaction of native prisoners given as a food gift by their countrymen to a group of Englishmen (p. 186).[17] The link between fear of man and man as worse than cannibal is made almost explicitly in *Farther Adventures* when Crusoe and his partner, who have inadvertently bought a ship stolen from the Dutch, become obsessed by fear of being mistaken for pirates. At rare intervals Crusoe plucks up his spirits and makes vigorous resolutions that he will die fighting rather than be

> barbarously used by a parcel of merciless wretches, in cold blood; that it were much better to have fallen into the hands of the savages, who were man eaters, and who, I was sure, would feast upon me, when they had taken me; than by those, who would perhaps *glut their rage upon me*, by inhuman tortures and barbarities; . . . for the savages, give them their due, would not eat a man till he was dead, and killed them first, as we do a bullock; but that these men had many arts beyond the cruelty of death. (p. 142, my italics)

In the end Crusoe conquers his fear of other people. His re-entry into society is prefaced by establishing an idyllic paternal and didactic relation with Friday. Crusoe re-enters society as an equal of the ship's captain he has rescued from mutineers and to whom he has revealed his whole history. Each of the two men embraces the other as deliverer (p. 273), the captain presents him with gifts and clothes him from head to foot in civilized garments (p. 274). Greeting the mutineers in his new clothes, Crusoe is now addressed as governor of his island rather than as emissary of an unseen governor (p. 275). Back in England, his fortune in order because of the loyalty and fair dealing of all the acquaintances of his pre-island life, Crusoe acts as father to two nephews, educating them and settling them in the world, then himself marries and has three children.

The unmitigated good fortune of the ending of Crusoe's narrative marks it as a perfect example of the side of Defoe that longed for an ideal world of peace, harmony, clarity, order, and simplicity.[18] Yet the wish fulfilment victory of Crusoe is not complete, for the restlessness that caused his original difficulties begins to reassert itself by the end of his narrative.[19]

In the section on the ideal world in Chapter 1, I pointed out that the plain-dealing Mr. Review suggests occasionally that a state of peace is not to be found in this world and even associates peace with the stasis of death. This association is made clearly in Mr. Review's comment on autarky. In a human condition where desire is absent and all are equal, we might be better off, but we would be impoverished, lacking excitement and social intercourse: 'There would be no manner of correspondence of one part of the world with another', and 'men would move in a very narrow sphere' (22:109–10).

The intense concentration in *Robinson Crusoe* upon the conquering of self and of nature by the protagonist is predicated upon a long period of solitude. Without the unusual absence of emotional and ethical complications introduced by interaction with other people, Crusoe's victory over himself could not have been the subject of Defoe's narrative. The incursion of others—cannibals, European sailors—on Crusoe's island is the signal for change in the narrative, a change perceptible even in the pattern of humour. Understatement and mock heroic descriptions that re-enact through self-deprecation Crusoe's effort to limit and contain his feelings are replaced by expansive games of hoax, masquerade, and hide-and-seek designed to fool others. As we will see in the other fictions I shall discuss, these motifs, subordinate in *Robinson Crusoe*, become dominant in fictions dealing with individuals in society.

NOTES

1. All quotations from Defoe's fiction, unless otherwise indicated, are taken from the Oxford English Novels editions. Here are the fiction editions published in London by Oxford University Press: *Roxana*, ed. Jane Jack (1964); *Colonel Jack*, ed. Samuel Holt Monk (1965); *A Journal of the Plague Year*, ed. Louis Landa and *Captain Singleton*, ed. Shiv. K. Kumar

(1969); *Moll Flanders*, ed. G. A. Starr (1971); *Memoirs of a Cavalier*, ed. James T. Boulton and *Robinson Crusoe*, ed. J. Donald Crowley (1972).

2. Arthur Secord, *Studies in the Narrative Method of Defoe* (Urbana: University of Illinois, 1924), p. 98.

3. G. A. Starr points out, 'In Defoe's novels, God and the Adam of Genesis 1:19–29 tend to become one: things are not called into being and then named, but often called into being *by* being named.' The description in question is an exception to this general rule. See 'Defoe's Prose Style: 1. The Language of Interpretation', *MP*, 71 (1974), 288.

4. Starr, 292–93.

5. I have borrowed the notion of adventure from Paul Zweig's *The Adventurer* (New York: Basic Books, 1974), but I disagree with his analysis of *Robinson Crusoe*.

6. Louis Landa (ed.), *A Journal of the Plague Year*, introduction, pp. xxix–xxx. The same kind of middle ground between total inactivity and excessive activity is advocated in *Memoirs of a Cavalier*. Three types of military campaign are described: Gustavus Adolphus' method is one that combines daring with strategy; Prince Maurice's method is one that sets up sieges and waits until the enemy is starved out; Prince Rupert's method is one that falls upon the enemy the moment he catches sight of him. It is not difficult to guess which method the Cavalier, as spokesman for Defoe, approves.

   Michael Boardman argues, in his *Defoe and the Uses of Narrative* (New Brunswick: Rutgers University Press, 1983), that Louis Landa, George Starr, and Everett Zimmerman are misguided in attributing a semantic function to H.F.'s decision about remaining in London during the plague. Analysing the *Journal* as pseudo-historical writing, Boardman believes that the narrator's decision is described by Defoe solely for the purpose of endowing H.F. with plausibility (pp. 80–96).

7. Even Bob Singleton, the pirate captain, is less bloodthirsty than one of his companions, Captain Wilmot. Manuel Schonhorn points out in 'Defoe's *Captain Singleton*: A Reassessment with Observations', in *Papers on Language and Literature*, 7 (1971), that Singleton reveals Defoe's characteristic minimization of violence. The same disinclination appears in *Robinson Crusoe*, where Crusoe 'repeatedly rationalizes himself out of retributive violence upon the natives'. Schonhorn concludes, 'Even in Defoe's military memoirs, something of the [same] kind occurs' (p. 47).

8. In *Defoe and Casuistry* (Princeton: Princeton University Press, 1971), Starr points out that Defoe is advocating in the *Journal* a frame of mind both rationalistic and religious, 'which can be brought to bear on perplexities of all kinds'. Accordingly, his narrator's 'characteristic manner . . . is to juxtapose and mediate between the claims of reason and faith', and his 'posture thus comes to seem a model of sustained moderation, at once deliberate and devout' (pp. 80–1).

9. Landa, p. xviii.

10. Ian Watt, *The Rise of the Novel* (Berkeley and Los Angeles: University of California Press, 1959), p. 65. Besides, as a mercantilist, not a capitalist, Defoe in his writings on economics consistently opposed the engrossing

of the market by one entrepreneur—he advocated retirement after a moderate success in business.

11. Everett Zimmerman's perceptive observation about the purpose of Crusoe's fortifications can serve as a summary of my interpretation: 'Although concealment is necessary to Crusoe's defense, fortifications never figure in it. Crusoe fortifies to restore his psychic equilibrium; whenever he has brought his defenses to seeming perfection, he is again disturbed.' See *Defoe and the Novel* (Berkeley: University of California Press, 1975), p. 26.

12. My discussion of Crusoe's temptation to become absorbed by his environment was originally written in 1971, before I saw the seminal article by Homer O. Brown, 'The Displaced Self in the Novels of Daniel Defoe', *ELH*, 37 (1971), 562–90, and should be regarded as independent confirmation of Brown's argument.

13. Brown discusses the conflicting desires of Defoe's protagonists to expose and to conceal themselves.

14. Starr discusses the description of Friday in 'Defoe's Prose Style', emphasizing the savage's attractiveness to Crusoe and Crusoe's attempt to make what he had anticipated as a terrifying alien creature acceptable (pp. 282–83). Neither of us finds the description objective, but my concentration is on Defoe's depiction of yet another attempt by Crusoe to prune his environment.

15. Both J. Paul Hunter (*The Reluctant Pilgrim: Defoe's Emblematic Method and Quest for Form in 'Robinson Crusoe'*, Baltimore: The Johns Hopkins Press, 1966, p. 137) and G. A. Starr (*Defoe and Spiritual Autobiography*, Princeton: Princeton University Press, 1965, p. 94), accept without question the captain's reaction to Crusoe, for they discuss *Robinson Crusoe* from the perspective of the traditions of spiritual autobiography, spiritual biography, and pilgrim allegory. Given the religious starting point of their analyses, questions about the exact nature of Crusoe's original sin are not in order. From my point of view, however, it seems significant that Crusoe feels like a pariah from the very start of his adventures. Not only is the feeling significant, but it is singular, for most sinners do not feel so radically cut off from other human beings.

16. Brown discusses cannibalism and Crusoe's fear of others. Anticipating him on cannibalism, however, was a section from Frank Ellis's excellent introduction to *Twentieth Century Interpretations of 'Robinson Crusoe'* (Englewood Cliffs, N.J.: Prentice-Hall, 1969), pp. 12–14. Ellis points out, 'Images of eating and being eaten not only predominate in *Robinson Crusoe*, they also give the work something of its literary shape' (p. 12). In addition, he suggests what cannibals stood for in Defoe's private life when he cites a comment from Defoe's 1712 *Essay on the South-Sea Trade* classifying loan sharks as 'cannibals' (Ellis, p. 8).

17. *The Farther Adventures of Robinson Crusoe* (Oxford: Shakespeare Head Press, 1927–28).

18. Paul Alkon's study of fictional time in Defoe leads him to an observation that seems to agree with my theory of Crusoe's representing Defoe's ideal world: 'Crusoe's life is perceived as a movement away from

historical time toward the encounter with private and sacred time on his island, followed by a return to participation in the era which he left.' See *Defoe and Fictional Time* (Athens: University of Georgia Press, 1979), p. 64.

19. I agree with much of John J. Richetti's analysis of Crusoe's 'successive elevation to higher and higher forms of mastery (the self, the environment, animals, natives, and . . . Europeans) . . .', and especially with his analysis of Crusoe's method of 'co-operating with events at the moment when they will serve'. See *Defoe's Narratives: Situations and Structures* (Oxford: Clarendon Press, 1975), pp. 60, 53.

But Pat Rogers reaches essentially the same conclusion as mine in his *Robinson Crusoe* (London: George Allen & Unwin, 1979) when he writes, 'The restlessness which drives Crusoe is the very spirit of his being. It will be extirpated not by the end of his actual travels, or by the accomplishment of any economic goal; it is part of man's fallen nature, and will survive until he achieves salvation in death. . . . For Crusoe the act of conversion brings insight, joy and a reanimated energy born of self-acceptance; but full release from the innate contradictions of his nature will come only with the "longer journey" out of mortal existence' (pp. 65–6).

3

The Real World of the Trickster

The Real World

In his descriptions of the real state of affairs in England, the worldly Mr. Review relegates the peace, harmony, and clarity of the plain-dealing Mr. Review's ideal world to the moon or to the mythical past:

> 'Tis from this Parliament the world expects to have knaves detected, fools abandoned, and honest men acknowledged; a time, which if it happens, this shall be called indeed the *Golden Age*, justice shall return again, honour shall revive, plenty shall flow, and peace follow.
>
> But what peace, while parties struggle, and the state divided, fluctuates with the unhappy alternatives of Whig and Tory, High and Low churchmen, moderation and madmen, it cannot be; to talk of peace or of prosperity, is to build forts in the upper regions, and planting colonies in the moon. (10:450)

The only people living in the present who enjoy the state of peace associated with the ideal world are the virtuous ignorant, the humble and uneducated. These are likely to be country people, distant from the turbulence of politics and public affairs (13:390).

Judging from Mr. Review's descriptions, what makes the real world a scene of continual strife is the unbridled emotions of human beings. England's party conflicts are simply an emblem of the natural state of man (10:442).

The 'wheel of circumstances' has afforded opportunity for

each madness of religion and of politics to take its turn upon the stage in England. The history of England, from the reign of Charles I to the present, is a history of mass hysteria (5:499). Under Queen Mary, Popery was mad, under the interregnum the Reformation was mad, and parties in politics have been as mad as parties in religion, from arbitrary power to the victors of the Civil War, to the heirs of the Glorious Revolution (5:499–500). Poor England has been 'hag ridden, priest ridden, and fool ridden', and now it is 'party ridden, which in its effect is worse than all of them' (10:450). Even in Parliament, party emotions make it impossible in matters of vital public concern for justice to be done in an impartial manner (10:450).

The cyclical recurrence of public hysteria is as irresistible as natural disasters (13:609). Not only can no reasonable individual stem the tide, but even those who have once succumbed to hysteria cannot apply their experience to the present and prevent themselves from behaving exactly the same way again at the first new opportunity (17:21).

Dishonesty is as much to blame as unbridled emotion for strife in the real world. This is nowhere more apparent than in matters of ethics, where discrepancies between principle and practice are the norm, and where private interests prevail over public concerns:

> Here are sneaking High Churchmen, mercenary Low Church, covetous and cowardly Dissenters, men of every side, of all parties; that call themselves this, but vote for that; a Whig tenant votes for a Tacking landlord; a Low Church nephew, votes for his High Church uncle, because he is his relation; as if the relation to our native country, and the preserving our religion and liberty to our posterity, were not nearer than humouring the civilities of a family. (4:126)

The outcome of lack of principle is chaos: 'We have here men of all principles voting for separate persuasions, men of no principles at all, vote for conscience sake; all are busy, and vote as retrograde as they talk . . .' (4:126). In this confusion, the base emotions of rancor and envy prevail over considerations of personal honour and decent behaviour to others (4:126).

Most important for understanding the chiaroscuro of the real world of Daniel Defoe is its ambiguity: 'A few honest men I must allow on all sides,' writes Mr. Review, 'but besides them, we have such a medley of amphibious monsters, that profess one thing, and act another; that look one way, and row another, that no man alive knows where to have them' (4:126).

Whereas the plain-speaking Mr. Review dealt with open enemies by arguing or taunting, the worldly Mr. Review must combat concealed enemies in an ambiguous world. He must supplement speech with action; he must fight duplicity with duplicity. From king to peasant 'all the world . . . are generally gulled by the misrepresentations of things, not by the plain and downright articles of force and oppression' (12:555).

Truth Hidden Behind Appearances

The plain-dealing Mr. Review, we will recall, wished to 'put plain things in a plain form, that a clear view may undeceive the people, and we may come all to understand the matter the same way' (19:199). The worldly Mr. Review is much less ingenuous. 'Can any man take the author of this paper', he asks, 'to be so shortsighted, as to think when he begun this work, all men should pay homage to his opinion, or that he should find the world all of the same mind?' (4:21).

Aware of the complexity of the real world, he knows that he can be sure of nothing if, professing to be a historian, he confines himself to external evidence alone. In the matter of fame or a good name, for instance, he points out,

> 'Tis a thing so nice, so full of counterfeits, so daubed over with false varnish, so much worn by hypocrites, coveted by men of vice, and neglected by men of ignorance that I do not care for embarking, in the search of what is so hard to be found; and what, when we have found it, we have so much difficulty to know, whether it be the true kind or no. (6:21)

To the question what makes truth so difficult to discern he offers no complete answer, but, piecing together scattered remarks, we may infer that the difficulty is partly due to our inability to see into the motives of others, and partly to our laziness and hypocrisy (19:110). In addition, pursuing self-interest when our private goal is unacceptable to others, we resort to excuses and disguises, usually managing in the process to hoodwink ourselves, if not others (6:202). (Defoe's perception here is relevant to debates among critics about how far the writer was cognizant of the self-deceptions of his fictional narrators.) Furthermore, the common human failing of envy is often more powerful than truth. 'Malice is born with its mouth open', writes the experienced Mr. Review (13:467). In an ironic vein about complainers in politics, Mr. Review points out that unqualified people take upon themselves judgements they are not equipped to make: parsons direct courtiers, lawyers correct generals ('War and law having so near a correspondence'), country gentlemen explain about trade, and 'honest clowns' examine naval and colonial affairs (10:406–7).

In addition, as always in Defoe, the difficulty of deciding upon the proper relation between a general truth and a particular example of that truth is emphasized. Moderation, for instance, he defines from Whig and Tory points of view (22:71–2). Peace he defines from the different points of view of five Continental rulers and some eight different English interests. In his discussion, Mr. Review explains the discrepancies by quoting Scripture: 'The ways of men are right in their own eyes' (4:94).

Unlike the plain-dealing Mr. Review, who envisions truth as a building foundation, the worldly Mr. Review uses bi-focal images of outsides and insides, outdoors and indoors (*ex camera*, *in camera*), and surfaces and depths. In addition, as in the fictions, masks, disguises, and doubles are significant motifs in his writing. Sometimes he advises his readers to become more perceptive about external signs (10:326). Usually, however, he reads for them, and despite his repeated observation that the searching of hearts is best left to God, Mr. Review frequently finds himself obliged to emulate his Maker, as he exposes the specious designs of anti-ministerial political factions (5:451).

Indeed, the worldly Mr. Review is indefatigable in exposing what lies hidden behind facades. In his allegory of the armies (April 1710), which may possibly have been influenced by Swift's *Battle of the Books*, he shows that although Presbyterians are the declared targets of the High Church attacks set off by Sacheverell's 1709 sermon, the real targets are the Queen, the Constitution, liberty and religion (17:36). Not only does Mr. Review lift the concealing curtain, but he also raises the volume of a sinister echo he claims to hear after the High Church cry against Dissenters:

> This is the sham, but not one word of truth in it.—This indeed is the popular cry, because they could not raise the mob without it.—But this is not *the bird they shoot at.*—Listen to the noise of the crowd, and hearken close, you'll hear *a double sound in it all*; and they came exactly from the two lines of the army I spoke of, the cry is raised in the first line, and answered like an *echo* in the second.—High Church raises the cry; Jacobite answers as *the echo.*—Thus:
>
> | | |
> |---|---|
> | *High Church.* | Damn the Presbyterians. |
> | *Echo.* | Damn the Bishops for Presbyterians. |
> | *High Church.* | Down with the meeting houses. |
> | *Echo.* | Down with the Bank. |
> | *High Church.* | Burn that dog Burgess, and all the fanatic ministers. |
> | *Echo.* | Burn the state ministry, and damn the whole administration |
> | *High Church.* | God bless the Queen, and Dr. Sacheverell. |
> | *Echo.* | God bless the King, and Dr. Sacheverell. |
>
> (17:39)

The figure of a tailor's coat that looks different from every perspective best expresses the notion of truth held by the worldly Mr. Review. The coat appears in the *Review* of 29 April 1710, a period when Defoe's writing shows the influence of polite Whig writers including Steele and Swift. (This is the period of Defoe's Palatine series, discussed on pp. 47–9 above.) Readers may be surprised by Defoe's use of a figure recalling the coat in Swift's *Tale of a Tub*, especially since his use of it is so different from Swift's, revealing his non-visual, essentially intellectual, perception of his surroundings:

> The coat was wonderfully made indeed, every side of it was singular; as you turned it *this way*, it looked one thing, *that way* another; to one eyesight it represented *one thing*, to another *quite contrary*; and all agreed, that never such a coat was made before. If you turned it this way it was a *fool's coat*, that way 'twas a

knave's coat; on one side it represented a Lord Bishop, on the other side a Lord Duke; on another a Lord M—r, on another a clergyman, on another a thief; worn this way, it made a man a statesman; that way a mountebank; this way a general, that way a coward; a strange coat it was indeed, *as ever I saw in my life.* (17:58–9)

Only occasionally does the worldly Mr. Review's tone suggest that he is weary of unveiling, unmasking, and exposing doubles, and wishes Heaven would come to his aid. These occasions occur during the last two years of the *Review*, a period when ministerial policy had become so tortuous that defending Harley's politics was increasingly difficult for Defoe. One such instance comes when Mr. Review envisages what would happen if false oath takers were blasted in the act of swearing allegiance to the government. Heaven's adopting such a measure would mean the end of masks and the end of hypocrisy in the real world, as all the shadowy doubles stood suddenly revealed: 'What strange double faces and double voices, double views, double outsides, and above all, what double insides would then be discovered?' (21:775).

Defending Complex Truth Through Argument

The worldly Mr. Review is sometimes cynical, sometimes witty, about the possibility of arriving at truth through reasoning or argumentation. In a cynical mood, he maintains that argument is irrelevant in the face of power, for might makes right: '. . . and he is the sacred prince that gets the stamp of his authority printed by the length of his sword' (10:314). In a witty mood, he wrote the supplements to the *Review* (which, unfortunately, ran for only five monthly numbers, from September 1704 to January 1705), on one occasion refusing to answer his correspondent's question by saying: 'No doubt of it, Sir, it must needs be a particular favour to reconcile impossibilities, and make contradictions agree; and when we do it for anybody, you shall be sure not to be left out . . .' (5:57). In spite of his disclaimer, Defoe was a master of that kind of argument; in the Mesnager *Minutes* of 1717, his French narrator, describing English pamphleteers, in this case Defoe himself, praises a writer he hired, who 'had an excellent talent, and words enough, and was as well qualified to prove non-entities to contain substance, and substance to be entirely spirituous, as anyone I have met with.'

The methods of reasoning most frequently resorted to by the worldly (and frequently humorous) Mr. Review are: turning the argument against the person making it, redefining terms or basic premises, reconsidering a basic premise in the light of mitigating circumstances, changing perspective or considering an issue from a new angle, and weaving together a number of different issues so that they seem to be connected to each other, when in fact they are separate matters.

In the first category, he explains: '. . . there is no better way, to overthrow any man in dispute, than first to grant the principles he advances, and from thence to deduce by just consequence the contrary to what he inferred; so I think I shall, fully and fairly, overthrow all that has been said from this head' (17:78). That this was the practice of the worldly Defoe is indicated by his letter of 27 May 1712 to Harley (now Earl of Oxford), asking for permission to say something 'without doors' that 'would take off all the edge of the popular surprise some people think they have raised in the nation' by publicizing secret government orders to the English commander in Flanders, 'and turn all the mischief against themselves' (*Letters*, p. 375).

In an ironical mood occasioned by his great disappointment at the passage of acts pertaining to Scotland, particularly one introducing the English Common Prayerbook into Scottish (Presbyterian) churches, the worldly Mr. Review argues in the same way as in a mooted passage from *Moll Flanders* to be discussed later. He affirms that the worst thing he can envision happening in Scotland, the introduction of Anglican rites into a Presbyterian establishment, will have the desirable effect of uniting Scots Dissenters (Episcopalians) and the Scottish Established Church (Presbyterian) against English interference:

> . . . and as to the Common Prayerbook, and the methods used to bring it in there, I verily believe, it will do more to reconcile the Episcopal people and the established Church together, than anything that ever that party did before; nay the very reading of the English liturgy there, and a little of the wise management of

the persons that espouse it, will make more Presbyterians in
Scotland, than any step that party ever took before. (21:704)

Mr. Review is always redefining terms so that he can construct an argument upon different premises from his opponents. The best known example of this procedure is his discussions of the peace negotiations in the War of the Spanish
Succession. Arguing on 13 October 1711 for a termination of
the war even though England has not yet conquered Spain,
Mr. Review must slip out of the noose he tied around his own
neck on 1 September, when he wrote that it would be ridiculous for England to give up Spain to France, or the House of
Bourbon. He asks his readers, 'What do you mean by Spain?'
extricating himself by distinguishing mainland Spain from the
Spanish Empire (20:350). Advocating the negotiation of a
peace treaty, even though England's allies are not yet willing
to make peace with France, he reinterprets the words of the
agreement with the Confederates, 'No treaty shall be entered
into, without the common advice and consent of the allies', so
that by a strict construction of the words 'common consent',
he can justify England's making peace without the allies
(20:447).

Alert to the possibility that opposing writers can also define
any term as they want to, he makes sure to accuse them of
distortion. Such instances occur frequently with the term
'moderation' that Defoe managed to preempt for Robert
Harley in his highly successful campaign of 1705 against High-
Flyers. The campaign had been preceded by unsuccessful
efforts made in Parliament in 1702 and 1703 to pass a bill
forbidding occasional conformity. In November 1704 the
leaders of the High Tories failed in a spectacular and desperate
effort to get the bill passed by the 'constitutionally dubious
expedient'[1] of attaching or tacking it to the war supply bill that
provided materials for the War against the Spanish Succession.
Henceforth the tactic of Harley, seconded at that time by the
Earl of Godolphin, was to isolate the leaders of the Tack as
extremists and to consolidate a coalition of moderate Whigs
and Tories offended by the method resorted to by the Tackers
and by the hazarding of the national interest in wartime over a
domestic political issue. Accordingly, propaganda inspired by

Harley in the ensuing parliamentary election campaign had to concentrate its fire on the Tackers, taking care at the same time not to alienate moderate Tories and Churchmen.

The High-Flyers claimed, with some justice, that 'moderation' was a cover for an anti-clerical political faction aiming to dislodge them from power, and that it was particularly appropriate to those who were lukewarm about their religion. The worldly Mr. Review points out that first the enemies of the virtue of moderation tried 'to persuade mankind, that moderation was an enemy to zeal, to faithfulness, and to the great and just concern we ought to have for our religion and liberty' (4:294). When they were unsuccessful in discrediting the term itself, they tried to discredit Harley's brand of 'moderation', labelling it hypocrisy. Once the campaign to defeat the Tackers succeeded, Mr. Review snatched back the word, attaching it firmly to the administration he was serving and ticketing the losing High-Flyers with the label of coercion (4:295).

In a more playful mood, the worldly Mr. Review manages to define the word 'Presbyterian' in such a way, 'resistance to princes', as to prove the whole English nation is of that persuasion, especially that 'the whole nation was Presbyterian, when at the time of the Revolution, they resisted King James, joined with King William, then Prince of Orange, and forced him (*to use King James's own words*) to fly out of the kingdom. And yet, Gentlemen,' adds Mr. Review, 'not a Parliament has yet thought fit to disown that Presbyterian doctrine, nor to condemn that *resistance*' (19:86). He goes on to prove that English acceptance of Scottish Episcopalian ministers fleeing the law in Scotland is tantamount again to Presbyterianism. Thus, High-Flyers are acting like the Presbyterians they abhor, and any true Church of England supporters who espouse the violence practised by Episcopalians in Scotland 'will embroil themselves with their own principles . . .' (19:87).

Aside from redefining terms, the worldly Mr. Review likes to look at the same issue from different angles, so that he can make different points about it. Defoe's figure of the tailor's coat perceived differently by each viewer suggests the same mental characteristic as does his figure of a compass in the 1713 pamphlet . . . *But What If the Queen Should Die?*, in which

Defoe surveys the points of view of several major groups potentially inimical to the Protestant Succession. Defoe and the worldly Mr. Review delighted in arguing from many points of view on any one issue, a practice that earned the writer the reputation of being completely unprincipled. Readers concentrating on literary devices as well as ethics, however, should be alert to this flexibility in order to avoid the mistake of constricting the lively and playful Defoe in the contours of the plain-dealing Mr. Review.

Lastly, the worldly Mr. Review, master of so many shifts and subterfuges in his argumentation, is as adept at synthesizing as the plain-dealing Mr. Review is at analysing. Enemies are rarely simply High-Flyers or hot Whigs. They are usually associated with Jacobites and with French interests, as in the echo example above. Friends are not simply good— they are intimately linked with all the virtues or all the political benefits of England. Thus, in . . . *But What If the Queen Should Die?*, Queen Anne's tenure of life is linked with all the benefits of peace, civil, and religious liberty enjoyed in England.

The worldly Mr. Review does a good deal of this kind of synthesizing in his writing, but perhaps the most striking example occurs in the pamphlet, *A Letter from a Gentleman at the Court of St. Germains*, summarized by Mr. Review in the issue of 31 October 1710. In that pamphlet, every extremist political position detested by Defoe is woven by the ingenuity of his Jacobite speaker into the service of a diabolic master plan designed to bring back the Pretender to the throne of England.[2] First a propaganda campaign should be instituted to discredit the Revolution and create conflicts among High Churchmen, Low Churchmen, Latitudinarians, and Dissenters. Doctrines favourable to Jacobitism—passive obedience, non-resistance, and divine right—should be promulgated widely. Among the ways the Jacobite suggests for dividing English Protestants is accusing the Dissenters of writing irreverent and atheistic books, representing them as fanatics, and making it difficult for them to worship in their own way by putting restrictions on the Toleration Act. Other methods are suggested for putting Low and High Church advocates at loggerheads. The Jacobite speaker of the pamphlet goes on to discuss the Reformation in England, criticizing it from Roman Catholic eyes as illogical, and tracing the growing vogue for Catholic ritual in Anglican churches as an indication that a reconciliation between the two churches would be easy if the Pretender were on the throne of England. This partial summary of a pamphlet almost certainly written by Defoe[3] and described with approval by the worldly Mr. Review should make clear what I mean by synthetic argumentation. Each of the activities mentioned by the Jacobite speaker was despised by Defoe, but the connection between people who accused Dissenters of writing anonymous heretical or atheistic books and people who had disliked King William is not convincing as history or as logic.

Defending Complex Truth Through Fiction

The Jacobite plot described in *A Letter from a Gentleman at the Court of St. Germains* was a fiction, yet Mr. Review used the letter in his journal as evidence of a Jacobite conspiracy to elect extremists to Parliament in the campaign of 1710. At one time during the campaign false letters about Jacobite plots had in fact appeared in London, but their spuriousness had been detected immediately, not least by Mr. Review, who offered instructions to his readers on how to identify counterfeits. His own letter, however, complete with two speakers, a plain-dealing publisher who sounded like the plain Mr. Review, and a devious and subtle Jacobite who sounded like the devious Mr. Review, was no hastily concocted potboiler; indeed, it was too clever and too complicated to enjoy a popular success.

The worldly Mr. Review, no longer a historian scrupulously recording events and actions, refraining from examining the motives of statesmen, eventually resorted to manufacturing his own evidence. Addressing himself to that issue, he points out that journalists have been accused of 'first writing letters to themselves, and then answering them in print'. Claiming that he cannot answer for other journalists, he says of himself, 'I have been so far from having occasion to do so, that I have thrown by a monstrous heap of such letters, wholly unanswered' (20:333). For readers who overlook the equivocation in his words, it may be helpful to point out that in Defoe's *Commentator* No. XV of 19 February 1720, he expresses his disbelief in the authenticity of letters to journals: 'Do you believe these people really receive all the letters they publish? Not one in fifty of them. But it is a way of writing, that has mightily obtained of late years, and is found to be of singular good use.'[4]

As Mr. Review began to manufacture his own evidence, his definition of a lie changed to one based upon motivation. He had explained that formula to Harley in a letter of 1704: ': . . as a Lye Does Not Consist in the Indirect Position of words, but in the Design by False Speaking, to Deciev and Injure my Neighbour, So Dissembling does Not Consist in Puting a Different Face Upon Our Actions, but in the further Applying That Concealment to the Prejudice of the Person' (*Letters*, p. 42). The example he supplies is incontrovertible—knowing a man likely to fall into convulsions if he is surprised, one should be smiling and pleasant as one prevails upon him to leave his house, which happens to be on fire. Such hypocrisy is a virtue.

Indeed, any lie for the service of public good, religion, liberty, and trade is a beneficial deception (10:351–52). In contrast, 'the rumours, the false news, the discouraging artifices of . . . home-bred and malicious party enemies' in England who complain about the power of the French are dishonest because the aim is 'to dispirit and discourage' the English in their war effort (10:282). Lying now resides in emphasis alone.

Mr. Review goes even further in the case of the Duke of Marlborough. In one of several dialogues with a madman, in August 1708 (Defoe was then employed by Godolphin), Mr. Review replies that it is a malicious design to depreciate the military victories of the Duke because he is unpopular with Tories (12:228). But in 1710, when Defoe was again employed by Robert Harley, he went along with the Tory campaign to discredit the Duke. He never lent himself to the excesses of Swift, confining himself in the *Review* and in anonymous pamphlets to innuendo, but he did accept the design of the Tories, agreeing that it had become necessary to remove Marlborough in order to negotiate with the French. What had in 1708 been a malicious design apparently now was a *raison d'état*.

Furthermore, Mr. Review used the definition of a lie as a malicious intention, to attack political opponents for their emphasis alone, even when what they were saying was true to fact. In one instance, he went so far as to object to a report that a Catholic church had been built in Hanover as 'one of those tales, which *though it were true in fact, may be a lie in design*, being calculated to suggest that the family of Hanover are not such zealous Protestants as we think they are' (21:835, my italics). Inserting this truth of fact in a list of outright lies, he confounds any distinction by concluding, 'Thus we are amused with shams on every hand, and the trade of coining lies is come up to such a height, that it is amazing to me how it should so equally affect both sides' (21:835).

The examples I have discussed to illustrate the difference between the plain dealer and the worldly Mr. Review on the question of truth and lies are all taken from the field of politics. The question is, how did Defoe apply his expanded theory of truth to the area of fiction? Several interesting indications are provided in the *Review*. The first of them is an excuse for reporting a dialogue on the Pretender between yeomen who speak in an illiterate style. Mr. Review admits that the dialogue 'is not indeed, a history personally' (22:56). He excuses himself, however, on the grounds of historical fact: '. . . yet the fact is historical, and I am an ear witness to it, not in one or two, but many places, where the people are thus possessed, and where the notion of hereditary right begins to revive in favour of the Pretender' (22:56). What he appears to mean is that he has heard similar conversations in many places and from those examples has concocted a representative conversation of his own.[5]

The second example is more complicated and more thought-provoking. It occurs in the issue of 17 May 1711 in connection with Mr. Review's discussion of the *Prophecies* or *British Visions*, a fabrication of Defoe's based on a popular genre of the time. The speaker in this issue sounds like Defoe himself, neither posing as a plain dealer nor inadvertently revealing himself to be a worldly man. He addresses himself to the question of a 'converse of spirits' discussed at length in his books on the occult of the 1720s. What he means by 'converse of spirits' is 'private notices, strong impulses, pressings of spirit, involuntary

101

joy, sadness, and foreboding apprehensions' (19:95) pertaining to our private lives. In addition, he refers to admonitory dreams, citing Biblical precedents but refraining from further discussion. For our purpose here it suffices to point out that without going to extremes, Defoe believed in the importance of giving heed to these warnings and impulses, which today we would regard as signals from our subconscious.

Because he discusses the *British Visions* and makes some comment on the function of authors' prefaces in the course of a discussion about the 'converse of spirits', we can assume that he sensed some connection between this 'converse' and his writing. It is apparent from his discussion that he had given thought to the element of inspiration in writing, and that this element was not clearly defined in his mind. He was also interested in the function of prefaces, supposedly written by someone other than the author, but from Defoe's own knowledge, probably often composed by the author himself. The difference between the commentator of the preface and the writer of a body of a work is the difference between critic and creative writer:

> The considering reader of the book, may evidently see there are two strains in it.—*One* the predictor, who ventures to say things of great consequence.—*The other* the writer or methodizer, for publication, which seems, in a preface particularly, to cover or colour the substance, with an air of banter, ridicule, and I know not what.—Borrows a *name* formerly jested with in the world; pretends to *the great age* of a person who is really *nobody*; talks of a *second sight*, and much such kind of stuff, perfectly wild and wide from the main design.

He goes on to list some of the reasons for writing such a preface. These reasons apply to all of the fictions he wrote later on:

> This was certainly done from some of these views; 1. A diffidence perhaps of the things spoken of.—Nor has it been altogether unusual, that men may have been pressed to say what they durst not own they had a full revelation of; or 2. To cover the serious part a little from the eye of every reader, that it might not have so solemn an aspect till it went a greater length; or 3. To suit the thing to the loose humour of the age, who sometimes must have a light loose way taken with them, to

introduce more serious things to their reading.—Or 4. Merely to make the book vulgar, and make the publication of it easy to the booksellers, or some such mean views, which I cannot account for. (19:94)

The first and second reasons are of particular interest to readers of Defoe's fiction, for they suggest that no matter how much or how little commercial considerations influenced his writing of fiction, the actual product, which he could not completely analyse, seemed somewhat uncanny to him. Furthermore, he was unwilling to dismiss it as 'forgery', 'lies', or 'fiction', because no matter what his theoretical notions about fiction and its drawbacks, these products, partly of his subconscious, seemed curiously significant to him. It is for this reason that I avoid discussing his general theory of fiction, for any such suppositious theory seems to me a generalization after the fact, not entirely convincing because Defoe himself was not sure of what he was doing or why.[6] As James Sutherland points out, Defoe 'had become so accustomed to living in a twilight world between fact and fiction that the two mingle imperceptibly in his mind'.[7]

Judges of Truth in the Real World

The plain-dealing Mr. Review, confident that truth is simple and easily discerned and that he himself has described, explained, and defended it satisfactorily, appeals to an audience of impartial judges to certify his efforts. In contrast, the worldly Mr. Review finds the world too complicated for him to be able to rely on the good will and perspicacity of an impartial audience. Not only is truth hidden behind facades, curtains, and masks, or drowned out by loud overtones; it is inextricably entangled with secret motives and at times, when it resides in malicious intentions or designs, contradicted by overt action or speech. To complicate even further the problem of finding witnesses who will testify to the truth advanced by the worldly Mr. Review, the personnel of the real world is not suited to the role of God-like judge.

For one thing, people are complex; they resist classification into simple categories of fool, knave, devil, and wise man. As Harley warned Defoe on 12 June 1707, during the campaign for the Union between England and Scotland, clamour about financial corruption in Parliament was exaggerated: 'The malicious World Reports & Names the Men & Summs of Money ventured by those in both Houses, but be sure You do not believe that, for it is impossible that persons of all Sorts, Colours & pretences can be such Knaves' (*Letters*, p. 228). Either Harley's hint was not the first of its kind, or the Manichean Defoe had already recognized his own weakness, for it is the worldly Mr. Review who warns his readers in December 1706 not to 'be imposed upon to believe things and people, worse than they really are' (8:591). In March 1707 Mr. Review admits that it was not really devils who opposed the union; the turmoil had been caused by a 'party feud' (9:63).

French intelligence about England is not the work of the devil; the French have an excellent spy network. 'Had our intelligence been as good as theirs, we should as well have known of their coming to sea, as they of ours. I have observed', continues the worldly Mr. Review,

> that at one time or other the dearest intelligence pays its own charge; Cardinal Richelieu expended two millions of livres yearly, merely upon intelligence, and by that means had his fingers in all the actions of Europe, was informed of every motion, insinuated himself into every cabinet, and in short managed all Europe; nor is there a greater argument of a finished statesman, that let it cost what it will, to have a certain and exact intelligence in all parts of the world, and by this to take his measures from the earliest motion or posture of the enemy. (11:470)

Even pro-Stuart tendencies among ministerial Tories should be understood in the realistic way of the worldly Mr. Review rather than in the eschatological way of the plain dealer. Since the law of self-preservation prevails with everyone, it is foolish to drive people upon desperate measures to preserve themselves. If rabid Whigs would stop threatening that once the Hanoverian successor to Queen Anne assumes the throne Tory ministers will be in danger of their lives, the Tories would not be tempted to favour the Pretender (22:44).

Self-preservation is the first impulse of every individual who finds himself in a condition of extremity, and Mr. Review is eloquent about businessmen pressed to the wall by debts (Defoe's own experience) and people faced with starvation. Even in less dire circumstances, however, self-interest and self-gratification are the dominant motives of human behaviour. In that case, where are the impartial judges called upon by the plain-dealing Mr. Review? 'Where dwell the honest wise men?' he asks (16:515). Of what use is kindness and good nature, which may make an impression upon some, but is regarded as weakness by others? For these others, one must direct one's arguments to appeal to their self-interest (14:45–6).

Even the appeal to self-interest is not a sure key to engaging one's audience, for audiences include as many separate interests as there are social classes and occupations. If we take the practice of donning mourning upon the death of princes, which the *Spectator* deplores as an example of the vanity of being thought to have Court connections, we see that 'this folly is founded upon party interest in trade, as much as the revolutions of the Court are founded upon parties in the state' (19:98). Arguing on moral grounds against such a practice is useless, therefore, since commercial self-interest is the real issue. In the following scene, the worldly Mr. Review dramatizes this generalization, using four characters, an alderman, a mercer, a country gentleman, and a grave and sensible Member of Parliament. Mr. Review's point of view is voiced by the M.P., and his own judgement of the alderman as pompous, the mercer (lower in social class) as impertinent, and the needy country gentleman as foolishly vain, is unambiguous. (It should be noted that in the pages of the *Review*, aldermen appear consistently as overbearing and pompous fools, a point to be remembered in Chapter 4 in the discussion of the scene between Moll Flanders and the alderman.[8])

> Going the other day into a coffeehouse, I found a very warm debate, that had it not ended in a peaceable wager, threatened the company with something fatal to the peace.—The case was this: Somebody had started that unhappy question at a public table—'Will the town go into mourning upon the death of the Emperor?' Alderman Woolpack, the Blackwell Hall man, who had a great many Gloucester whites on his hands, answers gravely, 'Ay, ay, there's no question of it, we must all go into

mourning to be sure, you can do no less.'—Tom Taffety, the
mercer upon Ludgate Hill, a little too pertly replies with a
question—'Mourning! For what?' 'For the Emperor,' says
Woolpack—'The Emperor! the Emperor!' says Taffety, repeating the word, 'What's the Emperor to us? None but fools,
fellows that can't go to the price of new clothes, and hangers by
on the Court, will go into mourning for the Emperor; what
relation was he to anybody?'—This provoked Esquire Needy, a
gentleman that lived near St. James's, and happened to sit
by.—'Sir,' says he, 'you take a great deal of liberty with your
betters, don't you see the whole Court goes into mourning? And
does not the Queen's order published in the *Gazette* say, "Such
persons of quality shall dress so and so, and all other persons so
and so, all in black?" Has not her Majesty thereby commanded
all people to go into mourning?'—Taffety grew hot, fell upon
the esquire: 'Pray,' says he, 'who gave you authority to expound
her Majesty's words? And how do you prove, that by "ALL
PERSONS" in the public order, was meant any other, than all
persons who appear at Court?' 'Let that be how it will,' says the
esquire; 'WE think at Court that all the people ought to conform
to the mode that governs there.'—'We at Court!' says Tom
Taffety, 'Pray Sir,' says he, 'What are you at Court?—I
suppose you was Gentleman of the Holdup? Pray when was
your black coat last scoured?'—Needy draws immediately, and
calling him rascal, demands satisfaction; Taffety, a brisk fellow,
gets up—'Ay, ay,' says he, 'I'll give you the satisfaction suitable
to your quality, though not to a gentleman,' and with that,
struck up his heels, took away his sword, and kicked him out of
the room. . . .

A grave gentleman that stood by, after the dispute ended,
coolly put in this question, 'Pray Gentlemen, what makes you so
hot on both sides about this matter, which seems to me of no
signification, one way or other?'—Taffety answers him pertly
again, 'It's of no signification to you, Sir, but it is quite otherwise
to us; this old gentleman deals in broadcloth, and he has ten
thousand pounds worth of white cloths by him, from Worcester-
shire and Gloucestershire, and he cares not who are ruined, if he
can but sell his cloth; I am a mercer, and I have laid in ten
thousand pound worth of fine new fashioned silks for the spring
trade, that the looms have been at work upon all winter; and if
this madness goes on, I am ruined, and all the mercers in London
are in a manner ruined; besides the many thousand families that
depend upon us, and upon the advancement of a spring trade.

These woolen drapers, and tailors, and callico men and such fellows, as soon as ever such a Court mourning appears, run into all company, and cry up a general mourning, and these poor wretches, such as that Needy there, that can't buy a new coat, or clothe their families, or pay the tailor, and yet will be thought modish, they all run into black; and thus they lead the town into black, though they destroy the whole trade of a nation, it's all one to them, if their present gain be but answered.—And this is the cause of our public mourning, when the government has no hand at all in it.'—The honest gentleman answers him thus:

'Truly, Sir, I have heard a great and long complaint against the public mournings, and as I am a Member of Parliament, I remember it once came before us there, as a grievance in trade; but I see now, what hindered its being stopped then, will hinder it still.—As some lose by it, so others gain by it.—They whose interest of trade lay in it, strove to keep up the custom—eagerly run into it themselves, and oppose any law made to restrain it.—And so it is still, and therefore you may conclude it will not be remedied, for interest lies at the bottom of it.' (19:98–9)

Self-interest is bad enough when it leads some people to gratify themselves at the expense of others, but Mr. Review, whose spokesman is the Member of Parliament, can retain a philosophical calm about the matter. He becomes a cynic, however, as he observes that self-interest in the form of envy and ill-nature drives people to overt abuse of others, even their benefactors:

I know, we had much rather hear our friends abused than praised; and 'tis always more agreeable to hear the services done us satirized, than acknowledged.—The reason is plain, because ingratitude is a natural principle, retribution all forced and acquired; one pleases our distempered spleen; the other suits nothing but our generous part, and that's long since departed from us. (14:126)

Ill-nature must be taken as a matter of course. The worldly Mr. Review has moved from sober recognition to outright cynicism about the reception truth can expect in the world when he rhymes:

The lucky scoundrel every man will prize,
Successless actions never pass for wise. (18:530)

From cynicism too he replies impatiently to a correspondent's question about what rules guide inaccurate almanac predictions: 'But to ask me what rules they go by, is a question much easier answered; *why the rule of picking your pockets, what rule should they go by?* And as long as there are fools to be deceived, there will never want knaves to deceive them, especially when they can get by it too' (6:52). The plain-dealing Mr. Review believed it 'much less dishonour for a man to be a fool than a knave' (9:169), but the cynical Mr. Review believes that the prevalence of fools is the cause of the hegemony of knaves. Accordingly, we find in the *Review* as many attacks upon fools by the worldly Mr. Review as attacks upon angry extremists and scheming devils by the plain-dealing Mr. Review.

Worldly innocence seems to have been one of the kinds of foolishness that exasperated Defoe. Annoyed by Truth and Honesty, the simple-minded brother of the plain-dealing Mr. Review, Defoe has a High-Flying parson protest, 'You pretend to Truth and Honesty, but not to much sense I find, and so you count all that know more than you hypocrites' (21 May 1705). In *Advice from the Scandalous Club*, the sophisticated Mr. Review points out in a tone of mock mourning that nothing in this world can bear the scrutiny of a simplistic perception of truth and honesty:

> For what can this author treat on, that will bear the test and balance of Truth and Honesty. Woe be to our Justices, the House had need make a law to qualify them. Woe be to our clergy, if their moderation, which is their honesty, and their principles, which are the test of their truth, come to be weighed in the balance of Truth and Honesty. In short, woe to our reformers, woe to our authors, woe to our ladies, woe to our youth, woe to our wise men, ay, and woe to our Society too, if we should all come to this scale and be weighed. . . . (2:355)

In the pages of the *Review* Dissenters, Scottish Presbyterians, and sometimes even European Protestants in general bear a family resemblance to Truth and Honesty. Book 8 of the *Review*, for instance, in a running dialogue between a Jacobite and a Scottish Presbyterian, refers to the latter as 'well-meaning but zealous', 'poor man', and 'honest Presbyterian'. Letters from

Defoe to Harley confirm that privately the former had a low opinion of the intelligence and worldly wisdom of the Dissenters and the Scottish Presbyterians, remarking of Dissenters on one occasion, 'Our Friends were allwayes Fools' (*Letters*, p. 68). He complained constantly about the Scottish Presbyterians during his 1706–7 sojourn in Scotland, concluding in January 1707: 'It is in Vain to go about to Excuse these people; they are proud, passionate, Ignorant, and Jealous' (*Letters*, p. 196). Speaking in the *Review* about European affairs, he observes, 'I can give some instances in the world, where the Protestants, *even before now*, in the abundance of their simplicity, *you may take the word to mean honesty or folly, which you like*, have set their hands to the supporting and upholding Popish powers . . .' (9:13). I have italicized the words that equate honesty directly with simplicity and folly to demonstrate that in the *Review* Defoe frequently uses 'honesty' in a pejorative sense, even when he is not explicit about it as he is in this example.

After Dissenters and Scottish Presbyterians, country people are the group most invariably mocked by Mr. Review. At one time he commends them for their ignorance of the larger world that constitutes their felicity (13:390), but otherwise his contempt, expressed through humour at their ignorance, is unmistakable. Country people are ludicrously ignorant about anything outside their own narrow competence; they make ridiculous mistakes in pronouncing names familiar to everyone aware of the European war (8:479). Of peasant mentality, country people are incapable of understanding abstractions, even in the matter of wealth, which interests them more than anything else. Having a hearty appreciation for money in the pocket and for other tangible assets, they run to invest in land instead of stocks, thinking that because it is tangible, it must be a better investment (22:117).

But fools are not confined to the ranks of provincials, farmers, and Dissenters by Mr. Review. Collating references from the *Review*, one discovers that credulity in any form is subject to the scorn of the worldly Mr. Review, and that credulity can afflict anyone from any class at any time. Mr. Review's condescension toward naïve people whose own honesty causes them to place too much weight on the words of other people is usually gentle[9]:

> The extravagant proceedings of the High Churchmen have been such ... that no wonder it has produced thoughts as extravagant in the minds of the people, especially of those honest, well-meaning persons, who judge of people's meanings by their words, and do not remember that these sort of gentlemen, are not always to be understood to mean as they say, nor always to mean anything at all. ... (5:345)

The same is true for those whose judgements are adversely affected by their good-natured desire to believe well of people. Mr. Review points out that anti-Union agitators have been aided in their efforts to foment dissension about the relation between the established churches of England and Scotland by 'some, *whose good will is a little stronger than their judgment*', and who 'have been imposed upon, and rendered uneasy', believing the agitators that 'designs were concealed in bringing these sisters [the churches] together'. (8:522).

The worldly Mr. Review is most contemptuous of all those whose credulity arises from conformity with vulgar opinion or general fashions in thinking (7:346). Their 'faith is made to follow, and not to lead' (14:202). The result of succumbing to the popular tide of opinion is that conformists are treated like 'mere engines or machines', screwed and worked up, and made subservient to the projects of others (15:413).

Expanding even further the ranks of fools are those who disagree with Mr. Review on theoretical issues about which he feels strongly. Thus, those in favour of the doctrines of non-resistance and passive obedience are fools (16:478). Not only non-jurors or High-Flyers, but also mainstream Whigs and Tories act like fools, the former because they are too narrow in their principles and too divided in their interests, the latter because they are too hot-headed to behave sensibly (18:347).

Perhaps most helpful for understanding the attitude of the worldly Mr. Review toward foolishness or ignorance is the following statement:

> Honest ignorance merits pity, wilful ignorance contempt, slothful ignorance, correction; but of all kinds of ignorance, conceited ignorance is a thing the most troublesome in the world; if in my endeavouring to inform the first, expose the second, and punish the third, I should make some sport with the last, you must not take it ill, till you can tell me a better way to cure it. (19:12)

Defoe's tone toward the different kinds of ignorance in the *Review* and other writings is not exactly in accordance with what he professes here. He makes sport with all kinds of ignorance, as we will see in *Moll Flanders*. Furthermore, his contempt is not carefully confined to the wilful ignorance best illustrated by his descriptions of Scottish Presbyterians. But his practice bears out the assertion that conceited ignorance annoyed him more than any other kind, and he does make contemptuous sport with that, frequently in the person of an alderman, throughout the pages of the *Review* (see 11:673–74 for a good example).

In addition to aldermen, 'coffeehouse politicians' belong in Mr. Review's classification to the category of conceited ignorance. His reaction to their criticism of his advising Dissenters to content themselves with the defeat of High-Flying Tories and not to ask for full political participation in government, rings with annoyance and contempt:

> But you give the enemy a handle, to fall upon the Dissenters, as persons not contented, says the coffeehouse politician. Give them no handles yourselves, Gentlemen, and I'll answer for all I shall give them; let them take hold of them at their peril; if I do not defend it, then 'tis time to censure.
>
> But what if I should say, everything has two handles, and I ought not to expect those people, who could not understand the *Shortest Way*, should understand this. (6:11)

With this annoyed observation, we come to the crux of the problem of the readership of the worldly Mr. Review. Unlike his plain-dealing brother, he cannot rely upon an audience of impartial judges. His world is more complicated, his truths less clear, his argumentation more supple and varied, and the people he is addressing are not particularly amenable to reason, come from a number of different social classes, and range widely in education, intelligence, and worldliness. From the point of view of a writer knowledgeable about the world of public affairs, far too many of them are fools. As the plain-dealing and plain-speaking Mr. Review was accused of covering anger and abusiveness with the mantle of truth, the worldly Mr. Review was accused of concealing his own double dealing and mockery of his readers with the same sacred mantle.

111

Defoe answers such a complaint from Dissenters in November 1711, explaining in an autobiographical passage how his desire to serve honest men has caused most of his difficulties. His superior perspicacity and his insistence upon bestowing the benefit of his insights upon fellow Dissenters have aroused their antagonism. It is clear from this and many other passages that if the Dissenters never forgave Defoe for the *Shortest Way*, Defoe returned the feeling heartily. When we consider how often 'honest' is equated with 'foolish' in the *Review*, how impatiently Mr. Review suffers fools, and how often the fools are earnest Dissenting types, we will not be surprised to find Defoe conveying mixed feelings in many of his works about Dissenters and other honest but ignorant readers (see 20:422).

Defoe's failure to find a fit audience is understandable in the case of the *Shortest Way*, for the genre of that pamphlet has been a matter of dispute since its publication, and it is still under discussion today. But a perfectly standard ironical satire of 4 December 1705, in which the worldly Mr. Review attacked Lord Haversham and praised the Earl of Peterborough was apparently misunderstood by some readers of the *Review*. Mr. Review reports on 20 December that he has been accused of attacking Peterborough, which, he writes, 'cannot but make me smile'. We must assume that again the imperceptive readers were Dissenters, for Mr. Review reminds 'one sort of people' to re-read the piece and compare it with the times, as they did with the *Shortest Way* (5:494).

But over-earnest and under-educated Dissenters are not the only imperceptive readers. The problem, as the worldly Mr. Review saw it, was that if the reader was responsible for determining the meaning of a text, then Mr. Review had to expect different reactions from different segments of his divided and warring readership. He illustrates this point on 25 May 1708, when discussing three possible reactions to his ironical advice of 22 May to elect Tories to Parliament: '. . . pray, Sir, who are you that ask this question? [why vote Tory?] For according to your character will be the application of this whole story' (12:97). Dividing Whigs into two groups, Court and Country (12:98), Mr. Review explains, 'If you are one of these [the first], the discourse is directly ironical', and its effect should be to caution against the evils of other people's electing

Tories. If the enquirer is of the second group, however, the discourse will be understood literally, for the second group is honest (i.e. stupid) in its opposition to any ministry. In a sequel to his argument, Mr. Review follows up the question of a third enquirer, an honest Tory who wants to know what is wrong with Tories or High-Flyers (12:101). For him Mr. Review retails the horrors that will ensue if Tories are elected, and, when he protests that such an outcome is not inevitable, rails at him for stupidity.

The problem of different reactions from three different types of reader is essentially the same encountered by Defoe with his *Shortest Way*. Yet the advice to vote Tory is good ironical writing, uncomplicated by the mimicry of a High-Flyer that caused so much confusion about the genre of the early pamphlet. With a normal example of ironical satire, we see that Defoe's problem is not lack of ability to write effectively in this genre; it is lack of recognition of the effect of his contempt upon some of his readers and the overly ambitious aim of writing to several audiences at the same time, with the intention of provoking different responses from each of them.[10]

Effective Action in the Real World: Dissembling, Concealing, Manipulating—Hoaxes and Masks

Mental alertness, repression of emotion, decisive action in a few cases, slow and patient endeavour in most, were the prescription offered by the plain-dealing Mr. Review for effective action in the ideal world. But the prescription offered by the worldly Mr. Review is better designed for the actuality he finds in his own day:

> This is an age of plot and deceit, of contradiction and paradox, and the nation can hardly know her friends from her enemies, men swearing to the government, and wishing it overturned, abjuring the Pretender, yet earnestly endeavouring to bring him in, eating the Queen's bread and cursing the donor, owning the Succession, and wishing the successors at the Devil, making the marriage, UNION, yet endeavouring the divorce, fawning upon the Toleration, yet railing at the liberty; it is very hard indeed under all these masks to see the true countenance of any man. There are more kinds of hypocrisy

than that of Occasional Conformity—and the whole town
seems to look one way and now another. . . . (16:523)

In such circumstances, the best way to proceed is by
concealing your designs, dissembling, and manipulating. King
James was '*too honest* to effect the glorious design he had laid of
restoring the Church of Rome in these nations, since had he
been able to dissemble, and proceed by ways of policy and
good management; had *he gone on moderately*, and been content
to have done it gradually, he had certainly effected it in
time . . .' (4:287)

This was the way pursued by Defoe in his 1705 campaign
for Robert Harley against the attempt to abolish occasional
conformity and his 1706–7 activities in Scotland on behalf of
the Union. Both these campaigns combined action and writing.
A third campaign, to exonerate Robert Harley, then Earl of
Oxford, from charges of treason, seems to have been waged
primarily with the pen; it culminated in the publication, on
17 June 1717, during the week set for Oxford's trial, with the
publication of Defoe's Mesnager *Minutes*.

The tactics the plain-dealing Mr. Review will use in following Harley's line in the 1705 electoral campaign are sketched
out in his issue of 17 April 1705: 'If you would know, gentlemen freeholders, who to choose in your approaching elections,
in order to secure the Church, to save the state, and protect
the Protestant religion, see their description here, *Let them be
men of peace* . . .' (4:75). High Tories are to be smeared as
infuriated fools and madmen, a lunatic fringe seeking to sow
dissension among the ranks of the peaceful English majority.
Every angry or foolish outburst occurring in England during
the course of a turbulent electoral campaign is to be cited by
Mr. Review as an example of High Tory behaviour. In
between his head-shaking reports to moderates of the latest
Tory or Tory-incited tantrum, Mr. Review addresses the
erring Tackers directly, lecturing them in the voice of a firm
but affectionate adult.

Particularly noteworthy in the 5 May issue of the *Review* is
Mr. Review's reproach to Tackers for their willingness to
endanger war-besieged England by proposing a measure that
they knew the House of Lords would refuse to pass: 'Can there

be any plea for these things? . . . For what can be said for Members sitting in the House to do nothing; making long speeches without meaning, and voting bills without design to have them pass?' (4:106). What makes the reproach of the plain-dealing Mr. Review interesting is that in a letter of 2 November 1704, the wily Defoe had urged Harley to get some trusty Parliamentary allies to introduce the Occasional Conformity bill he was certain would be defeated, in order to 'Brand the Party with the Scandall of Opposeing the Queen'. Defoe believed the High Tories' automatic support of such a bill would 'Sink their Character, and They would go home with Such a Fame, as would Cause Fewer of The Same Men to Come back Again Next session than may otherwise be Expected' (*Letters*, p. 69). The tactic he was suggesting was similar to what he had tried out on High-Flying Churchmen in his *Shortest Way*; not content with simply waiting for excited political opponents to make fools of themselves, Defoe preferred engaging in behind-the-scenes activity to incite them to their inevitable overreaching.

Another deceptive remark made by the plain-dealing Mr. Review on 5 May 1705 is his claim to be treating the Tackers 'like gentlemen, men mistaken, men unhappily misled into an error too black to be justified; and yet men, I would be glad to see retrieving the folly you have fallen into.' In support of this claim, he points out that he has not 'accosted' the Tackers with 'ballads, lampoons, or pasquinade' and so forth, 'nor have I wrote anything upon the subject, but what is to be found in the course of these [the *Review*] papers' (4:105). It is true that the plain-dealing Mr. Review had not written on the subject, but Anglipoloski of Lithuania, alias Daniel Defoe, had attacked various of the High Tories who later participated in the Tack in his hard-hitting Rochesterian verse satire, *The Dyet of Poland*, written in 1704 and finally, permitted publication by Harley, issued around May 1705. In addition, the author of the *True-Born Englishman* (commonly known to be Defoe) had 'translated' in March 1705 a political allegory (its machinery influenced by Swift's *Tale of a Tub*) called *The Consolidator: Or Memoirs of Sundry Transactions from the World in the Moon*. In this long prose work, Defoe had accused the Tackers ('High Solunarians') of acting 'in mere malice to the Low Solunarian

Party [moderate Tories], who had the government in their hands' (p. 288).

But few readers could have known in 1705 that Daniel Defoe, behind the scenes, liked to taunt excitable opponents into furious outbursts, while the plain-speaking Mr. Review, on stage, was chiding them for their bad temper. The coffee-house public heard only the plain-dealing and moderate Mr. Review's eminently reasonable voice, answered in a tone of impotent outrage by Charles Leslie a he defended the Tack in his *Rehearsal* of 12–19 May: 'TACKING! first introduced by the Whigs against King Charles II. And applied occasionally against even King William. But now *monstrous* to be mentioned (when all other ways are stopped) for the preservation of the Church, and of the Queen.'

A further contribution of Defoe to the 1705 campaign against Tackers was his creation of the character Truth and Honesty for the *London Post*. Truth and Honesty was a simplified version of the plain-dealing Mr. Review. Unlike Mr. Review, however, he was an uncompromising Whig who lumped all Tories together, refusing to distinguish between moderates and extremists. In this he resembled John Tutchin of the pro-Whig, pro-Dissenter, pro-urban *Observator*. Judging between the two competing plain dealer journals, Truth and Honesty notes that Tutchin's *Observator* is louder, but the *Review* is 'damnably sly and cutting by way of innuendo and retort'.[11] This remark would seem to be a private joke of Defoe's on the genuineness of Mr. Review's plain dealing.

By 1712 private jokes were unnecessary; it was clear that Mr. Review had lost his credibility with readers. The plain-dealing mask no longer covered the face of the worldly Daniel Defoe in his activities on behalf of Robert Harley, called 'Robin the Trickster' by many of his contemporaries. Even a reader of our own day can sense an incongruity in the 31 May 1712 issue of the *Review*. Amidst rumours that the government had sold out its allies, was making a separate peace with France, and that shameful orders had been sent to the Duke of Ormond, the English general, secretly instrucing him not to fight the French, the speaker sounds genuinely distraught about the possibility of civil war. Breaking off his description of England in ferment, he calls upon his readers to forget the individual statesmen involved and to fix their thoughts on Providence. It is God, not party, who reigns over the affairs of men: 'The fury of parties, the ambitions of princes, the envy of statesmen, the power of armies, what are they?' (21:746). The call to religion, an ideal realm beyond the strife, strikes a jarring note. The sudden audibility of the familiar voice of the plain-dealing Mr. Review sounds like a diversionary attempt to distract attention from malfeasance among statesmen. This is particularly so because the familiar voice is followed immediately by a worldly voice introducing wily reservations about the rumours that 'our General has positive orders not to fight—or, as it was better expressed in the Parliament House, *not to act offensively*, for I suppose nobody thinks so madly, that the Duke of Ormond should have orders, that if the French had attacked his army, they should have stood still and let the French have cut them to pieces' (21:747).

One mask, that of plain dealer, served Defoe in the 1705 campaign. In his activities in Scotland in 1706 and 1707, however, he availed himself of many different disguises in order to conceal his true status as a secret agent of the English ministry, working to promote the Union between England and Scotland. Defoe's activity was prodigious; not only did he publish many pamphlets on the Union and discuss it extensively in his *Review* from September 1706 to mid-1707; he also testified on taxes and economic development to committees of the Scottish Parliament, acted as propagandist in personal conversations with representatives of various Scottish interests, including the clergy, and finally, in 1709 published his *History of the Union*, still considered indispensable source material by historians of the twentieth century.

It is apparent from the enthusiasm with which he worked that Defoe very much enjoyed exercising the versatility required by his assignment in Scotland. (Indeed, the variety of duties he undertook may have been largely self-imposed; Harley was notorious for never completing his business in interviews, and in Defoe's letter of 13 September 1706 confirming the mission, he composes his own assignment list, much more detailed and specific than the one Harley finally dispatched in October.) It is also apparent that as an economist interested in the expansion of internal markets and the development of trade to stimulate potential industry, he was strongly committed to the cause of union. But above all, the necessity for disingenuousness in executing the mission in Scotland, the need to appear as a plain dealer, as an advocate of the union motivated honestly and simply by the cause of the common good, with no private axe of his own to grind, must have made the Scottish assignment one of the most personally gratifying of Defoe's political missions.

In *An Essay at Removing National Prejudices against a Union with England*, Part III (1706), Defoe, who was generally known as the author of these essays, writes:

> These things I humbly recommend to the Scots nation to consider of, I acknowledge, as a stranger it may be objected, why I engage in this matter; but as I have always professed a more than common regard to this nation, and am not come hither without some thought of settling amongst them, on the foot of trade and improvement, especially if the Union follows this treaty, so I have presumed with all the calmness and respect I can, to recommend impartially, not the imaginary, but the real advantages and securities of this Union, and I should be very sorry, if any person should mistake me.
>
> Nor am I afraid of being suspected here, the treatment I have met with from parties and power in my native country, I think will secure me from the scandal of being an emissary to a party I have no interest to pursue, no gain to make, no party to serve. I seek no advantages from the Union, other than in common with my native country. I condemn the suggestion, as I scorn the employment of an emissary, a spy, or a mercenary. My business is known here, which tending to trade, settlement, and general improvement, I never purposed to meddle in this affair, and I hope I have done it so as can give no offence to any. (pp. 33–4)

In this extract appear the major characteristics of the plain dealer: the public profession of ingenuous dedication to the common good, the denial of suggestions that he is personally concerned or employed as an interested party by the English ministry. Of further interest are the moral qualities and the epistemology associated with this plain-speaking, plain-dealing person. He is honest and open, impartial and calm, his concern is with the common good rather than with particular, selfish interests. He deals with what is real, not with the imaginary, and what is real figures significantly as trade and economic improvement. In contrast, the devious manipulator whose character he abjures is associated with factions, with self-interest, either because of mercenary considerations or involvement with a particular party, and with spying, or duplicity. By inference he is concerned with the imaginary world, rather than with the real world of trade or economics. The imaginary world, we may infer, is associated with emotion—calmness, or lack of strong emotion, characterizes the plain dealer.

All this is highly significant in view of Defoe's letter of 26 November 1706 to Robert Harley, in which he describes from behind the scenes his Scottish activities. Defoe presents himself to Harley not as a plain speaker and plain dealer, but as devious manipulator. Not at all a free agent, he is employed by Harley; he discusses trade and religion with Scotsmen, not because these are the real elements of a concrete world, but because his aim is to arouse emotions in behalf of his project: 'I am all to Every one that I may Gain some.' Most significantly, he is operating under a variety of disguises, and, far from being calm, Defoe is aroused by the prodigious dexterity required by all these disguises to a pitch of excitement revealed by the exuberant tone of the letter.

At the same time that Defoe was promoting the union publicly in pamphlets and in the *Review*, writing separately to English and to Scottish readers, his private activities included not only the constructive work of testifying to committees, but also the employing of secret agents and the deliberate setting of opponents against one another. He informs Harley in a letter of 2 February 1707 about 'Continuall Dispute with the Clamorous Clergy':

> If I have done any Service Since I Came hither I Think it is Now, for These Men are Really the Boutefeus [firebrands] of the Nation, and If they Talk against the Union Every body will do so also.
>
> However, I have Pick't Out Some who are for it; a Very Very few I have brought Over; and I have So Sett these against the Other that like Sathans kingdome Divided against it self the Furious Temper Can not Stand.
>
> These Reconcild parsons begin to Call the Other Mad Men, and they Call these Apostates, and the people Divide just as

119

their Leaders, but Peace will prevail and I hope gets ground. (*Letters*, p. 198)

In a letter of 18 March 1707 he reports to Harley:

> In my Mannagemt here I am a perfect Emissary. I act the Old part of Cardinall Richlieu. I have my spyes and my Pensioners In Every place, and I Confess *tis the Easyest thing in the World to hire people here to betray their friends.*
>
> I have spies in the Commission, in the parliament, and in the assembly, and Undr pretence of writeing my history I have Every Thing told me. (*Letters*, p. 211, my italics)

Defoe's behind-the-scenes activities in Scotland illustrate his ability at political intrigue. This ability may seem questionable to some, whose point of view is acknowledged by G. A. Starr when he writes, 'Defoe's readiness to assume a Pauline stance may indicate how far presumption and complacency could carry him in rationalizing shady doings.'[12] Indeed, it is the point of view of the plain dealer, as Mr. Review illustrates when he reproaches High-Flyers for engaging in the same kind of intrigue against the union that Defoe was undertaking behind the scenes in behalf of it. Mr. Review complains about the High Church party:

> They leave no stone unturned, they play Whigs against Whigs, and Churchmen against Churchmen, Presbyterians against Presbyterians; they amuse with jealousies on one hand, raise scruples on the other. In England they rail, gibe and banter; in Scotland they plead those very things for arguments, which they own their aversion to. (8:551)

The plain-dealing Mr. Review makes the same complaint repeatedly against Jacobites and emissaries of the Pretender:

> . . . the agents of this great work having their lesson thoroughly taught them, speak according to the persons they are speaking to; in Switzerland they were to restore the prince, but not to invade the laws or liberties of the Scots; at Rome, lest the Pope should go back from his contribution, the Holy Father was to be assured, the young gentleman would not renounce the Roman Catholic faith; in Scotland, to the Presbyterians, he was to preserve the Kirk, and make no alteration; to the Episcopal people he was to restore episcopacy; to the mere Jacobites he was to turn Protestant.

O the constant, steady hypocrisy of Jacobitism and High
Flying!

And O the stupidity, blindness and madness of those that
believe what they say! (12:76)

Not only do these enemies 'speak according to the persons
they are speaking to'; they act, as did Defoe behind the scenes
in Scotland, to foment divisions in England, 'setting the
Church against the Dissenters' (18:369).

Effective action in the real world of chiaroscuro, then, is
always subject to doubts and misgivings, for it is uncom-
fortably similar to the action of dangerous enemies, the 'subtle,
smiling, wheedling, cautious' ones (16:515). Such doubts and
misgivings can never afflict the plain-dealing Mr. Review, for
his ways are direct and open. Defoe's private resolution of his
moral quandary must have lain in the weighing of motives and
of design in lying, discussed on pages 99–103 above. His theory
of action, like his theory of fiction, rests not so much upon a
defence of lying as upon an expanded definition of truth, 'a
traditional distinction *between* lying and beneficial deception'.[13]

From the point of view of literature and of history, the most
significant contribution Defoe made to the Scottish campaign
was his *History of the Union*. It is a careful and scrupulous
account of the negotiations. From all the secret political
intrigue, from all the roles played and masks doffed and
donned by Defoe in the course of the campaign, what remains
today is a work of genuine historical value, a work appropriate
to the plain-dealing Mr. Review who claimed to be writing as
a historian in the first book of his *Review*.

The third campaign to be discussed under the rubric of
effective action in the real world was conducted entirely
through writing, as far as we know. We know little about
Defoe's behind-the-scenes activity to help exonerate the Earl
of Oxford from charges of treason brought after the accession
of George I to the throne of England. We do have a number of
pamphlets and a full-length book, the Mesnager *Minutes*, as
our guides to this campaign. Issued in 1714, 1715, and 1717,
the pamphlets examine Oxford's activities during his ministry
from the different perspectives of supposedly privileged insiders.
At times Defoe argues that Oxford had been reduced to

inaction by virulent Whig opposition, by opposition from extremists within his own party, and by Queen Anne herself, who dictated to him policy which he was forced to obey; at other times he argues that Oxford had acted energetically as Lord Treasurer and had succeeded in forcing the enactment of the measures he most cherished.

The Mesnager *Minutes* are discussed in some detail in my *Versatile Defoe*.[14] For our purpose here, it is sufficient to point out that the work is a hoax in genre and in organization. In genre, the *Minutes* was a fabrication by Defoe that purported to be a genuine inside account by the French participant in the negotiations leading to the Treaties of Utrecht. The forgery was designed to exonerate Oxford from charges of high treason occasioned by the role he had played in the peace negotiations and his purported dealings with the Pretender. In organization the *Minutes*, distorting actual dates and re-arranging and telescoping events, transforms history into fiction, making it appear that a diabolic Jacobite scheme was checkmated unexpectedly at the last minute by an omniscient and ever-alert Oxford, who had been waiting secretly behind the scenes for his chance to hoax the schemers, Abigail Masham, Queen Anne's Jacobite confidante, and the subtle and sinister Mesnager.

Ethics in the Real World: Principles and Practice

The practice of hoax and the motif of masks take on an importance in the real world of the sophisticated Mr. Review that they lacked in the ideal world of the plain-dealing Mr. Review. Even the question of principle and practice, running through almost all of Defoe's writings, is expressed in terms of masks by Mr. Review as he describes the contemporary state of England:

> I . . . have often been guilty of wondering, that we are not tired, in all this time, from the Revolution, with wearing masks, covering our faces, and smothering ourselves with disguises. . . . This is evident, in our constant concealing the principles we profess, and putting on a show of what we really neither love, serve, own or practice. . . . Why, the whole nation is one great masquerade.—All the people we see, from the greatest to the

122

least . . . ARE, or ARE MADE by others, to be mere maskers, and everything they do, they act in masquerade. . . . (19:81–2)

Mr. Review goes on to speak of masquerading in religion, from ancient times to the present, in politics, and in trade. He concludes his discussion by asserting, 'In short, the whole nation is now one great masquerade.—No men seem to act the part they aim at, or aim at the part they act' (19:83).

The worldly Mr. Review is aware of the methods of self-justification used by those who transgress their own principles. As he indicates at one point, 'the *secret part* we act, is neither to be seen or known, *hardly by ourselves*' (19:82). If a person does notice that he has violated his own principles, the usual excuse is that the action was necessary for effecting some beneficial design, and that circumstances made it necessary (16:446). In the *Family Instructor* of 1715, Defoe demonstrates in lively dialogues between rebellious young people and their parents his familiarity with the process of rationalizing transgressions of principle. As the worldly Mr. Review, he himself is not above this kind of rationalization, as I have observed in the section on defending truth through argumentation, nor does his own practice prevent him from castigating the same practice in others.

In a merry vein concerning the discrepancy that so exercises the indignation of the plain-dealing Mr. Review, the worldly Mr. Review describes ingenuously the dispute about passive obedience and non-resistance as a paradox, where those who are the most quarrelsome profess principles of unquestioning obedience, and those who are the least quarrelsome profess principles of resistance to tyranny:

> It was a mad kind of dispute; but that which was more strange than all the rest, was—that those people, who had the real design of quarreling with their neighbours, and were upon all occasions aptest to do it, were the people who ardently advanced and defended this *new position* (viz.), the utter illegality of quarreling one with another, upon any pretence whatsoever; and on the contrary, those who alleged it was lawful so to quarrel upon absolute necessities, and in just defence of right, life, property, law, etc., were the most peaceable and steady people in observation of laws, and in doing everything, that might conduce to the preventing those very quarrels, which they nevertheless judged to be so lawful. (17:62)

Two of the most successful of Defoe's ironical pamphlets are based upon the same technique as he used in the *Review* (see 16:438): a naïve speaker professes to disbelieve that honourable people or institutions could have behaved in a manner contrary to their professed principles. The first, *An Account of the Great and Generous Actions of James Butler* . . ., 1715, contains a long dedication to Oxford University, supposedly written by an elderly gentleman who is an admirer of the university. The gentleman is so respectful of the 'Right Honourables' of the venerable academic institution that he cannot be brought to believe that it has been the scene of anti-Hanoverian riots. Oxford has always professed allegiance to principles of divine right, of passive obedience, and of non-resistance to monarchy. Since it can easily prevent its members from participating in riots, and since its principles are opposed to rebellion, the university cannot possibly have been involved. To the gentle and unworldly speaker, principles speak louder than facts. In the case of the university, therefore, the facts must be wrong or misinterpreted by enraged enemies of Oxford.

The second highly successful piece of irony is the pamphlet, *A Declaration of Truth to Benjamin Hoadly*, published in 1717. Its speaker is a relentlessly logical Quaker, who addresses the Bishop of Bangor about the latter's unorthodox principles of religion. The Quaker demonstrates these principles to be similar to those of his own Dissenting sect. His deduction that Hoadly's next step, logically, should be to demolish the entire structure of the Church of England gives no pause to the imperturbable Quaker, who is so intent upon the logic of his argument that its practical consequences are irrelevant to him. With the greatest composure he proceeds to invite Hoadly to join the Society of Friends. The entire argument has been leading up to this impudent invitation, 'For why shouldst thou not cause thy life and thy doctrine to conform unto each other?', the ironic climax of the pamphlet which, like a good deal of the worldly Defoe's irony, rests upon the contrast between professed principle and actual practice.

The choice of speaker for the Hoadly pamphlet is particularly amusing because, as I mentioned above, the plain-dealing Mr. Review's interest in Quakers was based upon their conforming more closely than most to their professed principles.[15]

The worldly Mr. Review, recognizing that most people do not practise the principles they profess, frequently greets that recognition, not with the indignation of the plain dealer, but with the irony and humour of the sophisticate.

Personality: The Worldly Mr. Review and Daniel Defoe

The plain-dealing Mr. Review prided himself on his courage and blunt speech in the service of truth. Others—secret Jacobites, High-Flyers, French agents—were 'ambodexters... alternate swearers' (5:323). Others exhibited 'ambiguity and studied darkness of councils' (5:395). The Occasional Conformity bill, tacked to the money supply bill, was devised by the devil himself, and Mr. Review marvels at the ability of the Tackers 'so to model vice' that it resembles religion, and to dress up 'the Devil so like the Angel of Light, that they cannot easily be known asunder' (4:230).

On the other hand, we have seen that in Defoe's 1705 campaign against the Tackers, the plain-dealing Mr. Review was a mask behind which Defoe was inciting his enemies to the fury deplored by the calm and moderate Mr. Review. At the same time Truth and Honesty, a simplified version of Mr. Review, was characterizing his older brother as 'damnably sly and cutting by way of innuendo and retort'.

By 1710 Defoe had probably grown accustomed to thinking of himself in terms of doubles. His September 1710 pamphlet, *A Letter from a Gentleman at the Court of St. Germains*, consisted of two parts, a brief introduction by a fictional publisher, a plain-speaking plain dealer, and the body of the work, a complex scheme of propaganda to prepare England for the return of the Pretender and of Roman Catholicism, written by a complex and devious Jacobite gentleman. The central metaphor of the letter is the 'use of a double weight and a double measure' by the Church of England, which appeals to tradition to defend itself against other Protestant sects but rejects tradition for Scripture, to defend itself against Roman Catholics.

The publisher is a hero, a plain-speaking and simple man, who has nothing to gain from his warning to the English about the Jacobite plot. He wishes only to open the eyes of Englishmen, for once they see the truth, naturally a self-evident one, they will take appropriate action. The publisher's writing style resembles the most familiar one of Mr. Review: his syntax is casual, utilizing the loose connective 'and', clauses are sometimes out of logical order, and he relies upon the simple naming of concrete objects to set the scene in which he claims to have discovered the letter.

As I have written in *The Versatile Defoe*:

> opposed to the voice of the honest publisher is the voice of the Jacobite author of the letter, a man who has access to secret information, who advises concealing meaning by using ambiguous language, a man who relies upon complex logic rather than the common sense natural to honest and good natured people, and above all, a man who goes about in disguise. The Jacobite's writing style is characterized by formal syntax underlined by heavy parallelism. Individual clauses are closely articulated. . . . The diction of the Jacobite gentleman, who is discussing complex political and religious ideas, is precise and relatively formal.[16]

The style it best resembles is the highly worked writing cited in Chapter 1 above, pp. 52–3, addressed to the House of Commons.

It would be too simple, however, to think of only two Defoes—the worldly Mr. Review and his opposite, the plain-speaking Mr. Review. As we will remember from Defoe's letter to Harley during the Scottish campaign, he mentioned a number of different roles he enjoyed playing for a number of different audiences. With the return of Harley to power in the summer of 1710, an elusive Mr. Review appears in the journal, a Proteus whose true contours are difficult to discern. This is the way he presents himself in the first two paragraphs of the 12 August issue, a month during which he was making as smooth a transition in the *Review* as possible from the Whig ministry he had been serving to Harley's new Tory ministry:

> I believe no man will deny, that this is the most critical time that it was possible, for any man that writes of public affairs, to speak in.—It is impossible for the wisest man in the world, *or for aught I know that ever was in the world*, to speak to the points now in hand, so as to please you all.—If a man could be found, that could sail north and south; that could speak truth and falsehood, that could turn to the right hand and to the left, all at the same time, he would be the man, he would be the only

proper person, that should now speak, for all any other man can say, will signify just nothing. What you do not like, you will not hear, what you will hear, you will not practice, and what you will practice, no man in his senses can like.

He that will speak to please you, must say nothing to the purpose; he that will speak to the purpose, must not expect to give you any content, or to gain from you anything but reproaches. . . . (17:233)

This amorphous creature, not the plain-dealing Mr. Review, was the Daniel Defoe seen by contemporaries like Joseph Addison. Addison allegorized him in the *Trial and Conviction of Count Tariff* of 1713 as follows:

When the Count had finished his speech, he desired leave to call in his witnesses, which was granted: when immediately there came to the bar a man with a hat drawn over his eyes in such a manner that it was impossible to see his face. He spoke in the spirit, nay, in the very language, of the Count, repeated his arguments, and confirmed his assertions. Being asked his name, he said the world called him Mercator [the name of a journal Defoe was writing in favour of the commercial articles of the Treaty of Utrecht, opposed by Whigs like Addison]: but as for his true name, his age, his lineage, his religion, his place of abode, they were particulars, which for certain reasons, he was obliged to conceal. The court found him such a false, shuffling, prevaricating rascal, that they set him aside, as a person unqualified to give his testimony in a court of justice. . . .

After suggesting on 12 August 1710 what his new role is to be, however, Defoe quickly changes back to the old, plain-dealing Mr. Review:

Now, Gentlemen, I know but one man in the world, that is fit to speak of this matter.—And find him where you will, this must be his character: he must be one, that searching into the depths of truth, dare speak her aloud in the most dangerous terms; that fears no faces, courts no favours, is subject to no interest, bigoted to no party; that asks no protection, is afraid of no laws, hunts after no preferments, solicits for no place, and will be a hypocrite for no gain; I will not make such a panegyric upon myself, as to say *I am the man*, I leave that to the consequences.—(17:234)

In spite of his reversion to the old type, the argument of the 12 August issue of the *Review* illustrates rather the personality

of the man 'that could speak truth and falsehood' than that of
the plain dealer. Furious that Godolphin, Lord Treasurer and a
superb financial administrator, had been removed from office,
the Whigs were threatening to withdraw funds from the Bank of
England and in other ways to disrupt public credit. The new
Mr. Review points out that he is trying to be impartial when he
observes that, on the one hand, crying public disaster and
running down public credit will create that very disaster, but,
on the other hand, being brave and going on as usual will
strengthen the hands of those who want to see more Tories put
into office. Caught between these two evils, he does not, as one
would expect from his introduction, choose some middle way.
Instead, he advises Whigs to consider their financial interest
first and not to sell stocks at a loss, to be grabbed up by Tories as
a bargain. His preliminaries, therefore, are only a smokescreen
designed to conceal the opening move in his campaign to
protect public credit for the new Tory ministry.

The worldly Mr. Review does not make his first appearance
in 1710. On many occasions during his mission in Scotland he
equivocates about why he is really there, and throughout the
Review he denies charges of being a government writer. The
equivocations employed by the worldly Mr. Review to deflect
accusations that he is employed by the government are numerous and ingenious. He professes to be writing 'without doors'
or publicly on behalf of the Union, having no privileged inside
information (6:preface; 8:579, 682). He places the world 'only'
in a position that makes his sentence ambiguous: 'As to the
principle, from which I have acted, I shall leave to the issues of
time to determine, whether it has been sincere, or no. Hypocrites only make use of masks and false lights to conceal
present reserved designs; truth and sincerity only dare appeal
to time and consequences' (6:Preface). He answers the author
of the *Medley*, who claimed Defoe had taken money 'for writing
Reviews' by replying, 'Only let him remember his own words,
FOR WRITING REVIEWS' (21:841). (Defoe was paid a general
retainer, not a special fee for the *Review*.) One of his most
adroit equivocations contains both self-pity and insult:

> As to the charge of flattery, I despise it; I am making my court
> to nobody; I am seeking no preferments, nor asking places;
> retired and unknown to men of power, I seek to speak truth

rather than to please, and my reward is to be despised not preferred, abandoned, not supported.—Men flatter that hang about courts, and wait at the levees of their generals; that live in expectation, and pursue their private interest. To what end does a man speak that seeks nothing, and asks nothing.—But truth commands the pen of every honest man.—And if I have gone beyond truth, let me see one *honest* man contradict it. (14:8)

Significant to the consideration of role-playing and the splitting and multiplication of voices in Defoe's personality is his role in the Mesnager *Minutes* of 1717. On stage, as we will remember, are Mesnager and Abigail Masham. Behind the scenes is the Earl of Oxford, engineering a last minute hoax on them. Even further behind stage is the author of the Mesnager *Minutes*, Daniel Defoe. And the nameless Defoe is split into two different writers. Speaking about English pamphleteers, Mesnager describes Defoe as a writer he had once employed:

> My writer had an excellent talent, and words enough, and was as well qualified to prove nonentities to contain substance, and substance to be entirely spirituous, as anyone I have met with; I was no judge of his style, having but little of the tongue; but as I kept him entirely private, I found the people always eager to read what he wrote, and frequently his books were said to be written by one great lord, or one eminent author or other; and this made them be more called for at the booksellers than ordinary, and the man gained by the sale, besides what I allowed to him, which was not inconsiderable.

He adds, 'It was a great disappointment to me that this man fell sick and died.' The Defoe of many roles, 'one great lord', or 'one eminent author or another', is dead. Mesnager attempts through the Swedish representative in England to employ as a substitute another writer, the author of the October 1711 *Reasons Why This Nation Ought to Put a Speedy End to This Expensive War*, but he is balked in his attempt when that writer, accepting Mesnager's gift of money, lets him know he is in the service of the state. In 1717, at the publication of the Mesnager *Minutes*, it was unlikely that many people would have remembered Defoe as the author of *Reasons Why . . .*, even more so since he had had to disguise himself as a country gentleman in that popular pamphlet, going as far as to 'expostulate with the *Review*, or his party', because as late as 13 September, Mr.

Review the plain dealer had ridiculed in his journal the suggestion that Harley's ministry was considering giving up Spain to the House of Bourbon. The author of *Reasons Why . . .*, arguing on behalf of the ministry, which had now switched its policy, had to draw a distinction between the kingdom and the empire of Spain.

Defoe's dissembling of designs and donning of many different masks has by the time of the Mesnager *Minutes* pushed his elusive personality far into the background. At that remote point, the dissociating process has gone even further, splitting Defoe into two different people, one of them a government writer, the other, who played many different roles, deceased.

Style: Literary Devices of the Worldly Mr. Review

In contrast to the directness of the plain dealer is the obliqueness of the worldly Mr. Review, who frequently has recourse to innuendo, reservation, and equivocation. Much of the obliqueness in the *Review* cannot be recognized without detailed knowledge of the current events under discussion so that one can appreciate how Mr. Review is twisting or distorting an entire argument to point in a new direction.

One relatively easy to understand example of equivocation occurs during the successful Tory slander campaign under Oxford's ministry against the Duke of Marlborough. Defoe was never violently partisan in that campaign, but he did make innuendoes, both in the *Review* and in pamphlets. In the following excerpt, the worldly (and wily) Mr. Review takes the unaccustomed trouble of explaining how equivocal his remarks are[17]:

> But I am persuaded of this, that there is no general has, or ever will, merit great things of us, but he has received, and will receive all the grateful acknowledgments he OUGHT to expect.— When I say OUGHT, and put it in capital letters, I am objected against, as being ambiguous; and one side tells me, I mean OUGHT, if he considers the reason of his merit, and the duty of his performance. Another says, I mean, if he considers the people he serves, their national temper, and ancient usage.— But I shall leave this undecided, the reader may take it *hic* & *ubique*. (18:530–31)

Another example of equivocation from the *Review* can also serve as an example of the many witty remarks in Defoe's journal. To a letter inquiring how many people make up the 'Society' supposedly writing the *Little Review*, Mr. Review replies:

> You desire of *me* an account of what *we* are; but when a man talks of himself, he handles a subject ten to one he does not understand. However, as to the complication of the Society, I say we are *nomen multitudinis*, a number, but 'tis a singular one. We are one person, sometimes Mr. *Review*, sometimes the *Scandal Club*, sometimes one single body, sometimes a body corporate. So that, Sir, if you write or address yourself to *us*, *I* shall receive your letter; or if you send to *me*, *we* shall give you all the satisfaction *I* can, for *we* are your *friend and servants, nos ego*. (5: *Little Review*, 81)

An example of innuendo occurs in the discussion of disputes between landed (Tory) and monied (Whig) men. Referring to the monster of Glasgow, a Siamese twin, the worldly Mr. Review uses the words 'non-resisting' and 'passively obedient' to imply that landed interests reluctant to co-operate with monied interests are Jacobite in their sympathies:

> If one of their bodies dissenting from the other would go east, and the other obstinately insisting to go west, refused to yield anything; what could the legs do in this case? They are non-resisting, passively obedient things, and submit entirely to the arbitrary dominion of the will. . . . (19:70)

A reader must be on the alert for the concealed reservation, placed within or at the end of a sentence by the devious Mr. Review. Referring to the popular astrologer Partridge, he remarks, 'I know, many people have of late made themselves famous for prophesying, especially some that have told us of things after they are come to pass' (16:591). On whether or not England has made a secret agreement with France about the division of the Spanish dominions, Mr. Review's statement is true only of knowledge 'without doors'. As an employee of the ministry he possesses, but does not mention, accurate private ('indoors') information:

> *And yet I believe*, and am persuaded, as far as I can learn from fact, or see from consequence, *speaking without doors*, that there is not yet one word spoke, question asked, proposal made, or

scheme laid, between us and France, whether on one side or another, towards *how*, *which way*, or *to whom*, any parts of the said Spanish dominions shall be divided, or whether there shall be any partition or no; but that *all the partitions* publicly talked of, printed, and laid down, serve as so many testimonies to the authors, that they know nothing of the matter. (20:366)

Because he disapproved of a Parliamentary attack on England's Dutch allies following the publication of the figures of allied contributions to the war, he writes in the *Review*: 'I shall make no scruple to allow, *in compliment to Parliament veracity*, that the Dutch have, *as all the Confederates have been*, deficient in their quotas of troops, ships, etc.' (21:583, my italics). When Mr. Review reports the conversation of a Jacobite who takes the abjuration oath in between asides like, 'By God, I'll never keep that', the journalist concludes, 'and yet at the end, [he] kissed the book, and took the oath—and now he is *as loyal as other folks*' (16:447, my italics). Another reservation placed at the end of a sentence occurs after an ironical argument of 6 December 1709 against a member of the House of Lords who has proposed that Godolphin and Marlborough should be dismissed from the ministry. Demonstrating how ridiculous the argument is, Mr. Review concludes that he agrees the ministry ought to be changed and in his next issue will suggest replacements, 'in which I shall be as careful not to differ with his Lordship, as I have been here' (11:512).

Slyly the worldly Mr. Review replies to a furious letter from a French Jacobite, occasioned by the *Review*'s having quoted a printed ballad in which the Pretender was called a rascal. He claims he 'never pretended to be the author of [the ballad], nor did I publish it as my own, but as a quotation.' As to the accusation that he has called the Pretender a rascal, he continues, 'It has not been my method, to treat even my worst enemies with scurrility or ill manners. But I quoted this, as a proof of the national aversion that was in the people of England to the Pretender. . . .' (21:814)

Yet in a previous issue of the *Review*, he had objected to the rising Jacobite sympathy in the City of London, referring to the popularity of the song, 'The King Shall Enjoy His Own Again'. He admits that it was a song written in the days of exile of Charles II, and therefore literally 'can have no reference to this day', so that the Queen 'is in no way concerned in it now'. But he insists that there is an oblique way of affronting people, and if there is not, then people should not be complaining that Mr. Review himself often uses this method:

> But I must ask you, pray, Gentlemen, will you allow of no oblique affronts to her Majesty? Is nothing a just offence to the Queen, but downright calling her usurper?—if you will go by that rule, no man can justly be affronted at the author of this, for I speak not directly to anybody.—And 'tis hard that private men shall think themselves affronted by a method, which they will not allow their sovereign to think herself insulted by. (20:314)

This observation of the worldly Mr. Review about oblique affronts is a particularly striking example of the difference between his style and the style of the plain dealer. The contrast can be seen clearly in the case of Defoe's Truth and Honesty who, when rebuked for being too blunt in declaring that a certain journalist believes the Queen is a usurper, replies that 'softer words' will not do; he is 'always for speaking truth'.

The element of humour and of play in Defoe has been touched upon by scholars, but it cannot be too often emphasized. In a postscript to a letter of 28 November 1706 to Robert Harley, Defoe writes:

> I Could not Refrain sending you a piece of my Ld Beilhavens Poetry in Answer to the Ballad. I Daresay you will believ it a meer Originall and I believ he may Challenge all the World to match it or to Answer it. You will also see by it I have mannagd so in the Ballad that he does not suspect it but believs it my Ld Haddington. (*Letters*, p. 162)

According to George Harris Healey, editor of the *Letters*, the 'ballad' is 'doubtless Defoe's *The Vision*, in which Belhaven's speech is ridiculed'. The story of this particular literary hoax would thus appear to be that Belhaven had spoken against the Union, and Defoe had written, circulated in manuscript, and printed a ballad called *The Vision*, ridiculing Belhaven's speech. In its manuscript form, the ballad was appreciated by such notables as the Earl of Marr. Defoe had complicated the hoax by disguising his ballad as the work of a Union supporter, the Earl of Haddington, and then writing an answer to that ballad in the style of Belhaven, its original victim.

The Earl of Marr came in for his own hoaxing when, according to John Robert Moore,[18] Defoe's 1716 redaction of the journal of Marr, now a Stuart rebel, changed a few strategic words to make the Jacobite cause seem ridiculous. Defoe's rendition apparently pushed Marr's original right out of the market.

Defoe's pleasure in his versatility of style and consequent ability to confuse his readers is expressed in a self-revealing passage in the Mesnager *Minutes*, when Mesnager reports how rumours were spread and letters written about secret peace negotiations taking place between England and France:

> It was the pleasantest thing in the world, to see how all the Confederates were alarmed at those rumours. The envoys and residents at London, were tormented with the reproaches of their masters, who complained, that having sent them to reside at the British Court, to take care of their interest, they should sit still, and let a negotiation of that consequence go on in so public and open a manner, and give them no notice of any of the particulars, nor so much as write for further instructions, how to act on such an occasion. Upon this they came buzzing about the Court, were inquisitive, uneasy, and so importuning, that had it not been diverting to the ministry on another account, it would have made them very uneasy.

But the pleasure in his ability to confuse readers was not confined to political intrigue. In *Religious Courtship* of 1722, Defoe describes a curious personal foible that resembles his own practice as he distorted the words of rival writers, toning them up to make them more obnoxious, or substituting a few key words, as in the journal of the Earl of Marr, to make the writer and his cause sound ridiculous. The widow of an irreligious and mischievous husband complains to her brother about Sir James, her late spouse:

> *Sist.* . . . and every now and then he would paste a single printed word, that he cut out of some other book, just over another word in their books, so cunningly, that they could not perceive it, and make them read nonsense.
>
> *Bro.* Why, what harm was there in all that?
>
> *Sist.* Why, it shewed his general contempt of good things, and making a mock of them; otherwise the thing was not of so much value. (p. 95)

The effect of all the role-playing, mimicking, and construct-
ing of complicated arguments was twofold. First, in hoaxes like
the *Shortest Way*, Defoe was too clever for his own good. He
confused his readers completely and paid dearly for their
anger once they realized that they had been tricked. *A Letter
from a Gentleman at the Court of St. Germains*, of which he was
apparently fond, since he mentioned it several times in the
Review, including once long after he could expect to be adver-
tising it for sale, was so clever in design that it passed unnoticed by the general public in spite of its being excellently
written. As a result, what Mr. Review wrote about overly
clever addresses to Parliament and to the Queen, applied all
too often to his own writing:

> I cannot but liken these addresses to some late books written
> by Mr. B. against the Quakers.—Those they were wrote for
> would not read them; those they were wrote against did not
> value them; those that read them did not understand them;
> those that [understood] them did not like them; those that liked
> them would not buy them; his friends would not vindicate
> them, his enemies would not trouble themselves to answer
> them, and he that wrote them did not believe them. . . . (17:30)

Second, the innuendo, equivocation and mimicry that so
amused Defoe as he revealed, yet concealed, the shadowy side
of his personality[19] must have been major impediments to
developing a style as appropriate to the worldly Mr. Review as
the plain-speaking style was appropriate to the plain-dealing
Mr. Review. What remained for the worldly Defoe in place of
a suitable style was laughter:

> . . . I cannot but divert myself sometimes, to hear these bright
> politicians talk, and their way of management, when they have
> a mind to have a book they don't like, called mine.—*I know it by
> its style*, say they, *it is his way of writing*; and another guesses by
> the way of printing; and thus twenty Tory books are called
> mine, which I have no manner of knowledge of, or hand
> in. Well, *on the other hand*, I find them reading such a paper, and
> such a paper, and caressing it and applauding it, and quoting it,
> nay, upbraiding me with it, as an excellent piece, and yet that
> piece has been of my own writing.—Can any man but laugh at
> these wise judges of style, or would put any value upon the
> censures they pass? (21:581–82)

The Elusive Daniel Defoe

NOTES

1. Geoffrey Holmes, *British Politics in the Age of Anne* (London: Macmillan, 1967), p. 102.
2. Defoe's synthesis in this pamphlet should be seen in terms of traditional Whig political propaganda. Corns, Speck and Downie point out that the 'fictional [Tory] archetype' (p. 23) developed in the course of over 100 years, although the Jacobite ingredient was stressed increasingly after the accession of the Hanoverians in 1714.
3. See bibliographical discussion in *The Versatile Defoe*, ed. Laura A. Curtis (London: George Prior Publishers, 1979), pp. 128–29.
4. Cited by G. A. Starr, *Defoe and Casuistry* (Princeton: Princeton University Press, 1971), note 43, p. 18.
5. This technique seems to be a political form of the 'pilgrim allegory' described by J. Paul Hunter, who writes, 'By mixing the stories of individuals into a potpourri which suggested the typical in human experiences, writers like Bunyan remained true to the spirit of Puritan doctrine, but they violated the letter. Their stories were "true" only in the sense that the episodes conformed to the totality of human experience, but the use of allegorical names and places (which did not pretend to correspond to "real" names or places) circumvented the charge of "feigned history"' (*The Reluctant Pilgrim: Defoe's Emblematic Quest for Form in 'Robinson Crusoe'*, pp. 116–17).
6. Maximillian E. Novak maintains that Defoe's definition of lying 'can hardly be used to justify those parts of Defoe's fiction from which no moral whatsoever can be drawn, but his defense of lying establishes a basis for any type of fiction which contains serious ideas, social commentary, or even a tag moral' ('Defoe's Theory of Fiction', *SP*, 61 (1964), 663). Novak demonstrates that Defoe's definition of what constituted a serious idea could justify a great deal of his fiction.

   G. A. Starr explains that the notion of injurious intent as integral to a definition of lying is distinctive but not unique to Defoe; discussions of casuistry by eminent laymen and divines of the seventeenth century had covered this point. He goes on to observe, 'Defoe does not claim, however, that a distinction must be made between wholesome and pernicious falsehoods, and that only the latter should be called lies. Thus his theory of fiction does not really rest, as one recent critic [Novak] maintains, on a "defence of lying", but rather on a traditional distinction *between* lying and beneficial deception' (pp. 200–1 in *Defoe and Casuistry*).

   Everett Zimmerman points out that the preface to *Roxana* is different from Defoe's other prefaces; the author recognizes there is personal gratification from writing, not just the edification of others (*Defoe and the Novel*, Berkeley: University of California Press, 1975, p. 181).

   Davis Blewett maintains in *Defoe's Art of Fiction* that there is in the prefaces to the fiction from *Robinson Crusoe* through *Roxana* a 'shift in emphasis from the authenticity of the tale . . . to the "Performance", the "dressing up the Story", the "Words" which are used to puff Roxana's

136

story' (pp. 15–16). He believes that he can trace a development in Defoe's fiction and mood and that the increasing self-consciousness about fiction in the prefaces is one indication of such a development (Toronto: University of Toronto Press, 1979).

7. Sutherland makes this remark about Defoe's *General History of . . . the Pyrates* of 1724 (*Daniel Defoe*, p. 153), but the twilight world seems to have descended upon Defoe a good deal earlier than this date, probably about the time of Harley's 1710–14 ministry.

8. John Robert Moore explains in *Defoe in the Pillory and Other Studies* (Bloomington: Indiana University Press, 1939), pp. 3–38, that enemies of Defoe, specifically aldermen, were the judges responsible for the exorbitant punishment he received for his *Shortest Way*.

9. Starr discusses the question of equivocation in *Defoe and Casuistry*, pointing out that the use of this device in refusing to clear up someone's ignorance was acceptable to Richard Baxter, and that dovelike innocence or naïveté was not admired by Christian apologists for casuistry (pp. 45–6).

10. Leopold Damrosch, Jr. raises intelligent questions about this kind of confusing effect in several of Defoe's best-known works, *A True Relation of the Apparition of One Mrs. Veal . . .*, *The Poor Man's Plea*, and *The Complete English Tradesman*, in his 'Defoe as Ambiguous Impersonator', *MP*, 71 (November 1973), 153–59.

11. Cited by J. A. Downie, 'Daniel Defoe's *Review* and Other Political Writings in the Reign of Queen Anne'.

12. Starr, *Defoe and Casuistry*, p. 196.

13. Starr, p. 201.

14. *The Versatile Defoe*, pp. 341–49.

15. Starr emphasizes Defoe's interest in Quakers because of their insistence upon speaking the literal truth, yet their acceptance of 'Richard Baxter's doctrine that one can legitimately speak to others in such a way that "through some weakness of their own they will misunderstand . . ." ' (*Defoe and Casuistry*, p. 207).

16. *The Versatile Defoe*, pp. 124–25.

17. Starr observes that 'speaking in colors', connected with disguise and dissembling, is one of Defoe's characteristics, employed 'more frequent[ly] than is usually recognized . . .' (*Defoe and Casuistry*, p. 203). I have classified 'speaking in colors' as equivocation in the discussion on pages 130–31 above.

18. John Robert Moore, 'Defoe's Hand in *A Journal of the Earl of Marr's Proceedings*', *HLQ*, 17 (1954), 209–28.

19. My analysis of Defoe's writing style substantiates Homer O. Brown's thought-provoking discussion of conflicting tendencies to exposure and to concealment in Defoe's fictional characters. See 'The Displaced Self in the Novels of Daniel Defoe'.

4

The Real World:
Moll Flanders as Hoax

In Chapter 2 I traced two tendencies in *Robinson Crusoe* and in *A Journal of the Plague Year* that conflict with Defoe's compulsion to construct in his writing an ideal, clear, and simplified world of traditional morality, Christian belief, family hierarchy, and slow and patient work. The first tendency, as we have seen, is restlessness. In *Moll Flanders* the restlessness contained and controlled by Robinson Crusoe finds its outlet in aggression against society and against the reader. The fear of others overcome by Crusoe only after slowly mastering himself and his island and establishing a paternal relation with Friday finds expression in *Moll Flanders* in the quickly acquired reserve of the social outsider who rarely lets others see into her heart. The world view accommodating Moll's activities is described in Chapter 3: truth is difficult of access, reasoning is frequently unsound, judges of truth are unreliable, and effectual action requires dissembling of design, disguise, and manipulating and tricking other people. The real world is a realm of chiaroscuro where the disreputable jostles the respectable, humour vies with fear, and equilibrium is highly precarious.

The problem of equilibrium or pattern in *Moll Flanders* has been the subject of prolonged and heated controversy among scholars and critics. Although patterns from picaresque narrative, criminal biography and spiritual autobiography have been clearly identified and traced in this fiction, the crux of the still unresolved debate is irony: do the many individual instances of irony in the fiction harmonize to form a consistent and subsuming pattern? Is the fiction an example of stable irony, defined by Wayne Booth as a substitute system of meaning reconstructed by the reader from a series of incongruities in the literal sense of the text, a reconstructed meaning the reader is 'not . . . invited to undermine . . . with further demolitions and reconstructions', and which he is certain he shares with the author in an 'amiable community' of understanding?[1]

The conflict about ironic pattern is best expressed in the controversy between Ian Watt and Maximillian E. Novak. Watt, author of the influential *Rise of the Novel*, launches a powerful attack when he asserts that in spite of individual instances of patent and conscious irony, nothing in the fiction itself clearly indicates that Defoe viewed either his central character or his purported moral theme differently from Moll.[2] Maximillian E. Novak, author of three books and numerous articles on Defoe, and *C.B.E.L.* Defoe bibliographer, relies upon his extensive acquaintance with Defoe's vast written output, with his reading, and with his habitual thought patterns to explain those individual passages in *Moll Flanders* where modern readers are not sure whether or not the author was conscious of irony. As a result of his superior acquaintance with Defoe, Novak comes to exactly the opposite conclusion from Watt; there is indeed a consistent pattern of irony structuring *Moll Flanders*: 'the underlying irony of the work is to be found in Moll's blindness.'[3]

Although the debate between Novak and Watt dates back many years, the issue has never been settled, as I believe it must be if we are ever to understand the complex and evasive sensibility of one of the major figures in English literature. To summarize the following argument, I take *Moll Flanders* to be an unstable equilibrium of picaresque narrative, criminal biography and spiritual autobiography. What holds it together is not the stable irony defined by Wayne Booth and required by Ian Watt. Instead, the rubber bands encircling the warring elements in *Moll Flanders* belong to the realm of comedy, the secretive Defoe's most idiosyncratic form of humour, the hoax or put-on. Defoe uses irony as well as mimicry and innuendo to draw his readers into a position which appears to the inattentive to be his, but which in fact is only partially so. Thus he traps his gullible readers into accepting Moll for different reasons from his own, the wrong reasons, proving for his own private amusement, for the relief of his guilty conscience, and for some financial gain (novels were not as remunerative as the didactic manuals Defoe began writing in 1715), that his readers' morals and understanding are superficial; everybody falls for a success-ful rogue, but only Defoe recognizes the self-deception that permits each reader to accept her.

The comic pattern I am arguing for in *Moll Flanders* was originally suggested to me by an extensive study of Defoe's idiosyncratic sense of humour throughout his writings. The idea of hoax as genre comes from Miriam Leranbaum's study of *The Shortest Way with the Dissenters*. Professor Leranbaum described hoax as a deception perpetrated on a reader or a group of readers. The purpose of the deception varies, accord-ing to the particular work: it may aim at private amusement or at monetary gain for its perpetrator; but, especially in political writing, it may have the relatively disinterested intention of exposing to ridicule a single individual or group regarded by the hoaxer as pernicious to the public interest. Hoax contains only one level of reality, striving for an 'aura of authenticity'[4] in order to deceive its primary audience totally. If the hoax is to be detected at all, the task must be performed by a totally different audience, a secondary group not directly involved in the issue. Although the hoaxer uses many of the same techniques as the ironist, he does not exhaust his energy in verbal attack; instead, his hoax provokes action and reaction from different groups of readers as a result of their lack of intellectual sophistication or their possession of it.

Biography provides us with many instances of Defoe's recourse to hoax in his political writing, from the 1702 *Shortest Way* to the 1717 Mesnager *Minutes*. In Chapter 3 I discussed his 1705 campaign in the *Review* against the Tackers, describing the backstage activities of Daniel Defoe, taunting excitable opponents into furious outbursts, while on stage the imper-turbable Mr. Review was chiding them for their bad temper and reminding them how offensive it was making them to moderates. I mentioned also the complicated literary hoax he played on Lord Belhaven.

But Defoe's fiction cannot be defined as hoax in the same way as his political writing can; although his successful attempts to pass off fictional autobiographies as authentic memoirs by real people conform in many details with Professor Leranbaum's definition, these writings were not expected, like the *Shortest Way*, to provoke different political reactions from different groups of readers. Their ultimate design is closer to the 'put-on', classified by Wayne Booth as 'an "ironic" statement that the ironist does not expect to be reconstructed and may not himself even [fully] understand'.[5] An example of this covert baiting appears in the apparently autobiographical passage I cited in Chapter 3, from *Religious Courtship*,[6] contemporaneous with the 1722 *Moll Flanders*. The pleasure taken by Sir James in distorting the words in books read by his pious wife is akin to the pleasure taken by the narrator of the Mesnager *Minutes* about the effect of false rumours about peace negotiations on foreign envoys in London. Sir James's widow explains that her late husband's idiosyncrasy arose from 'a general contempt of good things, and making a mock of them', but this kind of teasing is as much directed against readers as it is against ideas. It is aggression that finds its outlet in puzzling or exciting others while remaining calm and concealed oneself, a variation of the same activity performed in public by the plain-dealing Mr. Review when he chided Tackers for bad temper Defoe had helped to provoke.

If the impulse to put on readers arises from a desire to mock respectable ideas and gullible readers, the device essential to Defoe as put-on artist is that of the mask. His central activity as writer of fiction is mimicry: making his disguise so energetic and so natural that few ever think of trying to penetrate to the schemer behind the disguise. Defoe's comic spirit, delighting in its own energy and elasticity, and revelling in masquerade, remains invisible to cursory modern readers because he took great pains to camouflage it from his contemporaries, who knew him better than we do and many of whom regarded him as a false, prevaricating rogue.

Defoe's favourite mask was that of the plain dealer and plain speaker of a world he desired, an ideal that had probably been inculcated into him in his childhood. He certainly wished to be recognized publicly as a man like Robinson Crusoe or the plain-dealing Mr. Review and must have made repeated private attempts to align the devious self required by the circumstances of the world he lived in and his own position in that world with his simple, childlike, principled public persona. The energy expended on this effort probably underlies his asseveration that *Robinson Crusoe* was true in the sense that it was an 'allusive allegoric history' of his own life. But for Defoe real life was more likely to be a masquerade, as he informed Robert Harley in the letter about his Scottish activities cited above,[7] and his enjoyment of this masquerade is apparent from the verve of that letter.

The passage I have chosen to illustrate how Defoe's habitual sense of comedy, carefully concealed from his public under the vigour of his mimicry, operates in the form of put-on in *Moll Flanders*, occurs shortly before Moll's last theft. Defoe has dispatched her for a short run outside of London so that he can supply a few typical examples of how city slickers prey upon country people. Moll is on her way back from Harwich, trying to avoid the most travelled routes in order not to bump into a Dutchman whom she has just robbed of his trunk:

> I WALK'D about two or three Mile, and then I met a plain Countryman, who was busy about some Husbandry work I did not know what; and I ask'd him a great many Questions first, not much to the purpose; but at last told him I was going for *London*, and the Coach was full, and I cou'd not get a Passage, and ask'd him if he cou'd not tell me where to hire a Horse that would carry double, and an honest Man to ride before me to *Colchester*, so that I might get a Place there in the Coaches; the honest Clown look'd earnestly at me, and said nothing for above half a Minute; when scratching his Pole, a Horse say you, and to *Colchester* to carry double; why yes Mistress, alack-a-day, you may have Horses enough for Money; well Friend, *says I*, that I take for granted, I don't expect it without Money: Why but Mistress, *says he*, how much are you willing to give; nay, says I again, Friend, I don't know what your Rates are in the Country here, for I am a Stranger; but if you can get one for me, get it as Cheap as you can, and I'll give you somewhat for your Pains.
>
> WHY that's honestly said too, says the Countryman; *not so honest neither*, said I, to myself, *if thou knewest all*; why Mistress, *says he*, I have a Horse that will carry Double, and I don't much care if I go my self with you; *and the like*: Will you, says I? Well I

believe you are an honest Man, if you will, I shall be glad of it, I'll pay you in Reason; why look ye Mistress, *says he*, I won't be out of Reason with you then, if I carry you to Colechester it will be worth five Shillings for myself and my Horse, for I shall hardly come back to Night.

IN short, I hir'd the honest Man and his Horse. . . . (pp. 266–67)

Both irony and comedy are present in this anecdote, but the major ironic techniques, innuendo, understatement, and verbal irony, play a role subordinate to Defoe's subsuming comic convention of the put-on. For this reason, much of the irony is fleeting; our attention as readers is captivated by his magical talent for mimicry. Thus we assume, like Virginia Woolf, that he lived his characters without exactly knowing how, and we find it difficult to decide whether or not his irony is conscious.

The description of Moll's encounter with the farmer is designed with great economy. Simply by noting the gesture of scratching his head, by imitating his speech, and by making him answer slowly with a restricted vocabulary, repeating some of Moll's words, Defoe suggests by mimicry and understatement the elephantine pace of the farmer's mental processes. Coupling the words 'honest man' and 'horse' just enough in this short passage, Defoe suggests by innuendo a parallel in mental ability between the two never directly stated. (Several times in the *Review*, when Defoe wishes to describe the simplicity of 'honest' uneducated people or of slogan-shouting mobs, he couples an abstract noun with the word 'horse' to emphasize that the uneducated are not capable of distinguishing between the two, of understanding abstractions.)

The yokel uses the words 'honest' and 'reason' in such a restricted sense—they apply only to the fee he ought to charge and the probability that Moll will pay this fee—that these abstractions become ludicrous in his mouth. Moll is aware of the verbal irony (*'not so honest neither*, said I to myself, *if thou knewest all'*), and enjoys using the same words to convey different meanings. 'Honest' to her means 'stupid', and 'reason' is her flattery of the yokel; she is implying that he can be addressed in the same terms as an urban shopkeeper, and he is quick to show her, by picking up the word 'reason', that he merits her distinction and would be at ease in that socially elevated circle.

In this encounter, Defoe dramatizes a generalization about language he frequently played with in the *Review* and in his pamphlets: words like 'honesty' and 'reason' impede communication because their abstractness invites different interpretations, depending upon individual experience. Yet readers unfamiliar with Defoe's other writings will hesitate to infer such a generalization because the momentum of the passage hurries them away from judgements about verbal irony to spontaneous laughter.

Here we should stop for a moment and refer to three passages above.[8] The first two passages discuss the low style of the plain-dealing Mr. Review, pointing out that it seems to be based on his observation that uneducated people are unaccustomed to dealing with abstract ideas, so that instead of supplying particulars to explain an idea, they simply repeat the noun that names it. The monotony of a conversation where the linguistic abilities of a speaker are insufficient to convey more than platitudes is apparent in the scene between Moll and the farmer. The third passage, 'Judges of Truth in the Real World', describes several sociological groups Defoe regarded as honest but stupid, pointing out that country people fall into this general category. Incapable of understanding abstract ideas, in compensation they have a hearty appreciation of tangibles like money.

All this, however, is lightly skirted over in the scene between Moll and the farmer.[9] The salient effect is comic rather than ironic; it arises from the yokel's failure to penetrate Moll's mask as an honest city tradeswoman, partly because he is stupid and partly because he is intent upon driving a shrewd bargain with her.[10] As a result of this failure, he unwittingly aids her in crime and thus becomes her dupe. Money is not the test of who wins the battle here. As the O.E.D., Johnson's *Dictionary*, and Norman Knox's *The Word Irony and Its Context, 1500–1755* all point out, 'hoax' and 'banter' in Defoe's period meant mischievous verbal fictions designed to bamboozle audiences, not necessarily to swindle them.

In another example of hoax, money is again not the central issue. After Moll has been reunited with her American son, who proves conveniently affectionate and unsuspicious, she receives a gift from him of a 'Deer skin Bag' and 'five and fifty *Spanish* Pistoles in it' (p. 336). During a subsequent visit she says,

> I made him one Present, and it was all I had of value, and that was one of the gold Watches, of which I mention'd above, that I had two in my Chest, and this I happen'd to have with me, and I gave it him at his third Visit: I told him, I had nothing of any value to bestow but that, and I desir'd he would now and then kiss it for my sake; *I did not indeed tell him* that I had stole it from a Gentlewomans side, at a Meeting-House in *London*, that's by the way.
>
> He stood a little while Hesitating, as if doubtful whether to take it or no; but I press'd it on him, and made him accept it, and it was not much less worth than his Leather-pouch full of *Spanish* Gold; no, tho' it were to be reckon'd, as if at *London*, whereas it was worth twice as much there, where I gave it him; at length he took it, kiss'd it, told me the Watch should be a debt upon him, that he would be paying, as long as I liv'd.
>
> A FEW Days after he brought the Writings of Gift, and the Scrivener with them, and I sign'd them very freely, and deliver'd them to him with a hundr'd Kisses; for sure nothing ever pass'd between a Mother, and a tender dutiful Child, with more Affection. . . . (pp. 337–38)

Moll is anxious to assure her readers that she has not cheated her son in terms of money—the watch she gives him is worth almost twice as much in the Colonies as in London. But she has hoaxed him by passing off a mischievous verbal fiction on him; his kissing a stolen watch in the belief that it is of sentimental value to his mother makes Humphrey look ridiculous to a reader of Moll's narrative.

The information that the watch has been stolen from a gentlewoman at a meeting-house looks like the addition of detail for the sake of simple verisimilitude. As Paul Alkon has noticed with chronological details in Defoe, however,[11] the additional fact sometimes served to suggest something more to Defoe's readers. In this case the something more suggested by the meeting-house may have been the genuinely warm and close family relations characteristic of Dissenting families in the late seventeenth and early eighteenth centuries.[12] Family structure in the ideal world of Mr. Review and of the *Family Instructors* is a form of the affectionate model pioneered by Dissenters, and the primary obligation of parents to children is education, religious and vocational. This duty Moll of the real world has shown no interest in at all. The additional detail about the source of the stolen watch, therefore, might have had the effect on Defoe's contemporary readers of an innuendo (at which, we will recall, he was a master), which could have drawn the attention of some to the ironic discrepancy in the last sentence of the above passage between the hundred kisses and the protestations of affection while receipt of deeds of property are Moll's main business. I do not insist upon the ironical interpretation, however, for my point is that Defoe's emphasis in this passage is on the hoaxing of Humphrey.

Other passages in *Moll Flanders* where Defoe touches lightly on irony, because his emphasis is elsewhere, include Mother Midnight's notorious rationalization of Moll's stealing from a gentleman whose inebriated lust has distracted his attention from her extra-sexual activities. Critics like Dorothy Van Ghent have waxed indignant over Defoe's failure to indicate that he disagrees with this blatant projection of blame onto the gentleman, and have therefore concluded that the irony of true and false evaluations of the crime was not apparent to Defoe. One can respond like G. A. Starr, by contrasting the liaison between Moll and the gentleman with a case of conscience in the *Athenian Mercury*, a publication that influenced Defoe's Scandal Club and *Supplements* to the *Review*.[13] Like Maximillian E. Novak, one can formulate generalizations about Defoe's beliefs on such topics as sex by reading all of the over 500 works he wrote, and checking each individual case against the generalization.[14] In line with this method one can add that fruitful sources of such evidence are the 1715 and 1718 *Family Instructor* and the 1722 *Religious Courtship*, not only very close in date to *Moll Flanders*, but also close in genre to fiction. The 1715 *Family Instructor*, in particular, addressed to lower social classes than the 1718 and 1722 works,[15] classes probably akin to Defoe's projected readership for *Moll Flanders*, includes an interesting passage in which a mother explains to an obedient younger daughter the method by which a disobedient older daughter will rationalize her misbehaviour and several exchanges dramatizing the actual excuses of rebellious young adults.

What I have chosen to do, however, is to reconstruct a context of Defoe's feelings and perceptions about the world from consistent patterns in a work he wrote over the course of nine years. I am convinced that if readers would stop thinking of the author of *Moll Flanders* as a plain dealer who made occasional divagations into unscrupulousness and would start thinking of him as a worldly, even cynical man with a rather peculiar sense of humour, they would find the fiction a great deal easier to understand. I believe this to be a fruitful way of approaching the problem of intention, a problem essential in all questions of irony, but particularly in the writing of Defoe. As Professor Novak observes in relation to economic ideas, the comments of Defoe's fictional characters 'merely scratch the surface of ideas. [I would emphasize attitudes rather than ideas] inherent in the situation'.[16]

When Moll brings home to Mother Midnight the loot she has taken from her gentleman lover, she reports:

> . . . and really when I told her the Story it so affected her, that she was hardly able to forbear Tears, to think how such a Gentleman run a daily Risque of being undone, every time a Glass of Wine got into his Head.
>
> But as to the Purchase I got, and how entirely I stript him, she told me it pleas'd her wonderfully; nay, Child, *says she*, the usage may, for ought I know, do more to reform him, than all the Sermons that ever he will hear in his Life. . . . (p. 228)

As modern readers, we react to Mother Midnight's remark as to sublime, explosive effrontery. If we doubt that Defoe expected us to react this way, we should turn back to Chapter III, pp. 95–6, to see how he thought people actually reasoned in this imperfect world. There we will find that, exasperated by the passage of the worst law he can imagine for Scotland, the introduction of Anglican rites into a Presbyterian establishment by order of an English Parliament, Mr. Review exclaims ironically, in speech patterns Defoe later simplified for Mother Midnight:

> . . . *and as to the Common Prayerbook, and the methods used to bring it in there,* I verily believe, it will do more to reconcile the Episcopal people and the established Church together, than

anything that ever that party did before; *nay the very reading* the English liturgy there, and a little of the wise management of the people that espouse it, *will make more Presbyterians in Scotland, than any step that party ever took before.* (My italics)

If we still doubt our reaction, we can return to the *Shortest Way*, a hoax against the effrontery of Sacheverell and the High-Flyers. By heightening Sacheverell's rhetoric,[17] Defoe induced different kinds of explosions among different groups of readers, but the Dissenters who were to benefit eventually from the hoax were not exempt in that pamphlet from the criticisms. In the same way, Moll is the major culprit when she robs a drunken lecher, but gentlemen who traffic with whores are not exempt from Defoe's scorn.

Since I am arguing that *Moll Flanders* is a hoax, I should remind my readers of Professor Leranbaum's observation that hoaxers may resort to irony, but they do not exhaust their energy in verbal attack. Like the late Sir James of *Religious Courtship*, Defoe had aggressive designs on his readers as well as ambivalent feelings about the 'good things' he was discussing in his fictions. We must not, therefore, expect him to take us fully into his confidence eventually, as if he were primarily an ironist; a hoaxer teases and irritates those readers who are aware of the tricks he is playing.

What other clues in the text of *Moll Flanders* suggest it is a hoax, or, near cousin to a hoax, a put-on? In spite of scattered didactic passages on criminals, on morality, and on religion, the language, hints, allusions, and theme of the fiction are not presented in a didactic form, as in *Robinson Crusoe*. There is no equivalent to Quaker William of *Captain Singleton* to resolve for the protagonist and the reader doubts and difficulties arising from accommodations necessitated by life in an imperfect world. Moll's reticence, even with Jemy, her favourite husband, parallels the reticence Defoe describes in an interesting passage from the essay on solitude in *Serious Reflections of Robinson Crusoe*. The passage may have some autobiographical significance; we know that Defoe ruined the fortunes of his family and must have suffered some reproach from them, for the family of his wife, who had been a wealthy young woman, did not trust him with money. We also know that although he mentioned his wife and children at times, he seems to have been close only to his daughter Sophia:

> I have heard of a man that, upon some extraordinary disgust which he took at the unsuitable conversation of some of his nearest relations, whose society he could not avoid, suddenly resolved never to speak any more. He kept his resolution most rigorously many years; not all the tears or entreaties of his friends—no, not of his wife and children—could prevail with him to break his silence. It seems it was their ill-behaviour to him, at first, that was the occasion of it; for they treated him with provoking language, which frequently put him into undecent passions, and urged him to rash replies; and he took this severe way to punish himself for being provoked, and to punish them for provoking him. . . .

> His children separated, some one way and some another way; and only one daughter, who loved her father above all the rest, kept with him, tended him, talked to him by signs, and lived almost dumb like her father near twenty-nine years with him. . . . [He falls ill.] He recovered of the illness afterwards, and frequently talked with his daughter, but not much, and very seldom to anybody else. (pp. 6–7)

This is an exaggerated account of the secretiveness of someone who has been mistreated or ostracized by others, as Moll and as Defoe had been. Although in *Serious Reflections* Defoe attributes the reticence to a fear of losing control of his temper, in Moll's case it is the fear of revealing guilty secrets to others who will then prevent her from getting what she wants. Whatever the source of reticence in author or protagonist, the fear of others expressed by this secretiveness found its vent, in Defoe as well as in Moll, in making fools of other people. This practice is appropriate to the imperfect real world of social interaction, but it occurs only intermittently in the ideal world of *Robinson Crusoe*, where fear of others is overcome through long and patient toil and prayer performed in isolation from society.

After Moll is betrayed by her first lover, she is never again trusting and ingenuous, and as her narrative proceeds, we find that she makes fools of a number of the characters she meets. I have already discussed how she makes fools out of the farmer and of her son. A third fool is Robin, younger brother of her first lover. In spite of his generous affection for Moll, Robin is a pert, sententious character with an authoritative manner not justified by his perspicacity. In fact, he resembles Swift's descriptions of the know-it-all John Tutchin and Daniel Defoe, whom Swift regarded as contemptible Grub Street hacks.[18] If we refer back to Chapter 3 above,[19] we will find that Robin's manner resembles that of the impertinent lower middle-class mercer, Tom Taffety, who appears in the dialogue on those pages. Among the fools castigated by the worldly Mr. Review, Robin, who refuses to listen to warnings about Moll, belongs to the category of the wilfully ignorant. In speech he comes somewhere in the lower middle range of the plain-dealing Mr. Review's colloquial style (see Chapter 1 above).[20]

Like the plain-dealing Mr. Review, Robin exemplifies the simplifying tendency. When Moll tells his mother, 'There was nothing between Mr. *Robert* and I', Robin replies, 'She's wrong there . . . for if there was not a great deal between us, we should be closer together than we are . . .' (p. 45). When the mother protests to her son that Moll is a beggar, Robin devises a measure extravagant enough to match that hyperbole, suggesting that he will therefore 'take her off of the hands of the Parish', and that the two of them will 'Beg together' (p. 46). Robin's language, like the language advocated in *The Complete English Tradesman*, reduces complexity by translating figurative into literal statements. As we admire the wit with which he does so, however, we should remember that he has strayed from the ideal world into the real world, and that his language reflects his mistaken confidence that he understands people and things. To deal with the imperfect Moll of the real world, one would have to use the language and reasoning of equivocation resorted to by the older brother, who tells Moll he will make her and himself 'happy' when he comes to his estate (it is the older Moll who supplies the word 'marry' for the vague generalization, p. 24), and who extricates himself from his promises by saying 'I did tell you I would Marry you when I was come to my Estate; but you see my Father is a hail healthy Man, and may live these thirty Years still . . .' (p. 38). In the end, Robin's language may be witty, but it is mistaken; in spite of the social snobbery underlying her reservations about Moll, Robin's mother is shrewder than he in mistrusting the young woman.

The simplified and concrete language that reflects the personality of the lively and plain-dealing Robin does not protect him from being duped by his calculating older brother and Moll. At the other extreme, as we have seen with the country yokel, abstractions like 'reason' and 'honesty' give rise to misunderstandings that lead to the same ignominious end. And when Moll admits to a Covent Garden mercer who has unjustly accused her of theft that his apology should be reparation enough without insisting upon damages for false accusation, yet nevertheless extorts a whopping settlement from him, her words are totally divorced from her action. In fact, the impotence of verbal communication and the omni-potence of non-verbal signals is demonstrated when Moll tricks her Lancashire gentleman into marriage by disclaiming the possession of wealth yet acting like a lady with a fortune. She makes certain at the moment of his discovery to elicit his admission that her words have not contributed to his decep-tion, but many years later, when she sees him in Newgate, she admits to herself, 'and tho' I never told him that I was a Fortune, and so did not actually Deceive him myself, yet I did encourage the having thought that I was so, and by that means I was the occasion originally of his Mischief' (p. 280). A final verbal indication that *Moll Flanders* is a hoax is the frequent repetition of words 'banter', 'bite', and 'deception' throughout the fiction.

Furthermore, Defoe hints in his preface that his readers should take Moll's professions with a grain of salt. The supposed writer of the preface admits that he has had to clean up Moll's language, mentions that after her final return to England she 'was not so extraordinary a Penitent, as she was at first', and uses the word 'pretend' to describe Moll's assertions that she is a penitent. In the course of the fiction, commenting about an affair she had with a married man, Moll says, 'But I leave the Readers of these things to their own just Reflections, which they will be more able to make effectual than I, who so soon forgot my self, and am therefore but a very indifferent Monitor' (p. 126).[21]

In his *Review* of 17 May 1711, Defoe lists four functions of prefaces, which I have cited in full in Chapter 3 above.[22] The first two items, that the writer himself may well not quite understand fully what he has written, and that he may wish to conceal its serious aspect from his readers, sheds light on a real conflict in Defoe's feelings about the value of fiction in general, about why he himself feels compelled to write it, and about how far its professed moral function can be justified. It seems apparent from his list that Defoe was puzzled about the final products of his fictionalizing imagination; he did not quite know how to analyse them but felt that they were important in some way obscure to him.

These uncertainties about the value of fiction, characteristic of Defoe's period, are explained by J. Paul Hunter,[23] but Defoe conceals his misgivings in *Moll Flanders* by punctuating his narrative with many fleeting touches of irony. Above all, the spirit of the cynical Rochester runs through the fiction. His words are twice quoted by Moll, he is alluded to, and his influence has been traced by John McVeagh, who points out that Rochester's poems most admired by Defoe 'disclose a gap between what should be or is thought to be and what is, which makes them slightly dangerous. Because they are dangerous Defoe finds them piquant,' writes McVeagh, 'for he too loved to take the lid off traditional thought. . . .'[24]

In addition, underlying all the subterfuges practised by Moll in order to make her way in an indifferent, even hostile world, is the theme that the opaqueness of our minds to one another sends us to external appearances for guidance in judging each other's intentions, and consequently makes us vulnerable to fraud. Moll's many disguises dramatize this theme, and the varied receptions she meets with in each outfit help sustain our interest in her essentially repetitive action of dupery. Even a City of London alderman and Justice of the Peace, experienced in recognizing shoplifters, is fooled[25] when Moll agrees to buy some silver spoons from a goldsmith she has been suspected of intending to rob:

> WHEN Mr. *Alderman* saw my Money, *he said*, well Madam, now I am satisfy'd you were wrong'd, and it was for this Reason, that I mov'd you should buy the Spoons, and staid till you had bought them, for if you had not had Money to pay for them, I should have suspected that you did not come into the

Shop with an intent to buy, for indeed the sort of People who come upon those Designs that you have been Charg'd with, are seldom troubl'd with much Gold in their Pockets, as I see you are.

I SMIL'D, and told his Worship, that then I ow'd something of his Favour to my Money, but I hop'd he saw reason also in the Justice he had done me before; he said, yes he had, but this had confirm'd his Opinion, and he was fully satisfy'd now of my having been injur'd; so I came off with flying Colours, tho' from an Affair, in which I was at the very brink of Destruction. (pp. 271–72)

If so experienced an observer could be tricked by professions of innocence and by the appearance of prosperity, it is highly probable that Defoe expected the same of the less sophisticated readership he probably projected for this fiction.

In the real world of the sophisticated Mr. Review, aldermen consistently arouse his contempt as examples of conceited ignorance, the kind that annoyed him more than any other. The alderman in *Moll Flanders* is too confident about the wisdom he has accumulated from his experience with 'the sort of People who come upon those Designs' that Moll has been charged with; his mistaken confidence makes him susceptible in this instance to the credulity that can afflict members of any class at any moment, but which in any form is subject to the scorn of the worldly Mr. Review. Like the farmer and Humphrey, in spite of his relatively elevated social class and education, the alderman responds with his senses and emotions to the simplest form of demonstration, proving with objects, which Mr. Review regards as most appropriate for the uneducated. By his readiness to believe in the appearance of respectability if it is backed up with money, he reveals that behind his own respectability as a solid citizen lies a gullibility engendered by his unimaginative and materialistic consciousness.

The theme of appearance and reality is expressed in *Moll Flanders* in terms of respectability and a hidden reality that differs with each character. G. A. Starr perceives a discrepancy in descriptions of the outwardly respectable baronet who conducts an affair with Moll:

> In a single paragraph we are told that 'he is as civil a gentleman, there is not a finer man, nor a soberer, graver,

modester person in the whole city,' but also reminded that 'your modest men in common opinion are sometimes no better than other people, only they keep a better character, or, if you please, are the better hypocrites' (pp. 264–65). Moll calls him 'a fop . . . blinded by his appetite,' and finds 'nothing so absurd, so surfeiting, so ridiculous' as the spectacle he makes of himself 'heated by wine in his head, and a wicked gust in his inclination.' Yet she also refers to him as 'a good sort of man in himself: a gentleman that had no harm in his design; a man of sense, and of a fine behaviour, a comely handsome person, a sober solid countenance, a charming beautiful face, and everything that could be agreeable' (pp. 260–61). Finally, the man himself, like his prototype in the *Athenian Mercury*, 'would often make just reflections . . . upon the crime itself, and upon the particular circumstances of it with respect to himself.'[26]

If we regard him as an example of a nature in reality inclined to drunken lechery but disguised by the respectable mask of a sober gentleman, the contradictory descriptions can be reconciled.

Even if we admit that characterization, language, hints, allusions, and theme in *Moll Flanders* suggest that it is a hoax, we have not proved it to be so; just as *King William and Queen Mary Conquerors*, the hoax cited by Professor Leranbaum as a source for Defoe's *Shortest Way*, *Moll Flanders* contains no hints in itself of its genre. Jacob Brackman, defining a variation of the hoax that he designates as the put-on, warns us, 'The put-on is an *open-end* form. That is to say, it is rarely climaxed by having the "truth" set straight—when a truth, indeed, exists. . . . Irony is unsuccessful when misunderstood. But the put-on, inherently, *cannot* be understood.'[27] It is here that we must turn to our knowledge of Defoe's readers and to our knowledge of Defoe himself, for as Wayne Booth points out, 'Our court of final appeal is still our conception of the author.'[28]

As we remember, at the end of *Moll Flanders* Defoe rewards Moll for a life of crime, immorality, and hypocrisy with financial prosperity and a semi-aristocratic husband. The fulsomeness of this reward is predicated upon Moll's religious conversion, but the quality of the conversion does not stand up to close scrutiny. It was presumably calculated to appease the consciences of guilt-ridden readers of novels. As J. Paul

Hunter explains, the literary and religious-moral establishment almost universally condemned the English novel in its beginnings: 'Despite dramatic increases in popularity, the novel remained underground reading throughout most of the eighteenth century, suspicion of prose fiction long proving dogged and influential if not triumphant.' In spite of this condemnation, Hunter goes on to observe, the readership of novels

> did include members of merchant families, footmen and servant wenches, country bumpkins newly arrived in London, and idle, mindless women . . . but they also included the most literate, best educated, and socially prominent Englishmen and English-women of the eighteenth century. The readership of early novels cut across economic and social divisions, and included people of all major political and religious persuasions, despite the literary and moral stigma. Readers were intimidated by the novel's detractors—and some, like Pope and Swift, seem almost to have kept their reading a secret from themselves, but they were not deterred.[29]

But Defoe was restless with this kind of appeasement of conscience. 'You pretend to *Truth* and *Honesty*, but not to much Sence I find, and so you count all that know more than you Hypocrites', remarks one of his political creations to Defoe's simple-minded persona, Truth and Honesty. Defoe's consider-able experience of crime and criminals, coupled with the negative capability by which he empathized with the fictional characters created from his observations, must have made him sceptical about the quality of reformation to be expected from a former whore and thief.[30] Moreover, his active public life during a time of considerable political turmoil made him cynical and at times even bitter about the truthfulness and intelligence to be expected of his fellow men, not to mention the particular social and educational class he must have pro-jected as most avid readers of a criminal autobiography. As Jacob Brackman observes of the put-on, it is 'a basically hostile means of expression, in a speaker, hostile to his own feelings and to his antagonist; in an artist, hostile to his materials, his audience, and his own talent'.[31]

In addition to Defoe's attitude to his audience, the gusto of his characterization of Moll indicates that he had mixed feelings as well about his protagonist. In a way, he was fond of her. He did not regard her as truly evil like Jonathan Wild, the corrupter of others; indeed, what triggers her repentance in Newgate is her mistaken belief that she has been responsible for her Lancashire husband's becoming a highwayman. Moll does no gratuitous harm, she is good-natured, even merry; above all, unlike Roxana, she does not lose control of herself except near the end of her criminal career when she can no longer prevent herself from stealing. For that lapse Defoe punishes her severely with incarceration in Newgate. His judgement of Moll probably resembled the attitude of the worldly Mr. Review, who warned his readers in December 1706 not to 'be imposed upon to believe things and people, worse than they really are' (8:591).

Defoe's reservations about Moll's reformation, along with his fondness for her and his feeling of superiority to his audience and malaise about his medium, would account for the curious ambivalence of the ending of *Moll Flanders*. It is as if with one hand he were giving what convention, even part of his own consciousness required, but with the other were secretly taking it away. By the sanction from his readers he expects for Moll's good fortune, Defoe is in effect implicating them as accomplices in his own secret hoax, a put-on that will not produce overt action among his readers, but will deceive them for his private amusement and financial gain. He knows, but does not expect his contemporary readers to recognize, that the facade of respectability, sufficient to win the approval of society, enables most of us rogues to conceal the feral nature of our instinctual drives behind abstractions like 'penitence', or 'moderation', or 'sobriety'. The consciousness that caused Defoe to shuttle restlessly between the proclamation of conventional values and the questioning of those values and ·of the structure and limitation they impose upon the world was complicated by his private comic sense, with its affectionate contempt for his readers, his sly and mischievous impulse to laugh at the complacency that accepts conventional formulas unthinkingly. As Brackman shrewdly observes,

> The embarrassment at one's own predicament or identity which produces theatrical tongue-in-cheek (spoof) and conversational tongue-in-cheek (put-on) issues from an intermediate level of

awareness—an awareness that reveals the inadequacy of a come-on but fails to suggest any useful alternative. The put-on, then, arises out of a *partial consciousness* of one's own ridiculousness, in the absence of sufficient courage or intellectual perseverance to see that ridiculousness through to its roots and to alter it.[32]

Defoe's abiding concern with questions of ethics and religion and his inability to reconcile the irreconcilable, suggest why this morally contradictory fiction is imbued with moral earnestness and why the expectation of ironical resolution aroused in readers like Ian Watt is so invariably disappointed.[33] Instead, *Moll Flanders* offers to the twentieth-century reader, removed by time, by education, and by the history of the novel from Defoe's contemporary reader, a peculiarly unsettling kind of paradox as resolution. As Wayne Booth points out, 'the whole engagement between author and reader depends . . . on at least three kinds of agreement', the third of which, a common experience of literary genre, necessarily is absent in this first English novel. And it is literary genre 'that finally determines the precise fixing of ironies and non-ironies . . .'. He warns us later in his discussion, 'We can poison our reading experience both by failing to reconstruct when stable ironies are intended and by insisting on literal translation when the whole point is to heighten instabilities.'[34]

Because Moll's vitality is inextricably linked with her quintessentially human hypocrisy, we are powerless to break her spell over us. This paradox of reluctant acceptance belongs to the welcoming realm of comedy, not the repudiating realm of irony. Moll embodies Defoe's comic spirit, an explosive and anarchic force capable of shaking up the social order, just as he was accused of 'setting the nation together by the ears' with his political hoax, *The Shortest Way*.[35] Irony is subsumed by Defoe's particular form of comedy in *Moll Flanders*, whose stress, as Martin Price observes, 'is more upon the energy of impulse than its evil'.[36]

NOTES

1. *A Rhetoric of Irony* (Chicago and London: University of Chicago Press, 1974), p. 6. I want to thank Professor Robert Ryley of York College for bringing this discussion to my attention and for reading and criticizing the original of this chapter.

2. Ian Watt, 'Defoe as Novelist: *Moll Flanders*', reprinted in *Twentieth Century Interpretations of 'Moll Flanders'*, ed. Robert C. Elliott (Englewood Cliffs, N. J.: Prentice-Hall, 1970), p. 25. Watt modifies his position (first expressed in 1957 in his *Rise of the Novel*) in 'The Recent Critical Fortunes of *Moll Flanders*' (*Eighteenth-Century Studies*, 1, 1967), so that he seems to be aligning himself with a compromise view, in between the one that Defoe was too muddled for irony and its opposite, that Defoe knew just what he was doing in *Moll Flanders*. But Watt's compromise seems reluctant, for he qualifies and modifies in Part III of his article, first suggesting further study about Defoe's attitude to writing and then speculating about excessive sophistication in contemporary critics of literature.

3. Maximillian E. Novak, 'Conscious Irony in *Moll Flanders*: Facts and Problems', in *Twentieth Century Interpretations*, p. 46.

4. Miriam Leranbaum, ' "An Irony Not Unusual": Defoe's *Shortest Way with the Dissenters*', *HLQ*, 37 (1974), 243.

5. Booth, p. 48, note 3.

6. See p. 134 above.

7. See p. 12 above.

8. See pp. 41, 45–9 and 108–12 above.

9. Defoe's refusal to clarify here, to translate abstract concepts into a medium common to reader and writer is the same mischievous refusal to clarify as in the *Shortest Way*. See Paul Alkon, 'Defoe's Argument in *The Shortest Way with the Dissenters*', *MP*, 73 (May 1976), S 21–3.

10. In the *Review*, 15:355, speaking about an artificial rise in the price of grain, Defoe alludes to the gulling of Londoners by country people: 'It's all nothing but the fraud and cunning of the buyers, who make Cockneys of the people in London, and make them believe, rain at Michelmas should make corn dear—and run them up to what price and upon what pretence they please.'

11. Alkon explains that the topographical allusions in *A Journal of the Plague Year* covered landmarks there both in 1665, the chronological date of the *Journal*, and 1720, two years before the publication of the book. By taking care 'to provide a background of buildings and places that belong to more than one instead of only one temporal setting . . . [Defoe] diminish[ed] his readers' sense of distance between themselves and 1665, thus enhancing the possibility of emotional response to a narrative whose events are by many other means also brought as close as possible for the sake of making a greater impact.' *Defoe and Fictional Time*, pp. 49–50.

12. A possible allusion in the reference to the meeting-house is to the genuinely close and warm family relations typical among Dissenting families of the late seventeenth and early eighteenth centuries. (See

Lawrence Stone's *The Family, Sex and Marriage in England, 1500–1800*, New York: Harper & Row, 1977.)

13. *Defoe and Casuistry*, pp. 157–59.

14. 'Conscious Irony in *Moll Flanders* . . .', p. 41. But see footnote 10, p. 137 above for Damrosch's reservation about this method.

15. Laura A. Curtis, 'A Case Study of Defoe's Domestic Conduct Manuals Suggested by *The Family, Sex and Marriage in England, 1500–1800*', pp. 420–24.

16. Maximillian E. Novak, 'Defoe's Theory of Fiction', p. 666.

17. Paul Alkon, 'Defoe's Argument in *The Shortest Way with the Dissenters*', *MP*, 73 (May 1976), S12–23.

18. In his 1709 *Letter Concerning the Sacramental Test* and his November 16, 1710 issue (No. 15) of *The Examiner*. Swift did not use the word 'pert', because in contrast to John Tutchin of *The Observator*, he found Defoe of *The Review* a 'grave, sententious, dogmatical rogue'. But pertness was an attribute Augustans objected to in 'dunces', and the merry, know-it-all Robin, along with his creator, in the eyes of Augustans belong among the 'dunces'.

19. See p. 106 above.

20. See the Palatine excerpt, pp. 47–9 above, also the Tom Taffety excerpt, pp. 105–7 above.

21. Maximillian E. Novak, 'Defoe's "Indifferent Monitor": The Complexity of *Moll Flanders*', *ECS*, 3 (1970), 351–65. The observation about the equivocal word 'pretend' comes from Paul Alkon's *Defoe and Fictional Time*, pp. 79–80.

22. See pp. 101–2 above.

23. See p. 155 above.

24. John McVeagh, 'Rochester and Defoe: A Study in Influence', *SEL*, 14 (1974), 340. I myself have made a count of literary references identified by Defoe in the twenty-two book facsimile edition of the *Review*. Out of about 123, twenty-three of them are by Rochester. The next contender is Milton, with ten references. Dryden is cited nine times; tied at eight are Marvell, Juvenal and, most significant to the argument I am making about Defoe's partial contempt for less educated or worldly readers, Butler, for *Hudibras*.

25. John J. Richetti writes of this scene that readers experience delight 'at the social aggression implicit in such disguises', and that also 'we have the sense as we read that Moll recognizes the social subversion implicit in her disguises' (p. 130, *Defoe's Narratives: Situations and Structures*).

26. *Defoe and Casuistry*, p. 158.

27. 'Onward and Upward with the Arts: the Put-On', *The New Yorker*, 24 June 1967, pp. 34 and 35.

28. Booth, p. 11.

29. J. Paul Hunter, 'The Loneliness of the Long-Distance Reader', *Genre*, 10 (1977), 457, 459.

30. Sceptics about Defoe's awareness of irony in Jemy's religious conversion as a result of Moll's providing an unexpected abundance of 'Horses, Hogs, and Cows, and other Stores for our Plantation' overlook the

reservation in her use of 'as': 'And from this time forward I believe he was as sincere a Penitent, and as thoroughly a reform'd Man, as ever God's goodness brought back from a Profligate, a High-way Man, and a Robber' (p. 339). Such sceptics should look back to pp. 131–32 above for examples of Defoe's habitual use of the concealed reservation introduced by 'as'. Everett Zimmerman's discussion of *Captain Singleton* in *Defoe and the Novel* reminds me of another example in that work. Zimmerman writes, 'The narrator comments ironically that a priest made him "as good a *Papist* as any of them in about a Week's Time" ' (p. 8 in *Captain Singleton*, p. 57 in Zimmerman).

31. Brackman, p. 72.
32. Ibid., p. 63.
33. Ian Watt, *The Rise of the Novel* (1957; rpt. Berkeley: University of California Press, 1959), p. 126. Actually, Watt revised his original position, as explained in footnote 2 above. Although he expresses approval of an interpretation that describes Moll's real self as a 'vegetable tropism', he is interested in Martin Price's position that in *Moll Flanders* Defoe is ultimately a comic artist. This is my own position: the work is muddled in terms of irony but unified in the more expansive realm of comedy. The difference is between a consistent rejection of human failings and an excitingly variegated ultimate acceptance. Defoe seems here to have absorbed Harley's advice: 'Do not be imposed upon to believe things and people, worse than they really are.'
34. Booth, pp. 100 and 277.
35. A contemporary comment on *The Shortest Way* cited by Maximillian E. Novak in his 'Defoe's Use of Irony', originally published in 1966 and reprinted in *Stuart and Georgian Monuments*, ed. Earl Miner (Berkeley: University of California Press, 1972), p. 204.
36. Martin Price, *To the Palace of Wisdom* (1964; rpt. Garden City, New York: Doubleday Anchor Books, 1965), p. 276.

5
The Real World: Disguises and Doubles

Disguises

As we saw in Chapter 3, the worldly Mr. Review discusses truth in bifocal images: insides and outsides, indoors and outdoors, and surfaces and depths. Disguises and doubles become important motifs in his discussions. Role-playing and manipulation of others become more conspicuous than the slow and patient work characteristic of the plain-dealing Mr. Review.

In the social world of Defoe's fiction, disguise is a vital necessity. As we will recall, the very thought of the existence of other living beings dictates to Robinson Crusoe, all alone on his island, the necessity for concealment. He camouflages his sea-side fortress so that 'if any People were to come on Shore there, they would not perceive any thing like a Habitation' (p. 76).

After he sees the mysterious footprint, Crusoe goes through a nervous crisis over the possibility of being discovered by cannibals. When he calms down again, he decides that since almost eighteen years on the island have passed undisturbed, the likelihood is that he can remain undisturbed for the next eighteen years 'as entirely conceal'd' as he is now, if he does not 'discover' himself to human creatures, which, he reasons, 'I had no manner of Occasion to do, it being my only Business to keep myself entirely concealed where I was, unless I found a better sort of Creatures than *Canibals* to make my self known to' (p. 166).

A magical and fantastic strain in *Robinson Crusoe* is suggested by Crusoe's description of the final appearance of the approach to his seaside habitation after the frenzied spurt of new forti-fying and disguising activities ensuing upon his discovery of the mysterious footprint: 'Thus in two Years Time I had a thick Grove and in five or six Years Time I had a Wood before my Dwelling, growing so monstrous thick and strong, that it was indeed perfectly impassable' (p. 161).

The strain of childhood fantasy receives its fullest develop-ment in the episode during which Crusoe tricks the mutineers who have landed on his island into believing that he is governor of the place and commands a whole garrison of men. The most elaborate scene in the episode occurs when Friday and the captain's mate, pretending to be mutineers them-selves, lead the real mutineers away from their boat on a wild goose chase through the woods. The disguise is so effective that it completely demoralizes the mutineers, driving them in their confusion to extravagant manifestations of distress like the wringing of hands, in a fiction which throughout is con-cerned with mastery over violent passions. The mythical dimensions of this *Tempest*-like scene are suggested by the deceived mutineers' references to enchanted islands, devils and spirits, and by the confusion of outline occasioned by darkness and the marked absence of visual detail accompanied by increased stress upon the noises of human voices (pp. 264–66).

The humour in the scene is of the whimsical and fanciful kind, manifesting the delight in its own prowess characterized by Huisinga in *Homo Ludens* as the essence of the spirit of play. The comedy rises to such freedom because there is no conflict in ethics. Crusoe and the legitimate ship's captain are engaged in an action regarded by Defoe as reasonable and therefore acceptable; they are seeking to preserve their own lives and property against the forces of violence and rebellion.

A similar rationale underlies the more sober humour of a scene from *A Journal of the Plague Year*, in which a group of Londoners of humble social class fleeing from the plague into the country are refused passage through the town of Waltham-stow. Since they cannot persuade the town authorities to allow their company to enter, one of their number invents a disguise for the group in order to frighten the townspeople into giving way. By cutting some poles from trees and shaping them to appear at a distance like muskets, building campfires at extended distances apart, posting a man in plain sight with the one real gun they possess, and setting him to march back and forth before a tent as if he were a sentinel, the company succeeds in convincing the townspeople that they are a large group of armed men. Accordingly, the Walthamstow residents send the group some provisions and permit them to pass through their town. None of them, remarks the amused narrator, 'had Courage so much as to look out to see them go, and, as it was Evening, if they had looked they cou'd not have seen them so as to know how few they were' (p. 139).

This episode is morally more complex than the one from *Robinson Crusoe*; both groups, the travellers and the townspeople, are in the right. Nevertheless, our sympathy as readers goes to the travellers, and we laugh with them at their victims, for their immediate need of physical self-preservation is more urgent than the need of the townspeople.

Even the potentially terrifying possibility of being locked against one's will into a disguise temporarily assumed is regarded by Defoe from a humorous perspective, as long as the motive for assuming the disguise seems clearly defined, and thus rational, to him. In *Memoirs of a Cavalier* the protagonist and two others, members of the routed Cavalier forces, disguise themselves as farmers in order to get into Leeds and learn some news of the fighting between Roundheads and Cavaliers. The narrator, dressed up with a white cap on his head and a pitchfork on his shoulder, is accosted by 'three Country Fellows on Horseback':

> One had a long Pole on his Shoulder, another a Fork, the third no Weapon at all, that I saw; I gave them the Road very orderly, being habited like one of their Brethren; but one of them stopping short at me, and looking earnestly, calls out, *Hark thee, Friend*, says he, in a broad North Country Tone, *whar hast thou thilk Horse?* [It was one of the horses taken by the Cavalier army from the country people of the area.] I must confess I was in the utmost Confusion at the Question, neither being able to answer the Question, nor to speak in his Tone; so I made as if I did not hear him, and went on. *Na, but ye's not gang soa*, says the

Boor, and comes up to me, and takes hold of the Horse's Bridle to stop me; at which, vexed at Heart that I could not tell how to talk to him, I reached him a great Knock on the Pate with my Fork, and fetched him off of his Horse, and then began to mend my Pace. The other Clowns, though it seems they knew not what the Fellow wanted, pursued me, and finding they had better Heels than I, I saw there was no Remedy but to make use of my Hands, and faced about. The first that came up with me was he that had no Weapons, so I thought I might parley with him; and, speaking as Country like as I could, I asked him what he wanted? *Thou'st knaw that soon*, says Yorkshire, *and Ise but come at thee. Then keep awa' Man*, said I, *or Ise brain thee.* By this Time the third Man came up, and the Parley ended. . . . (p. 209)

The parley ends because the third man refuses to 'give . . . Words'; instead, says the Cavalier, he 'laid at me with his long Pole' (p. 209). The reader is distracted from the potentially terrifying aspect of the scene by Defoe's humorous emphasis upon the amusing and picturesque dialect of Yorkshire, and upon the grotesquely rustic form of violence that ensues upon the failure of words.

A case similar in its humorous emphasis upon becoming locked unwillingly into a disguise and having difficulties with the language required by that disguise occurs in *Captain Singleton*. When Singleton and William decide to leave off being pirates, they assume the disguise of merchants of Persia, clothing themselves 'in long Vests of Silk, a Gown or Robe of *English* Crimson Cloth, very fine and handsome' (p. 264). Letting their beards grow, they pass for Persian merchants 'in View only', because they can speak only English and Dutch. In the course of their new trading ventures they pick up some of the language they need to complete their disguise. Settling themselves for a time in Venice, they become known as 'the two *Grecians*' (p. 272). By this time, Singleton remarks, 'We had gotten so much of the *Persian* and *Armenian* Jargon, which they talk'd at *Bassora*, and *Bagdat*, and every where that we came in the Country, as was sufficient to make us able to talk to one another, so as not to be understood by any Body', although, as he adds humorously, 'sometimes hardly by our selves' (p. 272).

When the pair decides to return to England, William

accepts Singleton's plan to retain their disguise as foreigners and never to speak English in public with anybody except William's sister. A real sense of constraint at being cut off permanently from the public use of his native language is emphasized by William as he agrees to Singleton's terms: 'the not speaking *English* would be the hardest' (p. 277). Defoe's subtle deviation into gravity here seems the result of a slight uneasiness about endowing two pirates with the full reward that he accords to a reformed sinner like Moll Flanders: the return to London and the taking up of a legitimate role in society. Such a role would naturally include speaking English, the beloved native tongue; in Singleton's case, however, this would not be appropriate, for William has not succeeded completely in reasoning away the ex-pirate's guilt about his past. The pair are not completely reintegrated into English society; the price of their return is permanent imprisonment behind the Armenian beards and language that they had previously adopted in a comic mood, imprisonment which is fearful to Singleton, yet funny to the reader of *Captain Singleton* who has a sense of justice.[1]

The loss of mobility, the end of the freedom to take up and to drop disguises at will, the possibility of being trapped inside one's mask, is a punishment suffered by certain of Defoe's protagonists. When Moll Flanders dresses herself as a woman of humble social status, as a prosperous bourgeoise, as a servant, or as a poor widow, luck and quick-wittedness enable her both to cope with unforeseen difficulties arising from each disguise and to move rapidly from one mask to another. Her quickest change of disguise occurs when, dressed in man's clothing, she is pursued home after a theft by a crowd. When a constable and search party go through the house they find Moll sitting in one of the rooms dressed in a morning gown and surrounded with props Mother Midnight has provided (pp. 215–18).

The portion of her narrative devoted to the variety of disguises Moll assumes in the course of her increasingly successful criminal career follows her admission that economic self-preservation is no longer her motive for crime: 'Thus the Devil who began, by the help of an irresistable [*sic*] Poverty, to push me into this Wickedness, brought me on to a height beyond the common Rate, even when my Necessities were not so great . . .' (p. 202). The incident in which the psychological implication of such an admission is most fully dramatized occurs when Moll assumes the 'Ominous and Threatening' garb of a beggar (p. 254). Not only is she frightened and disgusted by this depth of poverty and by dirt, but she discovers that a beggar is even more of a social outcast than she is, in effect, an untouchable: 'This was a Dress that every body was shy, and afraid of; and I thought every body look'd at me, as if they were afraid I should come near them, least I should take something from them, or afraid to come near me, least they should get something from me' (p. 253). The life to which a beggar's costume gives access is outside the pales of civilized society as Moll knows it:

> While I was in this Disguise, I fell in with a parcel of Folks of a worse kind than any I ever sorted with, and I saw a little into their ways too, these were Coiners of Money, and they made some very good offers to me, as to profit; but the part they would have had me have embark'd in, was the most dangerous Part; I mean that of the very working the Dye, as they call it, which had I been taken, had been certain Death, and that at a Stake, *I say*, to be burnt to Death at a Stake; so that tho' I was to Appearance, but a Beggar; and they promis'd Mountains of Gold and Silver to me, to engage; yet it would not do; it is True if I had been really a Beggar, or had been desperate as when I began, I might perhaps have clos'd with it, for what care they to Die, that can't tell how to Live? But at present this was not my Condition, at least I was for no such terrible Risques as those; besides the very Thoughts of being burnt at a Stake, struck terror into my very Soul, chill'd my Blood, and gave me the Vapours to such a degree as I could not think of it without trembling.
>
> This put an End to my Disguise too, for as I did not like the Proposal, so I did not tell them so; but seem'd to relish it, and promis'd to meet again; but I durst see them no more, for if I had seen them, and not complied, tho' I had declined it with the greatest assurances of Secresy in the World, they would have gone near to have murther'd me to make sure Work, and make themselves easy, *as they call it*; what kind of easiness that is, they may best Judge that understand how easy Men are, that can Murther People to prevent Danger. (pp. 254–55)

Darkness is suggested by the dangerous nature of the counterfeiting activity, indirectly by the mention of fire, and by the absence of any clearly defined physical detail in Moll's description. Her horror is suggested through the selection of details like burning at a stake and 'mountains' of gold and silver, details that come from a realm of nightmare, a realm of fantasy far removed from the enchanted island fantasy of the wild goose chase scene from *Robinson Crusoe* discussed above. The brutal willingness of the counterfeiters to resort to murder contrasts with the clever confidence tricks more characteristically the subject of her story. Finally, the illegal activity itself, counterfeiting, or the passing off of appearance for reality, regarded as so heinous a crime by Moll's society, is analogous to Moll's use of beggar's garb. Disguise itself, here associated with evil, threatens to engulf Moll's real being, obliterating the distinction by others between the real Moll and the disguised Moll. This potential obliteration of distinction is all the more frightening to Moll because it comes at a moment when, as she demonstrates through language, making a pun on 'Die' and questioning the phrase 'make themselves easy', she is still fully capable of perceiving distinctions.

The most significant instance of disguise in *Colonel Jack* occurs when a designing woman traps him into marriage. Jack's account is instructive because it is the only relatively long one in Defoe's fiction where disguise is described from the perspective of the puzzled victim, and is thus clearly seen from the outside.

The woman's motives, neither economic nor physical self-preservation, are mysterious. More than the prospect of trapping a rich husband is involved, for her behaviour, which at first seems simply calculating, eventually becomes strange and self-destructive. Her first tactic, an unsuccessful one, is to try the effect of sarcasm on Jack. As he reports, her failure somewhat perplexes her, but not for long, since she is 'a meer Posture Mistress in Love', and can 'put herself into what Shapes she pleas[es]'. Accordingly,

this Camelion put[s] on another Colour, turn[s] on a sudden the gravest, soberest, majestic Madam, so that any one would have thought she was advanced in Age in one Week, from Two and

Twenty, to Fifty, and this she carried on with so much Government of her self, that it did not in the least look like Art. . . .
(p. 190)

Jack becomes so confused by the woman's change of behaviour
that he begins to wonder if her original levity with him has been

a kind of Rant, or Fit; that either it was the Effect of some
extraordinary Levity that had come upon her, or that it was done
to Mimick the Coquets of the Town, believing it might take with
me, who she thought was a *Frenchman*, and that it was what I
lov'd; but her new Gravity was her real natural Temper, and
indeed became it her so much better . . . that it really brought me
back to have, not as much only, but more mind to her, than ever I
had before. (p. 191)

But Jack remains cautious, waiting to see 'whether this
Change was Real or Counterfeit?' (p. 191).

During the course of their courtship Jack several times
associates the lady and her wiles with the devil. He introduces
the whole episode with the observation that ever since he had
renounced his career as a thief, the devil had owed him 'a
Spleen', which he paid with interest 'by laying a Snare in [his]
way' (p. 186) that almost ruined him. In addition there is
witchcraft in the lady's conversation. It ensnares Jack, who is
suddenly 'so embarrass'd in [his] Thoughts about her, that
like a Charm she had [him] always in her Circle' (p. 187). He
points out that she must be one of 'the subtilest Women on
Earth' (p. 187) to draw him in, for he is of a wary nature. 'She
had always so much Witchcraft on her Tongue' (p. 192) that
she could easily placate him and force him to marry her.

The association between the lady's disguise as a sober
person and the influence of Satan or of witchcraft is suggested
not only by direct reference, but also by a certain amorphous-
ness in the surroundings, a kind of haziness of outline. No
objects intrude during the episode, and the conversations
between Jack and the lady before their marriage are so
divorced from the actual motives and intentions underlying
them that they seem sinister. Jack's very language describing
her actions circles back and forth sinuously with vertiginous
effect: 'She made me effectually Court her, tho' at the same
time in her Design she Courted me with the utmost Skill, and
such Skill it was that her Design was perfectly impenetrable to

the last Moment' (p. 193). Finally, the sinister mood of their relationshp is suggested by a paralysis of will with which Jack seems to be afflicted. We will explore these characteristics further in Chapter 6, on the world of nightmare.

After they are married the lady throws off 'the Mask of her Gravity, and good Conduct, that I had so long Fancy'd was her meer natural Disposition, and now having no more occasion for Disguises, she resolv'd to seem nothing but what really she was, a wild untam'd Colt, perfectly loose, and careless to conceal any part, no, not the worst of her Conduct' (p. 193), and proceeds to destroy their marriage by increasingly strange and self-destructive behaviour.

A final indication that her disguise is associated in Defoe's mind with all that is terrifying, is the after-effect of that disguise. Once their marriage breaks up, Jack employs spies to observe his wife's conduct. He is forced to stay in during the day and to venture out only under cover of night in order to avoid troublesome encounters with bill collectors to whom his wife owes money. At last he becomes the victim of a sinister attacker out for revenge for Jack's treatment of his wife and his failure to pay her bills:

> Being come out into *Grace-church-street*, I observ'd a Man follow'd me, with one of his Legs tied up in a String, and Hopping along with the other, and two Crutches; he begg'd for a Farthing, but I inclining not to give him any thing, the Fellow follow'd me still, till I came to a Court, when I answer'd hastily to him, I have not for you, pray don't be so troublesome; with which Words he knock'd me down with one of his Crutches.
>
> Being stunn'd with the blow I knew nothing what was done to me afterwards; but coming to myself again, I found I was wounded very frightfully in several Places, and that among the rest my Nose was slit upwards, one of my Ears cut almost off, and a great cut with a Sword on the Side of my Forehead, also a stab into the Body, tho' not Dangerous. (pp. 203–4)

Defoe's interest in disguise as a means of escaping from one life into another is most fully developed in *Roxana*, which includes a long passage devoted directly to the problem (Amy, Roxana's servant and confidante, outlines for her mistress the specific measures by which she can take up a new role immediately—pp. 208–10), as well as many indirect indications of this interest. But Roxana's attempt to escape from her past, symbolized by her donning a Quaker garb, is doomed to failure. As with Moll and with Jack's wife, disguise proves ineffectual if motivated by desires less rational to Defoe than those of economic or physical survival. No longer is Roxana seeking merely an economic objective as when, on a previous occasion, she 'made as gay a Show' as possible in the Mall (p. 165) with the aim of attracting a rich and generous lover from the aristocracy. Now she is in search of affection: the possibility of identifying herself to her children, the opportunity of forming 'Acquaintances in the World' (p. 208). With such an aim disguise is inappropriate; it cannot guarantee to Roxana the necessary freedom of mind to enjoy the affection of others. As Benjamin Boyce observes, by the end of her story, Roxana is 'haunted by those who surround her, who could befriend her, and unknown to themselves, terrify her'.[2]

An illustration of the way in which Roxana's past destroys her disguise of the present can be seen in the impingement of her Turkish costume upon the new life symbolized by her Quaker costume. As David Blewett points out, the Turkish outfit symbolized her life in England as an aristocratic courtesan[3]; it was in that costume that she made her debut into that life. The costume and dance, originally described in terms that stress their visual interest as picturesque exotica (p. 174), return with increasing stress upon their sexual suggestiveness. Even in the first description Roxana used fake diamonds for real on the girdle, where there was so much glitter that no one would notice the difference, but added a real jewel on the turban, where such an adornment would be conspicuous. At that period in her life she was able to manipulate real and artificial with the cunning of an artist like Defoe.

On the second occasion of Roxana's appearance in this outfit, two ladies dressed in authentic costumes of Georgia and Armenia preceded her in dancing. Ironically, the authentic costumes and dance pleased the audience less than Roxana's adaptation. The hint that there was something of cultivated vice in Roxana's Turkish counterfeit was affirmed explicitly by her statement:

> I wou'd have withdrawn, and disrob'd, being somewhat too thin in that Dress, unlac'd, and open-breasted, as if I had been in my

Shift; but it cou'd not be, and I was oblig'd to dance afterwards
with six or eight Gentlemen, most, if not all of them, of the First
Rank. (p. 181)

When Roxana next appears in this costume she is in the
midst of her new life, symbolized by her having moved to
another part of town, adopted the garb of a Quaker, and
married her honest Dutch merchant. It is Roxana herself who
introduces this relic of her past life into her present. She is
courting trouble by tempting fate when, jesting with her new
husband, she tells him she has one kind of dress in which he
would not know his wife when he saw her. When he declares
that this must be impossible, she dons the dress, making sure
to point out that 'it is not a decent Dress in this Country, and
wou'd not look modest', adding, for her readers, 'It was but
one Degree off, from appearing in one's Shift' (p. 247).

Forced later to receive the unexpected visit of her daughter
while clad in a 'kind of *Dishabille*', Roxana is upset because the
immodesty of this outfit recalls to the mind of the young
woman the Turkish costume of the Lady Roxana, her former
employer, and she describes the costume so exactly that
Roxana's former identity is all but revealed to her Quaker
landlady, while the girl, who is seeking to prove that the two
Roxanas are identical, is put into great excitement by her
discovery and becomes even more determined to pursue her
investigations.

Further evidences of the sense of guilt that prevents Roxana
from escaping from one life to another by means of disguise
and pins her down insider her Turkish costume, are the extraordinary amount of spying that takes place in her story and
the violent consequences attendant upon disclosure of guilty
secrets. Roxana herself sets a spy to watch the movements of
her legal husband, who has turned up inconveniently as an
officer in the French Horse Guards at a time when Roxana,
mistress to a foreign prince, is herself moving in the higher
social circles. The midwife hired by her prince to supervise the
birth of their first illegitimate child looks like a spy to Roxana,
and the old woman who accompanies her and the prince upon
their tour in Italy is described by her as an old witch or
harridan (pp. 102, 107). After Roxana's departure for Paris,
the diabolical Jewish jewel dealer spies on the Dutch merchant

and the prince who have been associated with her. Roxana's Quaker friend becomes her faithful spy on the whereabouts of her 'teizing' daughter (p. 309). Finally, Roxana's daughter, spying on her mother and her Quaker friend, hounding Roxana from pillar to post, assumes more than human dimensions as a spy, developing into a figure of Nemesis.

The results of exposure, of disguises being penetrated, of secrets being 'open'd' (p. 326), carry fatal consequences in *Roxana*.[4] The midwife provided by the prince to supervise the birth of his and Roxana's first illegitimate child looks not only like a spy to Roxana, but 'like one set privately to dispatch me out of the World, as might best suit with the Circumstance of my Lying-in' (p. 77). When Amy seeks out Roxana's legal husband, he is very startled to see her. '*Amy* believ'd,' says Roxana, 'if he had seen her at first, in any convenient Place for so villainous a Purpose, he would have murther'd her' (p. 87). This violent reaction, from a character who has been presented as an indolent fool, accords better with Amy's or Roxana's fears than with the nature of the man. Her good-natured jeweller 'husband' is angered enough by his sexual intimacies with Amy to 'hate her heartily, and could, I believe,' says Roxana, 'have kill'd her after it, and he told me so, for he thought this a vile Action' (p. 47). The vengeful and dishonest Jewish jewel dealer in Paris exemplifies the frightful consequences of exposure for Roxana. What should be involved in this episode is only the danger that his lawsuit might divest her of the property she inherited illegally by posing as the rightful wife of her first lover. Since she is now rich from the benefits showered upon her by her recently concluded liaison with the foreign prince, poverty is not really a danger to her. Nevertheless, the absurd threat of the Jew to have her convicted of the murder of her English jeweller is made to seem a reasonable possibility. The Dutchman himself, her ally, agrees that if French justice should put her to the rack, she would be made to confess that she committed the murder, whether or not she had done so (p. 118). Roxana later credits the Dutchman, who has saved her from being 'expos'd and ruin'd' by the Jew, with having saved her 'Life' (p. 121).

The Jew seems to Roxana a diabolical figure who jabbers in a foreign language:

> . . . the *Jew* held up his Hands, look'd at me with some Horrour,
> then talk'd *Dutch* again, and put himself into a thousand
> Shapes, twisting his Body, and wringing up his Face this Way,
> or that Way, in his Discourse; stamping with his Feet, and
> throwing abroad his Hands, as if he was not in a Rage only, but
> in a meer Fury; then he wou'd turn, and give a Look at me, like
> the Devil; I thought I never saw any thing so frightful in my
> Life. (p. 113)

After Roxana's hasty departure from Paris, he continues his
malicious persecution of everyone associated with her, the
Dutch merchant and the prince's servant, until he meets with
violent treatment for trying to penetrate what he senses to be
her disguise:

> . . . but he found out the Prince's Gentleman, and talk'd so
> saucily to him of it, that the Gentleman treated him, as the
> *French* call it, *au Coup de Batton*; that is to say, Can'd him very
> severely, as he deserv'd; and that not satisfying him, or curing
> his Insolence, he was met one Night late, upon the *Pont Neuf* in
> *Paris*, by two Men, who muffling him up in a great Cloak,
> carried him into a more private Place, and cut off both his Ears,
> telling him, It was for talking impudently of his Superiours;
> adding, that he shou'd take Care to govern his Tongue better,
> and behave with more Manners, or the next time they would
> cut his Tongue out of his Head. (p. 134)

The last and most serious victim of the results of trying to
penetrate Roxana's disguise is her importunate daughter. The
girl meets with even greater violence than her Jewish pre-
decessor; murder is the fate Roxana believes has claimed her
daughter, and at the close of her narrative, visions of the
murdered body of the girl haunt the tormented protagonist.

As we have seen in this survey, the need for disguise is vital
to almost all members of the society of Defoe's fiction. Even
when he is alone on his island, the very possibility of other
people's intruding upon his solitude immediately suggests to
Robinson Crusoe the necessity of disguising any trace of his
habitation so that tell-tale signs do not expose him to the eyes
of potential enemies. Almost anyone who wants something,
even to save his life from the plague, will be prevented by
others from obtaining it, unless he can outwit them by donning some form of disguise. Almost everyone who acts has

something in his past that he must conceal. Only those to whom the status quo is perfectly acceptable, those who neither want nor seek anything for themselves, the Christians of his ideal world who possess 'steadiness of mind, . . . awful gravity of behaviour, . . . calmness and sedateness of temper' (*Review*, 12:126), characters like Crusoe's Portuguese captain and Roxana's Dutch merchant, are free from the need for disguise.

The loss of freedom to doff and don masks at will is a punishment imposed by Defoe on characters whose role-playing becomes motivated by hazy and undefined emotion rather than by rational considerations of economic or physical survival. When Moll no longer knows why she continues to steal, when Jack's wife's motives for trapping him into marriage and mistreating him are hazy, when Roxana is driven by the desire for affection rather than for economic or social advancement, they become trapped inside their masks. Captain Singleton, the outstanding exception to this generalization, is redeemed from a nightmare world that obliterates the distinction between real character and voluntarily chosen appearance by his ethical assessment that he has after all got a great deal more than he deserves. More important, he is redeemed by the spirit of comedy infused into Captain Singleton by the Quaker pirate, William Walters.[5]

Doubles

The solitary condition of Defoe's protagonists has frequently aroused comment from literary critics. In his *Rise of the Novel* Ian Watt argued that this psychological and social condition was the natural concomitant of the growth of economic individualism. His analysis was so persuasive that it has perhaps contributed to the failure of subsequent criticism to observe distinctly that the 'absence of a stable and cohesive pattern of social relations'[6] occurs at the same time as the presence of patterns of character pairs. In *A Journal of the Plague Year, Colonel Jack, Robinson Crusoe, Captain Singleton, Moll Flanders* and *Roxana*, the protagonist appears with a companion whose characteristics supplement those of his own, in a complementary relationship that varies in length (some of the following are very short) and in intensity.[7]

The topical pair is best represented by H.F. and his older brother, who disagree about the best preparation for the plague. The older brother, as pious as H.F., argues from Scripture to prove that 'the best Preparation for the Plague [is] to run away from it' (p. 9). He laughs at H.F.'s interpretation of the various minor checks he has suffered in his plans to leave London as divine providences, warning him to remain where he is. A rationalist, the older brother equates such interpretations with the prejudices of the Mohammedans, who hold that because man's end is predetermined, they can therefore venture unconcerned into infected places. As a result, they succumb to the plague 'at the Rate of Ten or Fifteen Thousand a Week' (p. 11). H.F., unsettled by his brother's argument, decides on impulse to practise Biblical divination, asking the Lord to direct him. Coming upon the passage in Psalm 91 which says that the Lord will deliver him who trusts in Him 'from the noisom pestilence' (p. 13), H.F. resolves to remain in London.

The disagreement between the two brothers stems from the inconsistencies between two contemporary views of the plague as a divine visitation or as a natural calamity. By choosing to remain in London, H.F. accepts the divine visitation theory. And yet, as I mentioned in Chapter 2, the manner in which H.F. bears witness attests implicitly to Defoe's desire to accommodate the two views, describing a providential design by means of rationalistic techniques. Like his brother, H.F. is both rationalistic and religious.

Having served his limited topical purpose, H.F.'s older brother disappears at the beginning of the *Journal*, and H.F. proceeds on his solitary way for the rest of the narrative. In *Robinson Crusoe* a similar topical purpose is served by supplying the narrator with two older brothers, one lost sight of, the other a lieutenant colonel killed in a battle near Dunkirk. The admonitory function of his fate is lost on Crusoe, who is not interested in the less genteel but safer profession of law for which his father intends him. Defoe supplies Colonel Jack with two brothers, whose role in the novel, relatively well developed, is to illuminate Jack's character by serving as his negative foils.[8] Captain Jack, an unregenerate criminal, is the direct opposite of Colonel Jack. Major Jack, a specious gentleman, resembles the Colonel in his charm, but lacks the latter's solid moral virtues.

The next degree of intensity of relationship between two characters in Defoe's fiction is that of teacher and pupil. In *Colonel Jack* a former highwayman, transported as an indentured servant to America, serves for a short time as tutor to the protagonist, introducing him to learning and to elementary principles of religion. Although he does not become a religious convert, Jack is a good student and quickly perceives the similarity between his own previous life and his tutor's and their present position in the world.

The relationship between Captain Singleton and William Walters, the Quaker surgeon, although an earlier version (1720) of the pupil-teacher relationship than the colourless one of *Colonel Jack* (1722), is much more complex. It can most accurately be described as symbiotic: Singleton represents the hothead's simple and spontaneous response to experience, William represents the considered response of the shrewder person, and the pair become inseparable.

When William is willingly abducted by the pirates from the sloop in which he has been travelling, he makes certain to secure a document signed by the master of his sloop, attesting that the Quaker has been taken by force. In this way, as Singleton points out, if the pirates are ever captured, they are 'sure to be hang'd', while William is 'sure to escape' (p. 144).

William quickly becomes a trusted adviser to the pirates. He is much clearer in mind about when to fight and when not to, always for getting booty without fighting if possible, but quick to bring matters to the test if battle cannot be avoided. Opposed to the gratuitous cruelty characteristic of the pirates, William prevents Singleton and his men from murdering the Negro slaves they accidentally come across in a derelict ship. Yet his recognition that these men have been unjustly enslaved does not prevent him from solving the problem of how to dispose of them by selling them privately to planters in Brazil.

It is always William who copes best with business complications; when Singleton cannot decide whether or not to trust certain Chinese merchants, William explains to him in what ways it is in the interest of the Chinese to trade with the pirates, concluding shrewdly 'I would as soon trust a Man whose Interest binds him to be just to me, as a Man whose Principle binds himself" (p. 199), the same observation made by the worldly Mr. Review in the course of negotiations for the Union between England and Scotland.

Having a shrewder insight into hypocrisy than does Singleton, William dissuades the pirate captain from putting himself and his men into the power of 'Malabars' of Ceylon who wish to entice them on shore to parley with them. William's reply to Singleton's declaration that he intends to go ashore demonstrates again that the Quaker's customary preference for booty without bloodshed is the result of practicality, not of pusillanimity:

> Well, Friend, says *William* very gravely, if thou wilt go, I cannot help it; I shall only desire to take my last Leave of thee at Parting, for depend upon it, thou wilt never see us again; Whether we in the Ship may come off any better at last, I cannot resolve thee; but this I will answer for, that we will not give up our Lives idly, and in cool Blood, as thou art going to do; we will at least preserve our selves as long as we can, and die at last like Men, not like Fools trepann'd by the Wiles of a few Barbarians. (p. 223)

It is William who persuades Singleton that they are rich enough to leave off piracy, devises the means by which Singleton and he abandon the other pirates, invents a new role for the pair as merchants, and finally gets them back to England. In addition, he serves as religious instructor to Singleton, first suggesting the idea of repentance, then preventing Singleton from falling a victim to despair as the latter too heartily embraces the novel idea that he is a sinner.

William Walters is such a picturesque character that Bob Singleton, the supposed protagonist of *Captain Singleton*, pales beside his Quaker adviser. Nevertheless, the consistency of the contrast in reaction between the two men, Singleton acting on impulse, Walters after reflection, suggests that Defoe wished to dramatize a relationship between complementary temperaments rather than simply to use Singleton as a foil against which to illuminate William's character. By the end of the fiction the pirate captain is even more dependent upon the Quaker's guidance than he was at the beginning of their relationship; he can never cut the cord between himself and William. William's need for Singleton can only be inferred from the text. Never the subject of any of the episodes, it is presumably a function of the Quaker's paradoxical love of adventure (and to be explained, perhaps, as an expression of Defoe's own fascination with rogues and criminals). The pair in *Captain Singleton*, therefore, is more intimately linked together than pairs in *A Journal of the Plague Year* and *Colonel Jack*.

The version of teacher-pupil relationship between Robinson Crusoe and Friday, less symbiotic than that of Singleton and Quaker William, is more a relationship between idealized father and son than it is of reflective and impulsive temperaments. First Crusoe feeds, clothes, and lodges Friday, then he teaches him to speak and to participate in the labours of their household. Like Crusoe, Friday in the end possesses the physical tools for subjugating man, beast, and nature, and has been instructed in the Baconian rational process as simplified by Defoe. Crusoe can now continue his education as son and companion in the higher matters of life—religion, and the politics, economics, and sociology of Europe and England.

Unlike Singleton, who to the end of his narrative continues to require the guidance of Quaker William, Friday is now prepared to act as an independent entity. He demonstrates his ability by assuming the role of leadership in the incident of teasing the bear that occurs during his journey with Crusoe across Europe to England (pp. 293–97). Paradoxically, however, in spite of his ultimate potential for independence, Friday is a more pliable subject of Crusoe's tutelage than Singleton is of his mentor's.[9] Defoe portrays the relation between Crusoe and Friday as the extension into the sphere of personal relationships of Crusoe's impulse to fashion potentially inimical elements in his environment into usable shapes that has dominated his whole narrative. Even the physical description of Friday, as I explained in Chapter 2, reveals this intention. Friday too belongs to the environment around Crusoe, and the same ingenuity that harnessed the tide and fashioned the pots is employed in fashioning Friday, first as a servant, then as a son and companion.

In Friday's pliability, as well as in the curiously accommodating behaviour of many of Defoe's subordinate fictional

178

characters in *Colonel Jack, Moll Flanders,* and *Roxana,* there is a large element of fantasy. O. Manoni classifies the notion of a world without other people as a common childhood fantasy; when this fantasy is peopled with other beings, he points out, these beings are of two kinds: monstrous and terrifying creatures (Crusoe's cannibals or Shakespeare's Caliban), and gracious beings, bereft of will and purpose (Friday or Shakespeare's Ariel).[10]

If we reconsider the pairs of characters I have discussed from *Colonel Jack* and *Captain Singleton,* we will observe that relationships I have classified as topical or symbiotic can also be regarded as relationships between emotion and reflection. Both in *Colonel Jack* and in *Captain Singleton* the reluctance of emotion to yield to intellect becomes a source of comedy. When Captain Jack makes a fool of himself by insulting the kidnapper who has him in his power, when Major Jack's compulsion to become a gentleman drives him to his death in France, Defoe's tone is humorous in the first instance, ironical in the second. When Quaker William instructs Singleton how to postpone the gratification of immediate and instinctual reactions in favour of some future benefit, his advice is frequently comical. In these two fictions Defoe's creative imagination envisions the conflict between reason and emotion or mind and body, as funny.

Friday's pliability in Crusoe's hands can be regarded as the point of imaginative equilibrium in Defoe's treatment of teacher-pupil, or mind-body pairs of characters. This fantasied receptivity to instruction about how to control oneself and one's environment, this ideal accommodation of emotion to mind, is neither comical nor frightening.

But in *Moll Flanders* and in *Roxana,* Defoe's creative imagination envisions the accommodation between mind and instinct as a guilty one, giving rise to a world of nightmare. Both in *Moll Flanders* and in *Roxana* the second partner of the characteristic pair, the intimate companion, is a Satanic counsellor, whose advice echoes the most secret and illegitimate desires of the protagonists.

An expert at rationalization, Moll attempts to place the major responsibility for her second career, as thief, on the shoulders of her sinister governess, distinguishing Mother

Midnight as the more wicked of the two. Yet Moll's endeavour to present herself as clay in the hands of a Satanic teacher (or body subjected to mind) is complicated by the extraordinary affability of that teacher. Even Moll, who ordinarily accepts with complacency the affection she receives from others, wonders at times why the governess is so accommodating. As readers, we observe that Mother Midnight seems to be as much influenced by Moll as Moll is by her.

The mystery of Mother Midnight's connection with Moll is suggested by her assuming whatever role Moll requires during a particular episode. This rapid changing of shape, sometimes associated with the diabolic in Defoe's writing (Jack's description of his first wife and Roxana's description of the malevolent jewel dealer, for instance), perhaps reveals the imaginative influence of Milton's Satan, who, touched by Ithuriel's spear as he crouches 'Squat like a Toad, close at the ear of *Eve*', springs up in his true shape. When Moll needs a discreet midwife or disposer of unwanted children, her governess fulfils that role. When Moll needs a fence to dispose of her stolen items, her governess turns out conveniently to have established herself in that business. She intercedes for Moll while the latter is in Newgate, repents when Moll does, and finally acts as her London agent in obtaining equipment necessary for becoming a settler in Virginia.

In addition to Mother Midnight's ability to change her shape at will, an ability that impresses the reader of *Moll Flanders* as sinister, she is also sinister to Moll, who finds her quickness to sense what is in her mind, and to articulate it for her, unnerving. The super-rational quality of the relationship between the two women is suggested by Moll's fright when the governess asks her if she is sure she was nursed by her own mother: 'Sure, said I, to myself, this Creature cannot be a Witch, or have any Conversation with a Spirit that can inform her what was done with me before I was able to know it myself' (p. 175).

Despite all these clear hints that Defoe conceived of the governess as something of a doppelganger, he is content to allow her to become tangential to the story once Moll is reunited with Jemy, her Lancashire husband, and resumes a legitimate position in society, emerging from darkness to light. Moll hides from the governess upon her departure for America the information that this fellow prisoner is actually one of her former husbands, and the governess, at this point in the fiction divested by Defoe of her clairvoyant powers, never sensing the truth, loses her aura of supernatural suggestiveness.

It is significant that while the relationship between Moll and her governess has sinister implications, that between Moll and Jemy gives rise to humorous incidents like the one when Moll cuts short the polite ceremonials between the ship's captain and Jemy, placing a purse in the captain's hands as a tangible guarantee that the two will return to the ship after a brief visit ashore (pp. 318–19). The relation between Moll and Jemy is partly that between trading and genteel classes, partly between practical and impulsive temperaments. Like the one between Singleton and William, this is a complementary relationship, never arousing the reader's suspicion that Jemy may be Moll's double.

The relation between Roxana and Amy is the most important of those in all of Defoe's fictions. Since recent commentators agree that Defoe establishes Amy as Roxana's 'alter ego',[11] it would be superfluous to go through the fiction to demonstrate the relation. All that should be pointed out is that although the temperamental difference observed by Roxana— 'It is true, this Difference was between us, that I said all these things within myself, and sigh'd, and mourn'd inwardly; but *Amy*, as her Temper was more violent, spoke aloud, and cry'd, and call'd out aloud, like one in an Agony' (p. 126)—is a variation upon the Singleton–William combination of impulsiveness and practical common sense, the two women are more mysteriously linked than the men, and thus they strike the reader more like one character split into rational control and instinct than two individuals. 'We are reminded by Roxana', writes David Blewett, 'that Amy always encourages that side of Roxana that prefers the glamorous and immoral to the dull and conventional. . . .'[12]

Thus we observe that, far from being isolated individuals, Defoe's fictional protagonists frequently appear in pairs and that the relation linking them is usually that of impulse/passion and reflection, or instinct and mind. When the mind encounters no opposition to its control, as in the relation between Crusoe and Friday, a point of equilibrium is reached, neither funny nor fearful. This is Defoe's ideal state, discussed in Chapter 1. It is a state, which we have seen, Mr. Review associates with the past, the countryside, and with death. It is a state associated with childhood by psychologists, for gracious beings, bereft of will and purpose, constitute one half of the inhabitants of the child's world of fancy. When instinct rebels against control by the mind, as in *Colonel Jack* and *Captain Singleton*, the result is comedy of the real world. Jack's violent brother makes a laughing-stock of himself, and Singleton acts as straight man to Quaker William. When the instinct takes control of the mind, as in *Moll Flanders* and *Roxana*, the result is nightmare.

The pattern of pairing in Defoe's fictions, his treatment of characteristics of one individual as if they belonged to two, suggests that he found it difficult to integrate two important aspects of personality, the instinctual, potentially anarchic force, and the reasoning and willing, or restraining force. The pattern of pairing further suggests that when the former successfully conquers the latter, temporarily in *Moll Flanders*, permanently in *Roxana*, so that a pair becomes identical twins, Defoe's feelings of guilt and fear caused him to depict a world of nightmare.[13]

NOTES

1. Leo Braudy describes the scene in which Singleton sets up these conditions for the return of the ex-pirates to England as 'one of the most surrealistic scenes in all "realistic" literature' in his 'Daniel Defoe and the Anxieties of Autobiography', *Genre*, 6 (1973), 4. This seems an exaggerated reaction. See footnote 5 below.
2. 'The Question of Emotion in Defoe', *SP*, 50 (January 1953), 53.
3. *Defoe's Art of Fiction* (Toronto: University of Toronto Press, 1979), p. 141.
4. Everett Zimmerman makes a similar point in *Defoe and the Novel*: 'People in this book commit violence, even murder, to conceal themselves' (p. 156).
5. As Manuel Schonhorn observes, Quaker William 'modifies the nature of the expedition and makes of it a comic voyage: Quaker William brings comic relief to a situation rife with expected violence and

potential brutalities, and the measure of Defoe's delight in such a
discovery is clearly evident in the eagerness with which he has William
take control over the expedition and redirect the tone of the book'
('Defoe's *Captain Singleton*: A Reassessment with Observations', *Papers on
Language and Literature*, 7 (1971), 45).

6. *The Rise of the Novel*, p. 66.
7. H. G. Hahn, in a provocative general discussion of character development in Defoe's writing mentions, among other subjects, the 'helper'.
(He also touches upon changes of costume.) 'In a way the helper is an
externalization of the hero, but he is more a kind of extramental
conscience who articulates an ethic to which the hero responds positively.
The developmental technique of the "helper" is an attempt in the
direction of a kind of psychologizing that supports the interior mono-
logue in purpose of self-questioning.' See 'An Approach to Character
Development in Defoe's Narrative Prose', *PQ*, 51 (October 1972), 855.
8. Zimmerman notices this relationship of alternatives (*Defoe and the Novel*,
p. 134).
9. The confidence Crusoe has in Friday depends, however, on the latter's
complete openness with the older man. Crusoe is entitled to his secret
thoughts, but the childlike Friday is not.
10. O. Manoni, *Prospero and Caliban: The Psychology of Colonization*, trans.
Pamela Powesland (London: Methuen, 1956), p. 104.
11. Michael M. Boardman, *Defoe and the Uses of Narrative* (New Brunswick:
Rutgers University Press, 1983), p. 148. Boardman's discussion of this
point is only a summary; he takes it for granted it is generally agreed
upon. David Blewett establishes the point carefully in his 1979 book.
12. *Defoe's Art of Fiction*, p. 132.
13. Both Zimmerman and Brown interpret Roxana's depraving of Amy and
witnessing the act as a form of subduing the dangerous other person so
feared by Defoe's fictional characters (Brown, 'The Displaced Self in the
Novels of Daniel Defoe', p. 582; Zimmerman, *Defoe and the Novel*, p. 169).
Such an interpretation describes only the nightmare world of Defoe; in
comedy Singleton is not afraid of William's witnessing his worst actions
and in myth Crusoe is not afraid of Friday, once he is assured of his
loyalty.

6

From the Real World to the Nightmare World

I discussed in Chapter 2 how two opposing tendencies in Defoe conflict with his compulsion continually to construct an ideal and simplified world of traditional morality, Christian belief, family and social hierarchy, and slow and patient work. The first tendency is restlessness, which in the ideal world of *Robinson Crusoe* is generally expressed by Crusoe's temptation to run away from or to tear down his own work, and in *Moll Flanders* and other fictions of the real world of social interaction is expressed in attacks, often playful and comical, upon the fictional characters Defoe has created and upon his readers. The second, to which this chapter is devoted, is the temptation to relax all effort, surrendering passively to internal emotions and to external forces. The second tendency, indulged, leads into the world of nightmare, which is adumbrated in *Colonel Jack* and *Moll Flanders*, but not fully depicted until *Roxana*.

A passage from Defoe's 1726 *Political History of the Devil* illustrates in miniature the modulation of laughter into fear. Significantly, such modulation occurs upon Defoe's perception of the danger of a loss of control over the external world. The danger arises from complacency about human ability to domesticate the unknown. The passage, which begins in laughter but ends ominously, re-enacts Crusoe's fear of the mysterious footprint as a surrealistic symbol of an ever-present but consciously overlooked danger:

> In the next Place 'tis [the cloven hoof] understood by us not as a bare Token to know *Satan* by, but as if it were a Brand upon

184

him, and that like the Mark God put upon *Cain*, it was given him for a Punishment, so that he cannot get leave to appear without it, nay cannot conceal it whatever other Dress or Disguise he may put on; and as if it was to make him as ridiculous as possible, they will have it be, that whenever *Satan* has Occasion to dress himself in any humane Shape, be it of what Degree soever, from the King to the Beggar, be it of a fine Lady or of an *old Woman*, (the Latter it seems he oftenest assumes) yet still he not only must have this *Cloven-Foot* about him, but he is oblig'd to shew it too; nay, they will not allow him any Dress, whether it be a Prince's Robes, a Lord Cha———r's Gown, or a Lady's Hoops and long Petticoats, but the Cloven-Foot must be shew'd from under them; they will not so much as allow him an artificial *Shoe* or a *Jack-Boot*, as we often see contriv'd to conceal a *Club-Foot* or a *Wooden-Leg*; but that the Devil may be known wherever he goes, he is bound to shew his Foot; they might as well oblige him to set a Bill upon his Cap, as Folks do upon a House to be let, and have it written in capital Letters, *I am the* DEVIL.

It must be confess'd this is very particular, and would be very hard upon the *Devil*, if it had not another Article in it, which is some Advantage to him, and that is, that *the Fact is not true*; but the Belief of this is so universal, that all the World runs away with it; by which Mistake the good People miss the *Devil* many times where they look for him, and meet him as often where they did not expect him, and when for want of this Cloven-Foot they do not know him. (pp. 266–67)

The superstitious are ridiculed for translating something symbolic (a 'Token') into something concrete and physical, thereby simplifying it in a way ludicrous to the thoughtful. Defoe's comic treatment in this passage is extensive; he supplies a range of illustrative examples from a social world instead of the single one more characteristic of his writing. Thus, when speaking of class or 'Degree', he supplies the range of king to beggar, fine lady to old woman, and when speaking of different kinds of dress he chooses three examples from the highest echelons of society, not neglecting to include a lady as well as a prince and a Lord Chancellor. He thus suggests that vulnerability to Satan is not confined to men and that such vulnerability is prevalent in the upper classes, where it is easiest to disguise it by donning the robes of office, the prince's robes, the Lord Chancellor's gown, the hoop and long skirts of the society lady.

It is incongruous for vulgar 'Folks' to insist that so refined and subtle a presence as Satan's must be marked in a concrete physical way, as they would mark a house they intended to let. What they are doing is characteristic of those with little intelligence or imagination; they are translating and reducing the concept of evil, or of Satan, into terms suitable to their own coarse and limited understandings.

The second paragraph of this passage dismisses summarily and vigorously the conclusions popularly accepted in the first but goes on to suggest something about Satan a good deal more frightening than a cloven hoof: the very translation of evil into physical terms, the concretization of Satan, the notion of the devil's being captive to a humble foot, makes Satan actually more dangerous to human beings than he was before this superstition became popular. The notion of the cloven hoof, frightening to the unsophisticated, amusing to the thoughtful, misrepresents Satan's real nature, which is internal to the individual, intangible, and complex, and thus leads people astray; they are powerless to recognize the presence of evil when Satan does appear in their midst.

The central action of this passage from *The Political History of the Devil* is a caricature of the central action of Defoe's writing. The 'Folks' or 'good People' are translating the non-quantifiable aspect of life, in this case evil, into a humble physical equivalent, the cloven hoof, and thereby ejecting from their world, or refusing to consider, the uncontrollability and the complexity of evil. The cloven hoof exists only in the simplified and ideal world of their limited imaginations. Yet the ideal world is what most of Defoe's writing is fashioning, in Crusoe's reaction to the footprint he finds in the sand as well as in Defoe's most conspicuous vein of humour, the comedy of simplification.[1] The second paragraph of the above passage appears to be as much Defoe's warning to himself as it is to the 'Folks'. It suggests that the act of simplifying and ejecting the problematical may boomerang, leaving the simplifier face to face with Satan when he least expects it.

A modulation like that of the devil passage, from control to loss of control, occurs in the important pair of scenes marking Moll Flanders' first and second ventures into crime:

> WANDRING thus about I knew not whither, I pass'd by an Apothecary's Shop in *Leadenhall-street*, where I saw lye on a Stool just before the Counter a little Bundle wrapt in a white Cloth; beyond it, stood a Maid Servant with her Back to it, looking up towards the top of the Shop, where the Apothecary's Apprentice, as I suppose, was standing up on the Counter, with his Back also to the Door, and a Candle in his Hand, looking and reaching up to the upper Shelf for something he wanted, so that both were engag'd mighty earnestly, and no Body else in the Shop.
>
> THIS was the Bait; and the Devil who I said laid the Snare, as readily prompted me, as if he had spoke, for I remember, and shall never forget it, 'twas like a Voice spoken to me over my Shoulder, take the Bundle; be quick, do it this Moment; it was no sooner said but I step'd into the Shop, and with my Back to the Wench, as if I had stood up for a Cart that was going by, I put my Hand behind me and took the Bundle, and went off with it, the Maid or the Fellow not perceiving me, or any one else. (pp. 191–92)

Moll's first theft is set in the evening. The scene is described with much more visual detail than is usual with Defoe. The interior of the apothecary's shop is lit by the candle of the apprentice, which provides a physical chiaroscuro supplementing the chiaroscuro suggested by the description. The description is more detailed than usual in Defoe, highlighting the positions and gestures of the actors and objects in the scene: the small bundle in white on a stool, the maid with her back to it and to the door of the shop, looking up, the apprentice standing on the counter and reaching up to a shelf on the upper back wall of the shop, Moll backing into the scene, and with her face to the door of the shop reaching behind her for the bundle.

Growing bolder, Moll commits her second theft by daylight. Paradoxically, however, the visual quality of the first scene is lacking:

> I went out now by Day-light, and wandred about I knew not whither, and in search of I knew not what, when the Devil put a

187

Snare in my way of a dreadful Nature indeed, and such a one as I have never had before or since; going thro' *Aldersgate-street* there was a pretty little Child had been at a Dancing-School, and was going home, all alone, and my Prompter, like a true Devil, set me upon this innocent Creature; I talk'd to it, and it prattl'd to me again, and I took it by the Hand and led it a long till I came to a pav'd Alley that goes into *Bartholomew Close*, and I led it in there; the Child said that was not its way home; I said, yes, my Dear, it is, I'll show you the way home; the Child had a little Necklace on of Gold Beads, and I had my Eye upon that, and in the dark of the Alley I stoop'd, pretending to mend the Child's Clog that was loose, and took off her Necklace, and the Child never felt it, and so led the Child on again. . . . (pp. 193–94)

The theft of the necklace takes place in a dark alley. Moll describes her gestures: she takes the child by the hand, stoops, covers her theft this time by pretending to mend the child's loose clog, removes the necklace, leads her on again, turns her about, and directs her out of the alley. But these details are not caught and outlined as in the first scene. We do not visualize people caught and held in a gesture; the movements are furtive. How, for example, does one remove a necklace from someone's neck while manipulating her foot?

Whereas after the first theft Moll is so frightened that she does not notice the precise route by which she escapes but crosses and turns through back streets without consciously choosing a path until she finds herself in Thames Street near Billingsgate, after the second she names in a mechanical tone each street of her escape route: '. . . I went thro' into *Bartholomew Close*, and then turn'd round to another Passage that goes into *Long-lane*, so away into *Charterhouse-yard* and out into *St. John's-street*, then crossing into *Smithfield*, went down *Chick-lane* and into *Field-lane* to *Holbourn-bridge* . . .' (p. 194). This time Moll's mind is shown working efficiently and automatically on the conscious level.[2]

After the first theft Moll gets home to her lodgings about nine at night (place and time are specified), and examines her booty. In the bundle are 'a Suit of Child-bed Linnen . . . very good and almost new, the Lace very fine', 'a Silver Porringer of a Pint, a small Silver Mug and Six Spoons, with some other

Linnen, a good Smock, and Three Silk Handkerchiefs, and in the Mug wrap'd up in a Paper, Eighteen Shillings and Sixpence in Money.' After the second theft there is only a string of beads, which, Moll quickly calculates at some indefinite time and place afterwards, is worth about twelve to fourteen pounds. In the latter scene, Defoe's energies are scarcely at all directed toward the actual loot; the paragraph devoted to the necklace mentions its value in passing and quickly proceeds to what Moll imagines may have been the circumstances of its appearance on the unaccompanied child.

Moll's reflections after the first theft fall into two sections. The first long paragraph is concerned with her fears of the social consequences which may await her: now a thief, she will be caught and tried for her life at Newgate. Then she tries to imagine the circumstances connected with the bundle; her reflections lead her to fear that perhaps she has stolen from another human being related to her closely by sex and by a similar condition of desperate financial need (p. 193). After the second theft, however, Moll no longer empathizes with her victims:

> The last Affair left no great Concern upon me for as I did the poor Child no harm, I only said to myself, I had given the Parents a just Reproof for their Negligence in leaving the poor little Lamb to come home by it self, and it would teach them to take more care of it another time. (p. 194)

Moll imagines that the child's parents are negligent, that the mother is vain for having adorned her child with her own gold necklace (the necklace is now described by Moll as too big for the child, although at first she referred to it as a little necklace, perhaps transferring the tender diminutive from the child to her adornment), the hypothetical maid has been derelict in her responsibility of caring for the little girl. Other human beings have become to Moll either helpless objects, like the child, or creatures whose immorality causes them to merit her use of them as furniture in an environment she will manipulate for her material benefit. From other passages in Defoe's writing we learn that he did indeed feel incensed at potential victims who placed temptations in the path of thieves (see *Colonel Jack*, p. 54), but his indignation did not extend so far as to excuse malefactors for succumbing to these temptations. The fact that Moll excuses herself because the child's parents have exposed her to mistreatment is an indication of how she is becoming hardened by crime.

I mentioned above that Moll's reflections after the first theft fall into two sections, one concerned with the social consequences of her action to herself and to her victim. The second section deals with the question of Moll's relation with the metaphysical world, God and the Devil. She expresses regret for her wickedness, 'praying to God, as well as I could, for Deliverance', but her own necessities drive her to listen to Satan: 'Had I gone on here I had perhaps been a true Penitent; but I had an evil Counsellor within, and he was continually prompting me to relieve my self by the worst means' (p. 193). Her reference to Satan seems perfunctory in this scene, merely a convenient device by which to transfer responsibility for her own misdeeds to an external force. The reason for this is the contrast between her generalized statements about God and Satan and the vividly realized scene of the theft and the specificity of the stolen items. After the second theft there are no whole paragraphs treating Moll's relation with God or with Satan. But the whole scene is permeated by a sense of mystery, as the first scene was not. The new tone is underlined by the marked contrast between the two scenes. As Moll's relation to other human beings diminishes, her isolation suggests greater mystery about a lone individual in a dark background. Her increasing distance from other human beings is not compensated for by a closer relation to objects. In her reflections after the theft, the solidity of the gold necklace melts into a consideration of her distance from the human beings related to that necklace.

The shocking note in the second scene is the sudden impulse to murder that enters Moll's mind while she and the child are in the dark alley. It is significant that this impulse wells up from an obscure source: 'Here . . . the Devil put me upon killing the Child in the dark Alley, that it might not Cry' (p. 194), as contrasted to the sharp command issued by the voice Moll imagines over her shoulder during the first theft: ''Twas like a Voice spoken to me over my Shoulder, take the Bundle; be quick; do it this Moment' (p. 191).

Furthermore, in spite of Moll's growing tendency to manipulate other people without compunction for her own material benefit, she herself is depicted in this scene at the mercy of obscure impulses. During the first theft, rich in observed details, all of her senses were shown working at their height. During the second theft, she is almost in a somnambulent state as she proceeds along the alley. Much more is indicated at the pre-conscious than at the conscious level in this scene. One notes, for instance, the greater amount of repetition in her reflections after this theft than after the first, almost a monotony in her tone: 'As I did the poor Child no harm', and again, in the last paragraph, 'However, I did the Child no harm.' What appears to Moll as the intervention in her own mind of a disembodied spirit is called Satan by Defoe because it represented what seemed most evil and terrifying to him: the eruption of irrational and irrepressible urges to which post-Freudians have given technical names.

The origin of this scene was undoubtedly one of Defoe's own nightmares, for he refers to it in his *Political History of the Devil* (1726) and his *Essay on the History and Reality of Apparitions* (1727), published four and five years after *Moll Flanders*. In the first book temptation presents itself to a measurer and quantifier par excellence, a 'Tradesman' who, like Defoe, finds himself 'in great Distress for Money in his Business'. The tradesman, 'walking all alone in a great Wood' (p. 361), comes upon a child, whom he robs of a diamond necklace and a bag of gold. The dreamer is prompted by the devil to murder the child, for it might 'some time or other know him, and single him out' (p. 361). Satan suggests that the dreamer 'need do no more but twist the Neck of it a little, or crush it with his Knee' (p. 362). In the account of the same nightmare in the second book, theft, not murder, is at issue, and Defoe stresses the rationalization for the crime provided by Satan, a rationalization similar to that of Moll's.

For Defoe a twilight zone where good and evil impulses to control the external world were intertwined lay in the realm of the unconscious. This is illustrated by his effort in the *Essay on the History and Reality of Apparitions* to distinguish between apparitions of angels and devils. His general guidelines are as follows:

It is as difficult too to determine whether the Spirits that appear are good or evil or both; the only Conclusion upon that Point is to be made from the Errand they come about; and it is a very just Conclusion, I think; for if a Spirit or Apparition comes to or haunts us only to terrify and affright, to fill the Mind with Horror, and the House with Disorder, we cannot reasonably suppose that to be a good Spirit; and on the other hand, if it comes to direct to any Good, or to forewarn and preserve from any approaching Evil, it cannot then be reasonable to suppose 'tis an evil Spirit. (p. 7)

Concerning the dream about robbing the child, Defoe exclaims:

What was this but an Apparition of the *Devil*, a real visible Apparition! visible to the Mind, tho' not to the Body? and that in a double Capacity too; the *Devil without* in the Temptation, and the *Devil within* yielding to it. (p. 209)

Although the betrayal of a child is one of the few occasions of a loss of control by the protagonist in *Moll Flanders*, in general Moll's concern about responsibility toward her own children is limited to getting rid of them as expeditiously as possible. Indeed, Defoe's scepticism about the validity of Moll's expressions of maternal affection toward her children supplies the tone for a practical joke on her son Humphrey described in Chapter 4 above. On the contrary, responsibility for children is a central theme, along with marriage, in *Roxana*, where the protagonist's relation to her children, especially to one of her daughters, is darkened by a sense of guilt absent from the earlier fiction. Roxana's daughter Susan, at first a pitiable recipient of charity and seeker of maternal affection, later becomes a hound hot upon her scent (pp. 281, 317), a master to whom opening Roxana's secret would have rendered her 'forever after . . . this Girl's Vassal' (p. 280), Roxana's plague (p. 302), her tormentor (p. 302), an evil spirit who haunts Roxana (p. 310), a spy on Roxana's Quaker friend (p. 316) who watches the good woman's door night and day, who haunts her (p. 381), and a prophet who terrifies the Quaker by threatening that if she keeps her from Roxana 'a Curse wou'd follow her, and her Children after her' (p. 322).

When Amy, Roxana's servant and confidante, disappears after threatening to murder the girl, and then Susan herself drops from sight, Roxana concludes that Amy has done away with the girl. Since Amy has been treated throughout the fiction as if she were Roxana's double, related to her as body is to mind, the effect upon Roxana of the suspected murder is devastating. It is as if her own nightmares have assumed physical reality. Visions of the murdered body of the girl haunt her mother. The novel is unfinished, concluding with Roxana's departure from England with her Dutch husband and her settlement in Holland. The last paragraph, hastily bundled in, seems to promise further adversities for Roxana as the result of her complicity in the murder of her daughter.

Another recurring occasion for loss of control in Defoe's nightmare world is illicit sexual feelings. In the form of a suggestive dialogue between the narrator and a beautiful woman, it is the subject of one of the more memorable group of scenes in Defoe's *Political History of the Devil*. Here the narrator, who calls himself Jack in this episode, partly succeeds in convincing the wife of a Sir Edward that although she is an angel in appearance, in reality she is a devil. In the conversation the narrator first frightens the lady and finally makes her angry. The tone of his argument is so curiously insistent that it is difficult to decide whether or not Defoe was serious. Its flavour is best summed up by Sir Edward's introductory remark, that the word 'Devil' 'to a Lady in a Man's arms, is a word of divers Interpretations' (p. 300).

In Defoe's 1718 *Family Instructor*, conflict between a husband and wife, supposedly over family prayers, incites quarrels whose tone, as I have written elsewhere,

> suggests . . . the extravagant emotions of concealed sexual warfare. The husband's passion for his wife and her struggle not to be mastered by it underlie her opposition to his conduct of family worship and the excessive and irrational form taken by her rebellion. The basis of the husband's uxoriousness, except on the one issue of family worship, is suggested when his wife attempts to make him go to bed with her instead of conducting evening prayers at his usual hour. Breaking from her with a promise to return shortly, the husband overhears his wife say as he leaves, 'I'll promise you I'll desire you less than I have done' (p. 79). After the wife leaves home and has lived for some time with a dissolute friend whose favourite fashionable phrase is 'Poison it!' she becomes so obsessed with the desire for revenge

on a husband whose power over her emotions she cannot shake off, that the words take hold of her imagination, and she broods about applying them literally to her husband.[3]

Looking back upon the relation between Colonel Jack and his troublesome wife, we see that that episode belongs in the same category as these.

In sexual conduct, as we might expect, Moll Flanders' conscience troubles her very little. Her first lover gets his younger brother so drunk on the wedding night that he is unable to recollect 'whether he had any Conversation with [her] or no' (p. 58), and therefore never realizes that Moll was no longer a virgin when she married him. Her attitude toward 'Brother Robin', as she and his older brother call him, seems to be one of contempt for his gullibility in spite of recognition of his goodness. When Roxana agrees to become the common-law wife of the man who has rescued her from the depths of poverty, however, she tells Amy to stop rationalizing about the lawfulness of 'marrying' again: '. . . 'tis in vain to mince the Matter, I am a Whore, *Amy*, neither better nor worse, I assure you' (p. 40). Indeed, Roxana's conscience is so uncompromising on the matter that she absolves her common-law husband of any blame, taking all the guilt upon her own shoulders (pp. 38–9).

The shocking scene in which Roxana forces her maid into bed with her jeweller husband while she herself acts as voyeur is the enactment of what has often been suggested in conversations between Roxana and Amy; legitimatized by the precedent of Rachel and Jacob, the titillating notion of such a substitution has been repeatedly dangled before the reader. Amy's function as a double in the fiction suggests that Roxana is deliberately striving to degrade herself. Roxana herself explains that the 'hardness of Crime I was now arriv'd to . . . was owing to the Conviction that was from the beginning, upon me, that I was a Whore, not a Wife' (p. 45).

Similar incidents of the protagonists' tempting of fate by lying in bed with men occur in *Moll Flanders* and in *Roxana*. Although enough details are supplied in both fictions to suggest that Defoe was appealing to the pornographic interests of his readers, Moll's experience differs from Roxana's in being essentially comical. Moll's Bath gentleman professes so much respect for her that he claims to be capable of lying naked in bed with her all night without offering her 'the least injury'. When he successfully accomplishes this feat Moll is surprised and disappointed. She terminates this 'innocent' relationship herself when 'in Bed together warm and merry, and having drank, I think, a little more Wine that Night, both of us, than usual', she tells him that she 'cou'd find it in [her] Heart to discharge him of his Engagement for one Night and no more' (p. 116). The gentleman of course takes her at her word immediately, and in the morning they are 'both at [their] Penitentials' (p. 116). Even though later she informs her readers that she had resolved to seduce the man from the first, Moll's action is described primarily as the natural outcome of drinking and physical desire. The penitence expressed the next morning is described in a tone of humorous scepticism.

When a similar situation confronts Roxana, the merriness serving as a prelude to sexual intercourse is feigned on her part:

> But one Evening, above all the rest, we were very merry, and I fancy'd he push'd the Mirth to watch for his Advantage; and I resolv'd that I wou'd, at least, feign to be as merry as he; and that, in short, if he offer'd any-thing, he shou'd have his Will easily enough. (p. 142)

The result of Moll's experience is a six-year liaison with the gentleman. Once the affair is terminated, she never worries about it again. In Roxana's case, however, a painful series of discussions about why she refuses now to marry her Dutch lover follows her sexual intimacy. The man finally insists upon breaking off the relationship, because he 'cannot give up Soul as well as Body, the Interest of this World, and the Hopes of another' (p. 157). Roxana is very much upset by the affair; she does not wish to marry the Dutchman, but neither does she wish to let him go:

> Yet all the rest of his Letter was so moving, that it left me very melancholly, and I cry'd four and twenty Hours after, almost, without ceasing, about it; and yet, even all this while, whatever it was that bewitch'd me, I had not one serious Wish that I had taken him; I wish'd heartily indeed, that I cou'd have kept him with me; but I had a mortal Aversion to marrying him, or indeed, any-body else. (p. 161)

Roxana's unwillingness to let the Dutchman leave, her mixed emotions over this affair, are more complex than usual in Defoe's fiction, and the impression of a conflict between her reason and her emotions, her mood of uncontrollable irritability, is more clearly expressed when she finally marries the man later in her career.

Betrayal of children and illicit sexual union are not the only signals of Defoe's nightmare world. Above all what characterizes this realm is a feeling of helplessness of the protagonist confronted with the world. In Chapter 5 we saw that one trait of the nightmare world was the loss of the ability to make distinctions. When Moll no longer knows why she continues to steal, when Roxana is driven by the desire for affection rather than for clearly understandable social or economic advancement, they become trapped inside disguises they thought they could put on or off at will. When Mother Midnight can see into Moll's mind and Amy and Roxana are no longer distinguishable, a nightmarish feeling pervades the narrative.

The same feeling is present in the following section from the 1722 *Religious Courtship*, highly significant because it reveals in miniature most of the characteristics of nightmare as it appears in Defoe's writing. No longer, like the discussion of Satan's cloven hoof, a passage in transition from laughter to fear, this dialogue about the power of a Catholic icon over human beings, or the loss of control over the external world, is in the same key as the sombre *Roxana*. In the dialogue the recently bereaved Protestant widow of a Catholic husband describes to her horrified family the efforts of her loving husband to convert her to his faith:

> *Eld. sist.* Did he never go about to bribe you to it?
> *Wid.* Oh, Sister! very frequently; and that with all the subtlety of invention in the world; for he was always giving me presents upon that very account.
> *Fa.* Presents to a wife! What do they signify? 'Tis but taking his money out of one pocket, and putting it into the other; they must all be appraised, Child, in the personal estate.
> *Wid.* It has been quite otherwise with him, indeed, Sir; for he has made it a clause in his will, that all the presents he gave me shall be my own, to bestow how I please; besides all the rest that he has left me more than he was obliged to do.

Eld. sist. Then they seem to be considerable.

Wid. He has, first and last, given me above £3,000 in presents, and most of them on this very account; but one was very extraordinary, I mean to that purpose.

Eld. sist. I suppose that is your diamond cross?

Wid. It is so; he brought it home in a little case, and coming into my room one morning before I was dressed, hearing I was alone, he told me, smiling and very pleasant, he was come to say his prayers to me. I confess, I had been a little out of humour just at that time, having been full of sad thoughts all the morning about the grant point, and I was going to have given him a very unkind answer; but his looks had so much goodness and tenderness always in them, that when I looked up at him, I could retain no resentment; indeed, Sister, it was impossible to be angry with him.

Eld. sist. You might well be in humour indeed, when he brought you a present worth above six hundred pounds.

Wid. But I had not seen the present, when what I am telling you passed between us.

Eld. sist. Well, I ask pardon for interrupting you; pray go on where you left off, when he told you he was come to say his prayers to you.

Wid. I told him, I hoped he would not make an idol of his wife.

Wid. Why, he answered, he hoped he worshipped no idols but me, and if he erred in that point, whoever reproved him, he hoped I would not.

Eld. sist. Why, that's true too; besides, 'tis not so often that men make idols of their wives.

Wid. Well, while he was saying this, he pulls out the jewel, and opening the case, takes a small crimson string that it hung to, and put it about my neck, *but kept the jewel in his hand, so that I could not see it*; and then taking me in his arms, 'Sit down, my dear,' says he, which I did upon a little stool. Then he kneeled down just before me, and kissing the jewel, let it go, *saying something in Italian, which I did not understand*, and then, looking up in my face, 'Now, my dear,' says he, 'you are my idol.'

Yo. Sister. Well, but pray go on about the jewel; what said you to him?

Wid. Truly, Sister, I'll be very plain with you. When he kissed the jewel on his knees, *and muttered as I tell you in Italian*, I was rather provoked, than obliged; and I said, 'I think you are saying your prayers indeed, my dear; *tell me, what are you doing? What did you say?*'

Yo. Sist. Indeed, I should have been frighted.

Wid. Dear Sister, let me confess to you, fine presents, flattering words, and the affectionate looks of so obliging, so dear, and so near a relation are dreadful things, when they assault principles; *the glittering jewel had a strange influence*, and my affections began to be too partial on his side. Oh, let no woman that values her soul venture into the arms of a husband of a differing religion! The kinder he is, the more likely to undo her; everything that endears him to her, doubles her danger; the more she loves him, the more she inclines to yield to him; the more he loves her, the stronger are the bonds by which he draws her; and her only mercy would be to have him barbarous and unkind to her.

Yo. Sist. It is indeed a sad case, where to be miserable is the only safety; but so it is, no doubt, and such is the case of every woman that is thus unsuitably matched. . . .

Wid. It was my case, dear Sister; such a jewel! Such a husband! How could I speak an unkind word? Everything he did was so engaging, everything he said was so moving, what could I say or do?

Eld. Sist. Very true; and that makes me say, he would have conquered you at last.

Wid. Indeed, I can't tell what he might have done if he had lived.

Yo. Sist. Well, but to the jewel. What said you to him?

Wid. I stood up and thanked him, with a kind of ceremony, but told him I wished it had been rather in any other form. 'Why, my dear,' says he, 'should not the two most valuable forms in the world be *placed together?*' I told him, that as he placed a religious value on it, he should have it rather *in another place*. He told me, *my breast should be his altar;* and *so he might adore with a double delight*. I told him, I thought he was a little profane, and since I did not place the same value upon it, or make the same use of it, as he did, I might give him offence by mere necessity, and make that difference which we had both avoided with so much care, break in upon us in a case not to be resisted. He answered, 'No, my dear, I am not going to bribe your principles, much less force them. Put you what value you think fit upon it, and give me the like liberty.' *I told him I hoped I should not undervalue it as his present, if he did not overvalue it upon another account.* He returned warmly, 'My dear, the last is impossible; and for the first, 'tis a trifle; give it but leave to hang where I have placed it, that's all the respect I ask you to show it on my account.'

Yo. Sist. Well, that was a favour you would not deny if a stranger had given it you.

Wid. Dear Sister, you are a stranger to the case; if you had seen what was the consequence of it, you would have been frighted, or perhaps have fallen quite out with him.

Yo. Sist. I cannot imagine what consequences you mean.

Wid. Why, first of all, he told me, that now he would be perfectly easy about my salvation, and would cease to pursue me with arguments or entreaties in religious matters.

Yo. Sist. What could he mean by that?

Wid. Why, he said, he was sure that blessed form that hung so near my heart, would have a miraculous influence some time or other, and I should be brought home into the bosom of the Catholic Church.

Yo. Sist. Well, I should have ventured all that, and have slighted the very thoughts of it.

Wid. You cannot imagine what stress he laid on it; now, he said, every good Catholic that saw me but pass by them, would pray for me; and everyone in particular would exorcise me by the passion of Christ out of the chains of heresy.

Yo. Sist. What said you to him?

Wid. I put it off with a smile, but my heart was full, I scarce knew how to hold; and he perceived it easily, and broke off the talk a little; but he fell to it again, till he saw the tears stood in my eyes, when he took me in his arms, and kissed me again; *kissed my neck where the cross hung*, and then kissed the jewel repeating the word Jesu two or three times, and left me.

Eld. Sist. I would have obliged him to have forborne his little idolatrous tricks then, and used them on other occasions.

Wid. That had been to desire him not to be a Roman Catholic. Why, in foreign countries, that are Popish, as I understand, they never go by a cross, whether it be in the road, or on any building, but they pull off their hats.

Fa. So they do, my dear, and often kneel down, though it be in the dirt, and say over their prayers.

Wid. It is impossible to tell you how many *attacks* I had of that kind when I wore this jewel.

Fa. I do not doubt it, especially if he brought any strangers into the room. How did you do, Child, when the Venetian ambassador dined at your house? Had you it then?

Wid. Yes, Sir, my spouse desired me to put it on, and I could not well deny him. But I did not know how to behave, for the ambassador and all his retinue *paid so many bows and homages to me, or to the cross,* that I scarce knew what to do with myself, *nor was I able to distinguish their good manners from their religion, and it was well I did not then understand Italian,* for, as my dear told me afterwards, they said a great many religious things that would have given me offence.

Fa. These things are so frequent in Italy, that the Protestant ladies take no notice of them, and yet they all wear crosses, but sometimes put them out of sight.

Wid. I did so afterwards; I lengthened the string it hung to, that it might hang a little lower, but it was too big: if it went within my stays, it would hurt me; nor was it much odds to him; for if he saw the string, he knew the cross was there, and it was all one.

Yo. Sist. Did he use any ceremony to it after the first time?

Wid. Always, when he first came into any room where I was, he was sure to give me his knee with his bow, *and kiss the cross as well as his wife.*

Eld. Sist. I should never have borne it.

Wid. You could never have resisted it any more than I, for I did what I could; but his answer was clear: 'My dear,' says he, '*take no notice of me, let my civilities be to you*; take them all to yourself, I cannot shew you too much respect; believe it is all your own, and be easy with me.'

Eld. Sist. How could he bid you believe, what you knew to be otherwise? Why did you not leave it off and *reproach him with the difference?*

Wid. Dear Sister, I did for months together. But then he doubled his ceremonies, and told me, I only mortified him by obliging him to reverence the place where once the blessed Figure had been lodged, as the holy pilgrims worshipped the sepulchre.

Eld. Sist. He was too hard for you every day, Sister. (pp. 263–65, 266–69, 270–71) (My italics are designed to stress the inability to understand or to make the distinctions and analyses characteristic of Defoe's usual style)

The sombre atmosphere of this scene comes from the condition of the Protestant wife, who seems to have been trapped in a nightmarish state of paralysis while her husband was living. Vulnerable through her wearing a cross, to the 'attacks' of her husband, of Catholic passers-by in the street, of the Venetian ambassador and his retinue, she begins to feel that the object to which they all pay homage has some occult power over her, that 'the glittering jewel [has] a strange influence' on her. Concern in others about her religious salvation seems evil to her. The attempts of Catholics to convert her are presented as a form of persecution; even her husband's great affection for her is sinister and dangerous: 'The more he loves her, the stronger are the bonds by which he draws her.'

Her passivity is suggested by the very language of the scene, which is notable for the absence of concrete, homely nouns. The reasoning that takes place is of a different kind from that of the plain-dealing Mr. Review side of Defoe; attempts to analyse and to translate words or abstract ideas are resisted. We note, for instance, that the widow's father and older sister attempt to divest the dead husband's gifts to his wife of emotional influence, the father by observing they belong to an estate whose value can be calculated, the sister by assigning the necklace a monetary value. The widow, however, refuses to accept this point of view, which would demystify the gifts by considering them in their material aspect alone. She herself attempts, when reasoning with her husband, to separate the religious from the affective value of the jewelled cross: 'I told him, I hoped I should not undervalue it as his present, if he did not overvalue it upon any other account.' But her husband's subtlety is 'too hard' for her; he replies in an ambiguous and equivocal phrase that 'the last is impossible'.

The equivocation apparent in the husband's response is typical of the whole scene, in that the polite and ceremonious attentions of the husband, the Catholic passers-by, the Venetian ambassador, serve to disguise their designs on the Protestant's soul, and to make those designs more dangerous than usual because more subtle and difficult to counter: '. . . the ambassador and all his retinue paid so many bows and homages to me, or to the cross, that I scarce knew what to do with myself, nor was I able to distinguish their good manners from their religion.' The combination of equivocal motives—the husband means well by his wife, but conversion to Catholicism, good in his eyes, is evil in hers—and of a discrepancy between the ceremonious talk and the ulterior motives of such talk, is highly sinister.

Other indications of the nightmarish helplessness of the Protestant wife are first, her significant failures to understand what is being said: when the husband places the jewel around her neck he keeps the jewel in his hand so that she cannot see it, 'saying something in Italian, which [she] did not understand', and when the Venetians dine at her house, she cannot understand much of their conversation, for it is in Italian.[4] Second, Defoe's concentration upon the diamond cross serves to magnify this object, suggesting that it has some vitality of its own greater than the vitality of the human beings connected with it. Defoe usually mentions or lists many objects in his anecdotes; when he concentrates so insistently upon one, it tends to assume symbolic proportions and to evoke the sinister, as in the case of the footprint in *Robinson Crusoe*, the portrait of Queen Anne stressed in the Mesnager *Minutes*, and the Turkish costume in *Roxana*.

We should not be surprised to remark the reappearance of the sinister necklace in *Roxana* when the prince, leading his mistress to the dark side of the room, fastens a diamond necklace on her in an ambiguous and painful gesture of love:

> . . . at last he leads me to the darkest Part of the Room, and standing behind me, bade me hold up my Head, when putting both Hands round my Neck, as if he was spanning my Neck, to see how small it was, for it was long and small; he held my Neck so long and hard, in his Hand, that I complain'd he hurt me a little; what he did it for, I knew not, nor had I the least Suspicion but that he was spanning my Neck; but when I said he hurt me, he seem'd to let go, and in half a Minute more, led me to a Peir-Glass, and behold, I saw my Neck clasp'd with a fine Necklace of Diamonds. . . . (p. 73)

As we can see, the loss of power to understand and to act is depicted in Defoe's nightmare world by a special use of objects. Many readers have noticed the prominence of objects in Defoe's fictions. Dorothy Van Ghent shrewdly observed that in *Moll Flanders* 'these tangible, material objects . . . are not at all vivid in texture', concluding, 'What is important in Moll's world of things is the counting, measuring, pricing, weighing, and evaluation of things. . . .'⁵ What is important in *Moll Flanders* is important in all of Defoe's fictions; it would be superfluous to list passages from *Robinson Crusoe*, *A Journal of the Plague Year*, *Captain Singleton*, *Colonel Jack*, and so forth, where vigorous manipulation of objects demonstrates the power and prowess of his protagonists. In those passages depicting a nightmare world, on the other hand, Defoe's objects become sinister by exercising a paralysing effect upon his protagonists.

Roxana differs from Defoe's other fictions in that the whole work depicts objects and memories of objects and gestures dominating the mind of the protagonist and so paralysing her that growth in her external prosperity becomes an incontrovertible sign of decline in her internal mental state. Both Moll and Roxana are impelled into careers of illicit activity by the fear of poverty; the difference is that Roxana's fear is reinforced by her recurring memory of the scene in which she sat on the ground 'with a great Heap of old Rags, Linnen, and other things' about her, waiting for Amy to return with the 'small Breast of Mutton and two great Bunches of Turnips' she has been able to buy in return for a silver spoon (pp. 17–18).

The memory of this scene and of the abject poverty and helplessness symbolized by the dinner, arises in Roxana's mind on three later occasions, notably until her fear of poverty has been replaced by another, less innocent, anxiety. As she grows richer by the proceeds of her first two love affairs, her rise in affluence with the social position of her lovers is measured by the meals offered to her by each one of them. Her landlord begins paying his court to her by sending Amy out to buy meat. Amy brings 'the Butcher along with her, with both the things that she had chosen, for him to please himself; the one was a very good Leg of Veal; the other a Piece of the Fore-Ribs of Roasting Beef'; Roxana's lover bids her 'take them both, the rest, he said, would serve another time. . . .' (p. 25).

After her 'husband' has been murdered in France, his client, a foreign prince, charmed by Roxana's beauty, courts her to be his mistress by having his servant bring in a little table covered with a fine cloth,

> the Table no bigger than he cou'd bring in his Two Hands; but
> upon it, was set two Decanters, one of Champaign, and the other
> of Water, six Silver Plates, and a Service of fine Sweet-Meats in

fine *China* Dishes, on a Sett of Rings standing up about twenty Inches high, one above another; below, was three roasted Partridges, and a Quail. . . . (p. 62)

Roxana's gifts are not, like Moll's acquired object by object, as the reward for her shrewdness and energy; as in a dream they come flying to her of themselves, caught in the hypnotic field of her sexual attractiveness.

The turnips, ever-present in Roxana's memory of life reduced to its barest minimum, serve to comment adversely on the sinful luxury of the meal provided for her by her foreign prince, a meal climaxed by his pouring sweetmeats into her lap. The moral connotation of the shower of sweetmeats is apparent when we contrast it to the less sensuous shower of gold coins poured into Roxana's lap during her first, less culpable affair. The first affair was almost a marriage; her liaison with the prince, however, is sinful luxury. The turnips are rooted in Roxana's mind; her memory of the depths of misery represented by that original scene of poverty motivates her actions for a good portion of her career. Indeed, the recurrence of this memory provides a psychological continuity to her life that is lacking in *Moll Flanders*, a work much closer to the picaresque or novel of character.[6]

The grip of objects and gestures on Roxana's mind is one element contributing to the nightmarish atmosphere of paralysis in this fiction, an atmosphere similar to that described by Defoe in the scene from *Religious Courtship* described above. Another element contributing to this atmosphere is the prevalence of prison imagery in *Roxana*. At one point in her career, Roxana locks all her wealth into a great iron chest. Hiding places of this type are less significant in *Roxana* than in *Robinson Crusoe*, where cave imagery is an important motif. Yet Roxana herself is often to be found tucked away for safekeeping like a valuable object. In her affairs with the foreign prince, with the English king, and with the lecherous lord, her elected seclusion is almost airless. With the foreign prince, she goes beyond his request that she avoid conspicuous display of his largesse to suggest 'if he thought fit, I would be wholly within-Doors.' She rejects the prince's desire that she rent a house in the country and remains in the town: 'I made no Scruple of the

Confinement; and told *his Highness*, no Place could be a Confinement, where I had such a Visiter . . .' (p. 67). As if to underline the suggestion of airless seclusion Defoe inserts an incident where the prince resolves Roxana 'should be weary of his Company, and that he would learn to know what it was to be a Prisoner.' He tells his servants he is going away and instead stays indoors with Roxana for two weeks, never going out of her doors (p. 68). As James Walton shrewdly observes of Roxana's lodgings: 'Her only domain will be that erotic "no place" which Steven Marcus has called "pornotopia".' He points out that Roxana's role sometimes 'reads like a male fantasy of female compliance'.[7]

The old lord who takes up with Roxana after her affair with the King settles her in new and private lodgings with a handy back door and a prominent lock and key. During her affair with the King, Roxana lives 'retir'd' (p. 181). At the end of this 'Time of Retreat' (p. 181), the suggestion of airless seclusion is made more explicit by the metaphor in which Roxana describes her reappearance in society: 'I did not come Abroad again with the same Lustre, or shine with so much Advantage as before', she remarks, as if she were a tarnished piece of silver re-emerging from a chest.

If during her love affairs Roxana elects her own confinement and there is usually an escape hatch in the form of a back door, marriage offers no such option. *Roxana* contains five discussions of marriage, some of them so extensive that, combined with the related topics of extra-marital sexual activities and irresponsibility toward offspring, it could be regarded as the central theme of the novel.[8] Roxana's long explanation to her amorous Dutchman of why she is opposed in principle to marriage rests upon the analogy between marriage and imprisonment or slavery. She tells him:

> The very Nature of the Marriage-Contract was, in short, nothing but giving up Liberty, Estate, Authority, and everything, to the Man, and the Woman was indeed, a meer Woman ever after, that is to say, a Slave. (p. 148)

The Dutchman is the only man in the fiction that Roxana admits would make an acceptable husband. Middle-class brewers make poor husbands, servants make poor husbands, and gentlemen and aristocrats make the worst husbands of all—jailers. Indeed, Roxana turns down many marriage offers from gentlemen, arguing that '*while I had £2000 of my own, I was happier than I cou'd be in being Prisoner of State to a Nobleman*; for I took the Ladies of that Rank to be little better' (pp. 166–67).

References to prison in *Roxana* are not, however, confined to the marriage state or to love affairs. One reference to prison is to her poor daughters, subjected to the 'Bridewell of their aunt's house' while Roxana is in France. Most of the references, however, are to Roxana herself, to her imprisonment by her past. When she adopts her Quaker disguise, for instance, she wants a costume that will make her unknown so that she 'need not be confin'd like a Prisoner, and be always in Fear' (p. 213). After her marriage in England to the Dutchman, she persuades him

> to give me leave to oblige him with going to live Abroad; when in truth, I cou'd not have been perfectly easie at living in *England*, unless I had kept constantly within-doors; lest some time or other, the dissolute Life I had liv'd here shou'd have come to be known. . . . (p. 249)

Forced to accept a visit from her inquisitive daughter and a friend, Roxana

> durst not leave the Room by any means . . . ; so that, *in a word*, I was oblig'd to sit and hear her tell all the Story of Roxana . . . and not know at the same time, whether she was in earnest or in jest; whether she knew me or no; or, *in short*, whether I was to be expos'd, or not expos'd. (pp. 284–85)

Most significant of all, when ruminating about why she does not break her liaison with an English lord, Roxana concludes:

> . . . as Necessity first debauch'd me, and Poverty made me a Whore at the Beginning, so excess of Avarice for getting Money, and excess of Vanity, continued me in the Crime, not being able to resist the Flatteries of Great Persons. . . . These were my Baits, these the Chains by which the Devil held me bound; and by which I was indeed, too fast held for any Reasoning that I was then Mistress of, to deliver me from.' (p. 202)

The chains by which the Devil holds Roxana are so powerful that her reason cannot break this paralysis of her will.

Indeed, the ultimate end to which Roxana's loss of control seems to be driving her is a madhouse. In spite of the hurried conclusion of the fiction, several instances of foreshadowing suggest that Defoe may have had such a destination in mind for his protagonist.

Turning back to *Moll Flanders* to remind ourselves how different the nightmare atmosphere of the later fiction is from the generally comic atmosphere of the first, we note the striking difference in the treatment of objects and prisons. In the one incident where Moll's uncontrollable urge to steal even when she no longer needs to do so drives her to make off with a horse, we find that the reward of her enterprise, far from dominating her thoughts, seems to Defoe an amusing encumbrance. During the one marriage where Moll is obliged to live quietly at home, it is not a prison to her. She thinks of herself as 'landed in a safe Harbour, after the Stormy Voyage of Life past was at an end' (p. 188), and lives with her new husband in the 'utmost tranquillity'.

Prison as a motif in *Moll Flanders* appears comparatively rarely. In the first instance referring to Moll, when she takes lodgings in the Mint, we can sense the paralysis of will that Defoe described fully only in *Roxana*; Moll explains:

> These Men were too wicked, even for me; there was something horrid and absurd in their way of Sinning, for it was all a Force even upon themselves . . . and nothing was more easie than to see how Sighs would interrupt their Songs, and paleness, and anguish sit upon their Brows, in spight of the forc'd Smiles they put on. . . . (p. 65)

In the second instance, Moll herself becomes temporarily 'possessed' by the 'certain strange lethargy of soul' that afflicts Roxana throughout her account:

> On the contrary, like the Waters in the Caveties, and Hollows of Mountains, which petrifies and turns into Stone whatever they are suffer'd to drop upon; so the continual Conversing with such a Crew of Hell-Hounds as I was with had the same Operation upon me, as upon other People, I degenerated into Stone. . . . (p. 278)

But the central emphasis in *Moll Flanders* is social rather than psychological. Defoe seems intent in the earlier fiction upon tinging Moll's successes in love or in crime with irony and mischief about social classes and social conventions, targets proper to the genre of comedy.

At the end of Moll's story, comfortably well off from her successful farming venture in America, she returns to London with her last and favourite husband. Jemy is certainly not Moll's equal; less enterprising and industrious than she is, and less resilient, he is not worthy of becoming a complete confidante about her previous career. Nevertheless, he is a gentleman by birth, and with money plentiful, they can be expected to lead a good-natured, even merry, life together. Roxana's last days, days of material riches, even of titled honours, are shadowed by murder and madness; Moll's last days, days of a more modest prosperity, adorned by a gentleman husband of her earliest desires, are cloudless. Defoe abandons Roxana on the Continent; Moll he conducts safely back to his beloved London, haven of all his fictional wanderers, the site of his earthly paradise.

NOTES

1. See the discussion of Robin, pp. 149–51 and the joke about Presbyterian fish, p. 42 above.
2. David Blewett points out that seeing only verisimilitude in this list of street names is 'to miss half the point'. Defoe is drawing attention here to Moll's *deviousness*, not her accuracy of memory or his own knowledge of London's streets' (*Defoe's Art of Fiction*, p. 21).
3. 'A Case Study of Defoe's Domestic Conduct Manuals Suggested by *The Family, Sex and Marriage in England, 1500–1800*' in *Studies in Eighteenth-Century Culture, Volume 10*, ed. Harry C. Payne (Madison: University of Wisconsin Press, 1981), pp. 421–22.
4. Note that Roxana is in the same condition when she is terrified by the malevolent Jewish jewel dealer, jabbering in a foreign language.
5. Dorothy Van Ghent, *The English Novel: Form and Function* (1953; rpt. New York: Harper Torchbooks, 1961), p. 35.
6. Michael Boardman goes further in his 1983 *Defoe and the Uses of Narrative* in classifying Roxana as a psychological novel in embryo than does David Blewett in his 1979 book.
7. 'The Romance of Gentility', *Literary Monographs*, 4 (1971), pp. 126, 127.
8. See Spiro Peterson, 'The Matrimonial Theme of Defoe's *Roxana*', PMLA, 70 (1955), 166–91.

Epilogue

Had Defoe stopped writing fiction after the publication in 1724 of the sombre *Roxana*, he would have greatly facilitated the task of literary analysts eager to organize his work into a neat pattern, as the plain-dealing Mr. Review tried to organize the world around him. Critics would have agreed with Michael Shinagel that Defoe gave up fiction because he realized his 'fictions were leading him to excesses of the imagination over which he could not exercise the same control as in his other forms of writing, or as in his earlier works of prose fiction.'[1] The path of least resistance has been to regard *Roxana* as a watershed for Defoe: Everett Zimmerman argues that he clarified and developed issues, characters, and motifs in the years between *Robinson Crusoe* and *Roxana* and accordingly prefers the latter to the former work because of its more penetrating moral perception as illustrated in its novelistic form[2]; David Blewett argues that *Roxana* is the first of Defoe's novels to explore 'a problem of central concern for the English novel, that of human relationships' and finds emotional progress in his 'darkening vision of the human lot'[3]; finally, Michael Boardman locates in the conclusion of *Roxana* the 'formal possibilities that became the traditional English novel'.[4]

Aside from overvaluing *Roxana*, such theories overlook the lack of evidence for darkening vision in Defoe's non-fiction of the 1720s. His books on the occult, dealing with Satan, show no sign of deepening emotional perception, other than two short descriptions of the nightmare of robbing and murdering a child and one description of sinister dalliance between the narrator and an attractive woman. Rodney Baine points out in *Daniel Defoe and the Supernatural*, that with the exception of certain ideas about guardian angels, Defoe was in the mainstream of Protestant tradition on the supernatural. Even Defoe's beliefs in the immateriality of Satan, the disguises he assumed in order to appear to humans and his using people's own passions to tempt them, were quite traditional. Baine writes:

> The more subtle media through which the Devil now exercises his power, it seemed to Defoe's predecessors and contemporaries, are far more effective; and gradually writers came to center almost exclusively upon such subtle temptations as the Devil effects in dreams, evil impulses, and passions.[5]

In spite of Defoe's lifelong interest in diabolic motifs, *Roxana* is the only one of his fictions that conveys throughout its entire length the feeling of hell, which I have previously described as a state of nightmarish paralysis, consisting of the loss of control over emotion and over objects, and of the loss of the power of analysis and of the ability to understand what is being said. The non-fiction works in which I have located a similar atmosphere come before *Roxana*: the 1717 Mesnager *Minutes*, the 1718 *Family Instructor*, and the 1722 *Religious Courtship*. It is significant that all the episodes dealing with evil actions or obsessive psychological states are confined to characters of great wealth or social status, as is much of *Roxana*[6]; in addition, the conversation of these characters lacks concrete nouns and is so polished and sinuous that the discrepancy between its surface and the design of the speaker appears sinister.

I have not been able to locate any passages of this kind in other non-fiction works by Defoe after 1722. Significantly, his 1724 *Great Law of Subordination Consider'd* includes a potentially terrifying story of a devilish house servant who disorders a whole family and succeeds in getting the housekeeper fired and the master of the house permanently smeared by slander. Yet the story is recounted in a slipshod manner with frequent confusion of pronouns; it is merely an uninspired account, with no atmosphere at all, of how the elaborate scheme was carried out and discovered. *The Protestant Monastery* of 1726 by the crotchety Andrew Moreton (Defoe's old man pseudonym) describes movingly the mistreatment of an old father by his ungrateful daughter and son-in-law, but the married couple are simply disagreeable and ill-natured; they are not described in the diabolic terms we would expect after *Roxana*.

After *Roxana* Defoe returned to his two central preoccupations, the organization of the world into an ideal state (in his social and economic tracts) and the participation in the real world of disorder and impulse (in his fictional works). An outstanding example of the second category was his creation of a false reputation of military genius for the Earl of Peterborough by doctoring heavily the military memoirs of Captain George Carleton (1728). Imposing order and participating in disorder are the two impulses I have been tracing through the pages of the *Review* and can be seen in many passages from early works. In the spirit of the plain-dealing Mr. Review, Defoe attacks dissimulation as the sinister, yet dominant characteristic of the whole period around 1709 in his *Letter to Mr. Bissett* (quoted in Chapter 3), which concludes: 'and the whole town seems to look one way, and now another. . . .' In the spirit of the worldly Mr. Review, however, Defoe writes a pamphlet in 1710, *Instructions from Rome, in Favour of the Pretender*. In this work we hear the subtle and worldly Defoe, who indicates that his plain-dealing brother is an artificial entity, to be exploited for literary and polemical purposes. The author, supposedly the Pope, instructs his English followers to behave like the sinister disguised manipulator Defoe publicly excoriated in his Scottish pamphlets while privately celebrating the manipulator as himself in his letters to Robert Harley. The Pope recommends that his English followers disguise themselves, assume differing shapes, and become all things to all men:

> Study profoundly humours and interests; to the poor magnify Popish charity, and to the noble, housekeeping of old; to young scholars, the learning of the Jesuits, and the excellent method and discipline of their schools beyond the seas; to the debauched, represent the moderation of our Church in voting the wanton sallies of nature (as whoredom, adultery, incest, and sodomy) but venial peccadilloes, and granting indulgences at easy rates, for greater crimes. . . .

> In the meantime let your emissaries alter their shapes; be one thing today, another tomorrow, now a courtier, by and by a formal Cit[izen], or a soldier; sometimes a tailor, other times a shoemaker, or valet-de-chambre; a beau among the ladies; and atheists among wits; or any other variation or transposition, agreeable to our interest. (pp. 9–10, 12)

The speaker concludes the above passage by adding, 'Endeavour to suppress that damn'd Review, that's a plaguey fellow. . . .' Defoe thus interjects the plain-dealing Mr. Review as dramatic antagonist of the disguised manipulator.

It would be simple to maintain that the solution to the puzzle of Defoe's elusive personality is that he pretended to be a plain dealer, while in reality he was a disguised manipulator. This position would require arguing that the public was demanding plain dealers and that Defoe, a hack writer, was eager to satisfy this demand. An unsympathetic critic would add that Defoe, being an accomplished liar and hypocrite, was qualified by personal characteristics to conform to the expectations of his age. This argument would be simple to sustain—but it would be incorrect, as well as unfair. The consistency with which traits of the plain dealer appear in all of Defoe's writings argues that this character was more than a literary fabrication; it was an integral part of Defoe's private consciousness. The ambivalence in his attitude toward the disguised manipulator argues that Defoe was sometimes aware that this too was a part of him and occasionally became frightened, though usually amused, by this other aspect of his personality.

In spite of the disappearance of the diabolic from his later writings, it is doubtful that Defoe ever came to accept without puritanical guilt the humorous outlook of the worldly Mr. Review. Even if he himself could have adopted Harley's attitude fully—'Do not be imposed upon, to think things and people worse than they actually are'—other people made such acceptance difficult for him. Cut off from his family, in hiding from creditors, he died 'from a lethargy'.[7] The isolated writer left us the legacy of the two divided sides of his personality, in *Robinson Crusoe* and *Moll Flanders*.

NOTES

1. *Daniel Defoe and Middle-Class Gentility* (Cambridge, Mass.: Harvard University Press, 1968), p. 196.
2. Everett Zimmerman, *Defoe and the Novel*, pp. 185–86.
3. *Defoe's Art of Fiction*, p. 145.
4. *Defoe and the Uses of Narrative*, p. 155.

5. *Daniel Defoe and the Supernatural* (Athens, Georgia: University of Georgia Press, 1968), p. 45.

6. By tracing a source for Roxana's Moorish costume, the dance, and the masquerade in Madame de La Fayette's *Princesse de Monpensier*, Joseph A. Kestner III also emphasizes that the social classes described by Defoe in this fiction would have to be of higher rank than those in his other fictions ('Defoe and Madame de La Fayette: *Roxana* and *La Princesse de Monpensier*', in *Papers on Language and Literature*, 8, 1972, 297–301).

7. James Sutherland, *Daniel Defoe*, p. 273.

Index

215

Index

P